# Off Duty

# Off Duty

## The world's greatest chefs cook at home

Photographs by
James Merrell

HarperCollins*Publishers*

**American measures and terminology are given in brackets after the UK ones - e.g. 250g ($1^3/4$ cups) plain (all-purpose) flour.**

**American cooks should measure unsifted flour by dipping the cup measure into the bag, scooping up the flour, and levelling the surface.**

First published in 2005 by
HarperCollinsPublishers
77-85 Fulham Palace Road
Hammersmith
London W6 8JB

11 10 09 08 07 06 05
7 6 5 4 3 2 1



This book was produced by Here+There for THE NICHOLLS SPINAL INJURY FOUNDATION
Art Director: Caz Hildebrand
Designer: Julie Martin
Editor: Jane Middleton
Photographer: James Merrell
Processing and Scanning: Metro Online at Metro Imaging, London
Indexer: Hilary Bird
**www.hereandtheregroup.com**

A catalogue record for this book is available from the British Library.

ISBN 0-00-775202-4

Printed in Thailand by Imago

# Contents

# Dedication

**To Daniel, knowing that you will one day walk again.**

# Foreword

On 30 December 2003, my nineteen-year-old son, Daniel, was enjoying his fifth week of a gap year (year off between school and college) in Australia. Standing on Bondi Beach, water up to his knees, he dived into a wave. Dan had no idea that a sandbank lay beneath. He broke his neck and is now paralysed from the arms down, with very little movement in his hands.

The effects of such a simple and tragic accident are devastating, not only in terms of Daniel's future but also for those close to him, our family, friends and associates. I guess that when such a life-altering accident occurs, you can go two ways: one route would be *not* to cope or come to terms with it. The other would be to look forward, decide quickly what needs to be done, and set about dealing with it. I chose the latter.

I flew down to Australia to be with Dan and to arrange his return to the UK, which we completed just over two months after the accident. Dan then spent all of 2004 at Stoke Mandeville Hospital in Aylesbury, England, a leading centre for spinal injury, undergoing extensive physiotherapy and occupational therapy to prepare for his discharge back into the community in March 2005.

Paralysis is something that most of us don't know very much about. When we see someone in a wheelchair, we often see just the chair, not the person in it. We don't think that a few months ago, that person might have been living a perfectly normal life and now, through no fault of their own, is at the mercy of the health service, the medical world and the government for survival and hope.

There are so many people living with spinal injury who are less fortunate than Daniel. Now that I am aware, I feel compelled to do whatever I can for my son and others like him. I am not alone in this. The response from my colleagues and associates in the food industry has been phenomenal. Every chef I have approached has responded with huge generosity and agreed to write a menu, in their signature style and cuisine, which the reader can cook at home.

With the proceeds from this collection of recipes, I am setting up a charity, The Nicholls Spinal Injury Foundation, to raise money to support research into treatment for spinal injury, stem cell research and development and rehabilitation for patients with spinal injury. I believe that a breakthrough will come in the not too distant future, and my goal is to do everything humanly possible to help make it happen.

This book is the beginning of that goal.

**David Nicholls**

In compiling this extraordinary cookery book with some of the world's finest chefs, there are so many people I would like to thank. I am so eternally grateful for their help, support and encouragement, without which I do not think it would have been possible. However I must specifically thank the following: Caz Hildebrand, James Merrell, Natalie Vorster, Adriana Gelves, Chris Tombling, James Campbell, Gordon McDermott, Anton Mosimann and finally Liam Lambert.

# Introduction – Thomas Keller

When David first approached me about becoming involved in *Off Duty*, my initial reaction to his son's horrific accident was pity, but thoughts of challenge and hope soon replaced that feeling. I knew I could play a role in helping David find a definitive cure for spinal injuries.

He and his family's strength throughout this ordeal have been amazing and inspirational. Their story and their determination have made me stop and think. It's too easy to get caught up in the daily burdens of running restaurants and, though this will always be important, what truly matters in life becomes clear in these moments of reflection. We take breathing for granted – until we can't breathe on our own. We can't possibly be reflective about how lucky we are to breathe every day, but we can't forget it either. Dan's story has renewed my gratitude for what I have and has doubled my desire to be of as much help as possible.

People tend to gather together to eat when an important event occurs, whether in jubilation or in tragedy. Besides providing nourishment, food draws us together so that we can find joy or solace in each other's company. Chefs, by the nature of their business, share an innate camaraderie because of this. They bring people together to celebrate food, and to celebrate life. It's appropriate, then, that David has culled his friends from the restaurant world to share in this project.

It was both an honour and a pleasure to have been a part of this mission. Although I expected nothing in return, I've been hugely rewarded. The ties of our friendship are stronger than ever, and the moments I took to reflect on life and hope have been profound.

To the readers and supporters of this cause, may these recipes provide you with great enjoyment and durable memories. May you continue to share them throughout the years with the people you love and care about.

To David, thank you, not only for opening my eyes to the devastating effects of spinal injury but for giving me the opportunity to offer my gift of cooking to such an important and worthwhile cause.

And to Dan, you are surrounded by friends and family who continue to support you. May this knowledge provide you with some relief and comfort while we fervently await your cure. This is for you.

**Thomas Keller**

# Introduction – Gordon Ramsay

When I was asked to contribute towards this book and write an introduction, I was delighted to assist.

I have known David for many years, as a chef and as a friend. When I first heard about his son Daniel's accident I felt despair as I began to understand the enormous challenges and devastating changes that were happening to David and his family, but most importantly to Daniel. I simply cannot imagine how a nineteen-year-old comes to terms with such a tragic injury. In all my time spent in kitchens, I don't know anyone who could deal with this challenge. However, I decided that I would do everything possible to support David in his dedication to a single goal: to get Daniel walking again.

As part of this goal, David has set up the Nicholls Spinal Injury Foundation, to support the latest research into stem cell surgery, spinal research and development, and patients with spinal injuries. The proceeds from this book will go directly to the Foundation.

The strength and drive of David and those around him has been impressive. We all take good health for granted, and if we have healthy children we assume that that is the way it will always be, never realising what might be around the corner. But Dan's story has made me aware that life is so precious we should be grateful for what we have. His condition has made me vow to do everything I can for him and to share David's vision.

On the day that Daniel walks again, I will feel immensely proud to have contributed, like all the other chefs in this book, to that goal. We share a common optimism to see Daniel and others like him recover from their tragic experiences. Such a simple thing for us – such an amazing achievement for them. What a gift from the culinary world when we can say we were part of that dream.

The recipes in this book will provide you with a real insight into chefs' lives 'off duty' – what we cook and eat with our families and friends at home. I hope you will get as much pleasure out of cooking these recipes as we have had in helping David compile them.

Daniel, thank you for giving me the chance to be involved in this project and for allowing me to support you throughout your healing process.

**Gordon**

# one

# HERBERT BERGER

## 1 Lombard Street

Regarded as a master by many of his peers, Herbert Berger has presided over London's 1 Lombard Street since it opened in 1998, where he has become celebrated for his imaginative, skilful cooking. Throughout his career, he has been keen to pass on his knowledge not only to members of his own brigade but to schools, aspirant chefs and professional bodies. He has been a member of the Academy of Culinary Arts since 1986, and in 2003 was presented with the Maitrise Escoffier Medal by the Association Culinaire de France. He has been awarded a Michelin star for three of his establishments.

**What are your favourite foods/flavours?**
I love all game but grouse, pheasant and jugged hare are my favourites. Otherwise, truffles, wild mushrooms and wild strawberries from the Alps, foie gras, scallops, crab, lobster, bitter chocolate, coffee and all artisan cheeses. My favourite cheeses are Vacherin, Comté and Cheddar from the Isle of Mull (very peaty), and I am also partial to Quargel and Bierkaese from back home in Austria. I would die for a great roast rib of beef with lots of marbling and I like suckling pig with caraway, coriander and sauerkraut. I really like everything fresh – superb produce simply cooked. I like all stews and braised dishes, from Irish stew to cassoulet, blanquette, oxtail and goulash. Cooking a joint of meat or fish outside over an open fire and baking potatoes in the hot ashes (without foil) is so simple but the taste is amazing. Flavours need to be clean and clear. I like all oriental and other spice and flavour influences from around the world.

**What are your favourite utensils?**
A non-stick pan and induction cookers.

**What is your most useful piece of kitchen equipment and design?**
The stove, work surface and flow and, of course, the ventilation.

**What is your favourite season?**
Autumn.

**What is your favourite meal?**
A full English fry-up (eggs, bacon, sausages), including kippers; otherwise a long, civilized lunch.

**How do you decide what to cook?**
The mood, the seasons, the market, travel and talking about great meals and places.

**What inspires you?**
Fresh, full-of-taste and cared-for produce.

**What is your favourite drink?**
Great red wines – it is a fantastic experience from buying to getting it from the cellar, planning the dinner, decanting it, putting your nose to it, tasting and drinking it and enjoying all the wonderful flavours and aromas.

**What are your likes and dislikes?**
I like perfection in simplicity. I hate all products of intensive farming. My pet hates are lollo rosso and cheap table salt.

**How can you inspire others to enjoy great food and cooking?**
By introducing them to real food and flavours and the benefits one gets from it.

**How did you become a chef?**
I grew up on a little farm in the Austrian mountains, where everything we ate was fresh and home grown or from the rivers, forests and land. For winter my parents did lots of preserving. I wanted to be a

cook when I was nine and it was also very fashionable then in the late Sixties.

**What are your top ten ingredients?**
Maldon salt, great oils and vinegars, fresh herbs and spices, wine, butter, cream, eggs, onions, garlic.

**What are your kitchen secrets?**
I keep no secrets. When I pass on a good idea, another one develops in my head.

**What are your top tips?**
If you use alcohol or wine in cooking, it must be very good quality – it is just like any other ingredient.

**Do you have any favourite junk food?**
A great shish or doner kebab in pitta bread.

**How do you feel about cooking for children?**
Frustrated and angry. They are spoilt, misguided by the environment they are in, TV and food ads, and they are missing out in a very big way, which could be damaging to their health in the future. I try my best to coax my daughter and others to learn about and eat real food; some of it will stick.

**Can you give one piece of advice for the domestic cook?**
Keep it simple, buy the best, do only a few things at a time, but do them well. Enjoy it. When you get frustrated and stressed, you do not cook well.

* Salad of Artichokes, French Beans and Wild Mushrooms with Pumpkinseed Oil and Balsamic Vinaigrette
* Poached Fillet of New-season Lamb with Summer Vegetables and Minted Broth
* Warm Strawberries in Sauternes with Black Pepper

## Salad of Artichokes, French Beans and Wild Mushrooms with Pumpkinseed Oil and Balsamic Vinaigrette

**Apart from tasting wonderful, the pumpkinseed oil has many medicinal qualities and is especially good for men's health.**

**Serves 4**

**250g (9oz) extra-fine French beans**
**150g (5oz) wild mushrooms, such as ceps (porcini), girolles, morels, mousserons, pieds de mouton**
**1 tablespoon corn oil**
**50g (2oz) shallots, finely chopped**
**4 large cooked artichoke bottoms, cut into thin wedges**
**175ml (3/4 cup) pumpkinseed oil**
**2 tablespoons mature balsamic vinegar**
**Maldon sea salt and freshly ground black pepper**

**To garnish:**
**sprigs of chervil**
**fried artichoke crisps (chips), optional**

Cook the French beans in heavily salted boiling water until tender, then drain, refresh in iced water and drain again. Split each bean lengthways in half by pulling it apart.

Sauté the mushrooms quickly in the corn oil until tender, then season with salt and pepper. Mix the beans, mushrooms, shallots and sliced artichokes together but keep some nice artichoke wedges aside for garnish.

Make the vinaigrette by whisking the pumpkinseed oil and balsamic vinegar together with a little salt and pepper, then dress the salad with just enough vinaigrette to coat. Adjust the seasoning and arrange the salad on a plate, surrounded by the reserved artichoke wedges. Dress with a little more vinaigrette and garnish with chervil and fried artichoke crisps, if using. It is best served while the mushrooms are still slightly warm.

**Opposite: Poached Fillet of New-season Lamb with Summer Vegetables and Minted Broth**

# Poached Fillet of New-season Lamb with Summer Vegetables and Minted Broth

**Serves 4**

**1 pair of best ends of lamb – ask your butcher to remove the fillets (tenderloins) and trim them; keep all the trimmings and bones, but not the fat, for the stock**
**16 asparagus spears, trimmed**
**50g (1/3 cup) shelled broad (fava) beans**
**50g (1/3 cup) shelled peas**
**12 baby turnips, trimmed**
**12 baby carrots, trimmed**
**8 baby leeks, trimmed**
**12 small Jersey Royal (or other new) potatoes, scrubbed**
**12 button (pearl) onions, peeled**
**50g (2oz) girolle mushrooms, trimmed**
**salt and freshly ground black pepper**

**For the lamb stock:**

**the bones and trimmings from the lamb**
**1 tablespoon oil**
**2 litres (2 quarts) water**
**200ml (7oz) white wine**
**a bouquet garni, made up of 2 parsley stalks, 1 bay leaf, a sprig each of thyme and rosemary and 5 white peppercorns, all enclosed in 2 pieces of celery and tied with string**
**1 small onion, cut into quarters**
**1/2 small carrot, chopped**
**1 garlic clove, bashed with the side of a knife**

**For the mint oil:**

**6 tablespoons mild virgin olive oil**
**a small bunch of mint**

First prepare the lamb stock. Season the lamb bones and trimmings lightly with salt and pepper. Heat the oil in a heavy roasting tin (pan), add the bones and trimmings and cook until beginning to colour. Then transfer to an oven preheated to 200°C/400°F/Gas Mark 6 and roast until golden brown. Drain off the fat and transfer the bones and trimmings to a small stockpot. Put the roasting tin on the hob (stovetop), pour in a few tablespoons of water and stir over a medium heat to deglaze the tin. Add these juices to the bones. Pour in the water and wine and add the bouquet garni, onion, carrot and garlic. Bring to the boil, skim any scum from the top, then reduce the heat and simmer gently for 3–4 hours, letting it reduce to about 1 litre (1 quart). Adjust the seasoning and strain through a piece of muslin (cheesecloth) or a very fine sieve.

For the mint oil, blend the oil and mint together in a food processor. Let it infuse for about 30 minutes, then pass through a fine sieve and set aside.

Put one-third of the stock in a pan and bring to the boil. Cook all the summer vegetables separately in it until just tender (this can be done well in advance).

To finish the dish, season the lamb fillets with salt and pepper. Put the remaining stock in a pan just big enough to hold the fillets and bring to the boil. Add the fillets (they must be covered by the stock) and simmer gently for 6–8 minutes (do not allow the stock to boil); the lamb should be pink in the centre. Take out of the pan and leave to rest in a warm place for 5–10 minutes. Meanwhile, reheat the summer vegetables in the stock in which they were cooked, if necessary.

To serve, cut the lamb into 4 portions and place in the middle of 4 deep plates. Arrange the vegetables around the meat and then flood the plates with the stock in which the lamb and vegetables were cooked. Drop a few pearls of the mint oil into the stock.

# Warm Strawberries in Sauternes with Black Pepper

**This is a simple and fantastic way of serving strawberries and very easy to prepare.**

**Serves 4**

**2 glasses of Sauternes or other good sweet white wine**
**4 pinches of cracked black pepper**
**600g ($1^1/_4$lb) strawberries**

To serve (optional):
**vanilla ice cream**
**double (heavy) cream, lightly whipped and flavoured with vanilla extract and a touch of sugar**

Warm the Sauternes and black pepper together in a pan and leave to infuse for about 5 minutes. Drop in the strawberries and bring to the boil, but do not overcook. The strawberries should still be quite firm and almost cold in the middle.

Serve the strawberries immediately, just as they are or with ice cream or lightly whipped cream flavoured with vanilla – or both. Shortbread is also very good with this dish.

# two

# VINEET BHATIA

## Rasoi Vineet Bhatia

**Vineet Bhatia arrived in the UK from the Oberoi Hotel (India) in 1993 and quickly became disillusioned with the state of Indian cookery in the country. He set his sights on improving the quality of his national cuisine, and in 2001 was rewarded with a Michelin star – the first Indian chef ever to have received this prestigious award. He opened his own restaurant, Rasoi Vineet Bhatia, in London in 2004. As a consultant, he advises British Airways in-flight (First and Business Class), Safran restaurant at Le Touessrok Hotel in Mauritius, Indego restaurant at the Grosvenor House Hotel in Dubai, and Agni restaurant in Moscow.**

**What are your favourite foods/tastes/flavours?**
I like my food to be in small portions but bursting with intense, well-balanced flavours.

**What are your favourite utensils?**
Something simple to use – for instance a non-stick pan works wonders for me.

**What is your most useful piece of kitchen equipment?**
The tandoor. It is such a simple piece of equipment, yet it can be notoriously hard to handle if you get the basics wrong. It is one magical clay pot, capable of dishing out a variety of healthy foods.

**What is your favourite season?**
Winter – not just for the variety of ingredients but for the feeling of cuddling up and wanting to eat all this food over a mug of hot chocolate.

**What is your favourite meal?**
A relaxed dinner of simple, home-cooked food eaten with my wife and kids.

**How do you decide what to cook?**
I go with the flow of my thoughts.

**What inspires you?**
A variety of things – the weather, my mood, a visual of a dish in a magazine, plates ...

**What is your favourite drink?**
Fresh mint tea.

**What are your likes and dislikes?**
I like to read about restaurants and their history. I dislike arrogance and rude behaviour.

**How can you inspire others to enjoy great food and cooking?**
By showing them that great food doesn't have to be complicated and layered but a simple, correctly spiced and balanced dish.

**How did you become a chef?**
As a failed pilot, really. When I couldn't make it as a pilot, I went for my second choice!

**What are your top ten ingredients?**
My spice box, oil (sunflower and olive), yoghurt, onions, tomatoes, ginger, garlic, fish, chicken and rice.

**What are your kitchen secrets?**
Well, if I tell them, they won't be secrets any more!

**What are your top tips?**
Keep it simple.

**Do you have any favourite junk food?**
Fish and chips.

**How do you feel about cooking for children?**
It's a real pleasure. I am so fortunate to be able to cook for my boys, though I must admit that they are my most difficult customers.

**Can you give one piece of advice for the domestic cook?**
Keep it simple, approach with confidence and then build on that to explore new cuisines and tastes.

BOROUGH OF CHELSEA
LINCOLN STREET
S.W. 3
YAMAHA
SHOEI

**✱ Quails with Tamarind Glaze**
**✱ Lobster Khichdi**
**✱ Kesari Ananas (Tandoori Saffron Pineapple)**

# Quails with Tamarind Glaze

**Serves 4**

**1 tablespoon royal cumin seeds, or ordinary cumin seeds, roasted in a dry frying pan (skillet) and crushed**
**50ml (3½ tablespoons) vegetable oil**
**8 quails, skinned**
**salad leaves, to garnish**

For the tamarind glaze:
**100g (3½oz) tamarind paste**
**250g (9oz) jaggery**
**3½ tablespoons coriander seeds**
**2 teaspoons cumin seeds**
**2 teaspoons fennel seeds**
**2 teaspoons green cardamom pods**
**1cm (½-inch) piece of fresh ginger, roughly chopped**
**1 green chilli, roughly chopped**
**1 teaspoon red chilli powder**
**½ teaspoon chaat masala**
**½ teaspoon ginger powder**

First make the tamarind glaze. Place all the ingredients except the chaat masala and ginger powder in a deep pan. Add 750ml (3⅓) cups water, bring to the boil and boil for 30 minutes or until reduced by half, stirring very frequently. Strain immediately to remove all the spices, then stir in the chaat masala and ginger powder. Leave to cool; if not using straight away, it will keep in the fridge for a month.

Pour the tamarind glaze into a large bowl and add the crushed cumin seeds and oil. Whisk together, then add the quails. Leave to marinate for 6 hours.

Cook the quails on a barbecue or a ridged griddle pan for about 4 minutes on each side, basting with the marinade as you cook. Serve garnished with a few salad leaves.

# Lobster Khichdi

**Serves 4**

**2 live lobsters**
**a sprig of curry leaves**
**2.5cm (1-inch) piece of fresh ginger, finely shredded**
**1 tablespoon chilli and garlic paste**
**a little vegetable oil**
**30g (2 tablespoons) butter**
**salt**

For the broccoli chips (optional):

**3 broccoli florets, very finely sliced**
**chaat masala**

For the lobster jus:

**20ml (4 teaspoons) vegetable oil**
**1 tablespoon mustard seeds**
**1 fresh red chilli**
**1 teaspoon black peppercorns**
**1 garlic clove, coarsely chopped**
**2.5cm (1-inch) piece of fresh ginger, coarsely chopped**
**1 green chilli, coarsely chopped**
**2 shallots, sliced**
**the shells from the lobsters, except the tail shells**
**1 teaspoon ground turmeric**
**1 teaspoon red chilli powder (cayenne pepper)**
**2 tomatoes, coarsely chopped**
**400ml ($1^3/_4$ cups) water**
**4 tablespoons double (heavy) cream**
**20g (4 teaspoons) butter**

For the broccoli rice:

**$^1/_2$ head of broccoli**
**2 tablespoons vegetable oil**
**40g ($2^2/_3$ tablespoons) butter**
**1 tablespoon mustard seeds**
**1.5cm ($^3/_4$-inch) piece of fresh ginger, chopped**
**1 garlic clove, chopped**
**2 green chillies, finely chopped**
**a sprig of curry leaves**
**2 shallots, sliced**
**160g (heaped $^3/_4$ cup) basmati rice**
**400ml ($1^3/_4$ cups) lobster or shellfish stock**
**2 tablespoons chopped coriander (cilantro)**
**20g (4 teaspoons) butter**

If you are making the broccoli chips, spread the finely sliced broccoli florets out on a baking sheet and sprinkle with chaat masala. Put in a very low oven until dried out, then set aside. Put the lobsters in a large pan of boiling water for about 15 seconds, then drain: this is in order to kill them instantly, not to cook them. Remove the meat from the claws and set aside. Cut each lobster tail in half lengthways and loosen the meat from the tail. Place the curry leaves and shredded ginger in the shell, then return the meat to the shell.

Rub the lobster meat with salt and the chilli and garlic paste. Heat a little oil in an ovenproof frying pan (skillet), add the lobster tails, flesh-side down, and the lobster claw meat and leave until lightly coloured. Put the butter on top of the lobster and place the pan in an oven preheated to 190°C/375°F/Gas Mark 5 for 7–8 minutes to finish cooking the lobster. Remove from the heat and set aside.

For the lobster jus, heat the oil in a deep pan and add the mustard seeds. When they crackle, add the whole red chilli, black peppercorns, garlic, ginger, green chilli and shallots. Cook for 2 minutes, then add the lobster shells. Sauté for 3 minutes, stirring constantly and making sure the shallots don't colour. Add the turmeric and chilli powder, cook for a minute, then add the chopped tomatoes and the water. Bring to the boil and simmer for 15 minutes. Strain the stock into a clean pan and boil until reduced by half. Add the double cream and butter and whiz with a hand blender. Keep warm.

To make the broccoli rice, cook the broccoli in boiling salted water until tender, then drain thoroughly. Whiz to a smooth purée in a food processor and set aside. Heat the oil and butter in a heavy-based pan and add the mustard seeds. When they crackle, add the ginger, garlic, green chillies and curry leaves. Sauté for 2 minutes, then add the shallots. Stir in the rice and sauté for 2 minutes, then add the stock, bring to the boil and simmer for 5 minutes. Add the broccoli purée and cook, uncovered, until the rice is tender and the liquid has been absorbed. Stir in the lobster claw meat, chopped coriander and butter, then season with salt.

To serve, put the rice in the centre of 4 large soup places and pour the lobster jus around. Place the halved lobster tails on top of the rice and garnish with the broccoli chips, if using.

# Kesari Ananas (Tandoori Saffron Pineapple)

**Serves 4**

**$^{1}/_{2}$ small pineapple, peeled, cored and cut into 4cm ($1^{3}/_{4}$-inch) cubes**
**mango ice cream, to serve**

For the marinade:
**25g (2 tablespoons) pure ghee**
**25g (2 tablespoons) gram flour (also called besan)**
**1 teaspoon fennel seeds**
**a large pinch of saffron strands, soaked in a little warm water to release its colour and flavour**
**125m ($^{1}/_{2}$ cup) milk**
**50g ($^{1}/_{4}$ cup) granulated sugar**
**$^{1}/_{2}$ teaspoon ground cardamom**

For the pineapple halwa:
**2 tablespoons semolina**
**25g (2 tablespoons) ghee**
**250ml (9 oz) pineapple juice, warmed**
**30g ($2^{1}/_{2}$ tablespoons) granulated sugar**

For the marinade, heat the ghee in a small pan, stir in the gram flour and cook, stirring, for a few minutes to make a light golden roux. Add the fennel seeds and saffron water, stir vigorously, then add the milk. Remove from the heat and stir well to prevent lumps. Add the sugar and ground cardamom. Place the pineapple cubes in the marinade and leave for 2 hours.

Meanwhile, make the pineapple halwa. Dry-roast the semolina in a pan over a moderate heat until it is very lightly coloured and has a nutty aroma. Stir in the ghee and cook for 2 minutes. Add the warm pineapple juice and cook until it has been absorbed by the semolina, then stir in the sugar. Cook, stirring, until the halwa has thickened enough to leave the sides of the pan.

Remove the pineapple cubes from the marinade and thread on to 4 skewers. Cook under a very hot grill (broiler) or on a barbecue – we use a tandoor oven at the restaurant – turning until lightly charred.

Shape the warm halwa into quenelles and divide between 4 serving plates. Place the cooked pineapple cubes around the halwa, or simply place the skewers on the plate, if you prefer. Serve with mango ice cream.

**Opposite: Lobster Khichdi**

# three

# RAYMOND BLANC

## Le Manoir aux Quat' Saisons

Raymond Blanc is acknowledged as one of the finest chefs in the world. His hotel and restaurant, Le Manoir aux Quat' Saisons, is the only country-house hotel in the UK to have achieved two Michelin stars for a total of 21 years. He also co-owns five successful Le Petit Blanc brasseries and a cookery school, L'Ecole de Cuisine. He has written numerous bestselling cookery books and regularly appears on television and radio.

**What are your favourite foods/flavours?**
As a good Frenchman, I was taught to eat everything, so I did and still do! Although the basis of my cuisine is French, I use lots of flavours and textures from other countries.

**What are your favourite utensils?**
I am particularly fond of my black granite pestle and mortar and a very old filleting knife; both of them are twenty-five years old.

**What is your most useful piece of kitchen design and equipment?**
The *plancha* very much fits the principles of modern cuisine. I find that thermo circulators are excellent to cook with and control the temperature.

**What is your favourite season?**
The best moment of any season is when one finishes and the other begins, offering choices from both.

**What is your favourite mealtime?**
Refer to the first question above! I love them all, but perhaps favour dinner, which I share with my family twice a week.

**How do you decide what to cook?**
The seasons have always played a vital role in what I cook. The organic vegetable and herb garden at Le Manoir aux Quat' Saisons plays an essential part in what I serve to my guests.

**What inspires you?**
Inspiration for most people comes in all sorts of guises – for example, the market, a conversation, something you read about, a new flavour, a new texture. But mostly inspiration comes from your ability to reinvent yourself at all times: opening your mind, constant searching and being curious are the motors of creativity.

**What is your favourite drink?**
*Café au lait* at breakfast time and, like every good Frenchman, a great glass of classic French wine with my dinner.

**What are your likes and dislikes?**
I dislike junk food, and pretentious food in pretentious surroundings with OTT waiters. I also dislike food that is heavy and leaves you ready to fall off your chair with a *crise de foie*!
I like meeting my friends and loved ones around the table to eat either a simple dish or the most elaborate gastronomic feast, as long as both follow a criterion of good-quality ingredients.

**How can you inspire others to enjoy great food and cooking?**
All my professional life I have shared all of my knowledge with anyone who would listen, whether it be a commis, an apprentice, a great chef, a waiter or a guest.

**How did you become a chef?**
I am totally self-taught; I never had one single hour of tuition or a mentor.

**What are your top ten ingredients?**
The best chocolate, with a minimum of 70 per cent cocoa solids, Tahitian vanilla, organic eggs that create all sorts of miracles, any poultry from Bresse (they look like over-decorated generals!), lemongrass, the last of the summer vegetables, the first winter black truffle

mixed with the humble leek, a whole grilled wild baby turbot, Angus beef and a great sourdough loaf.

**What are your kitchen secrets?**

- Each dish has a secret of its own – for example, with a crème brûlée you can achieve the same richness if you replace double cream with milk. The secret will be in the cooking, when the egg yolk barely coagulates, giving that illusion of richness, yet the crème will melt like snowflakes in your mouth. Understanding what is happening in the pan (the secrets) will help you become a better cook and a better teacher.
- Don't cook when you have just had a row with your girlfriend or wife!
- Talent is never enough for complete success. You need practice and more practice, which will take you a long way towards success.

**What are your top tips?**

- 'Experience is what we call our mistakes.' Oscar Wilde.
- Honesty must come first in all that you do.
- Enjoy what you are doing.
- Always be curious and learn better ways.
- Once you know a technique, immediately share it with someone else. This will help to make you a better teacher and the other person will be richer.
- Have a deep knowledge of your ingredients: 'strawberries in winter have the taste of the graveyard.' Paul Bocuse.
- Sharp knives.

**Do you ever eat junk food?**

Without sounding virtuous, I do not juxtapose junk and food together. I will always prefer an omelette with a glass of red wine to a sandwich made with white sliced bread and processed ham. Occasionally I enjoy a pizza.

**How do you feel about cooking for children?**

Children are part of my French culture and we actively welcome them at Le Manoir. To achieve that, I had to fight against food and travel writers who could not associate children with gastronomy, and even harder with my general managers and maître d's, who were not prepared to welcome these 'little hooligans', and the chefs who did not want to cook real food for them. Seven per cent of our turnover is generated from families. If I didn't welcome them, I would be a bad businessman and failing my culture.

**Can you give one piece of advice for the domestic cook?**

Never cook a meal for your guests that you do not know intimately. On the other hand, practise on your long-suffering family, as they are more likely to forgive your mistakes.

* Fricassée of Cockles and Clams with Wakame Seaweed and Jerusalem Artichokes
* Roasted Duck Breasts with Butternut Squash, Braised Chestnuts and Plum Sauce
* Gâteau à la Crème Fraîche et au Sucre

# Fricassée of Cockles and Clams with Wakame Seaweed and Jerusalem Artichokes

**A healthy and delicious starter (appetizer), with great textures and flavours from the land and sea. Wakame seaweed is very nutritious. It can be obtained dried from good Asian supermarkets.**
**Fresh shellfish such as mussels, clams and cockles should be heavy with seawater and tightly closed. If any are open, give them a light tap, and if they do not close on their own accord, discard them.**

**Serves 4**

**1 small shallot, finely chopped**
**1 garlic clove, crushed**
**30g (2 tablespoons) unsalted butter**
**$3^1/_2$ tablespoons dry white wine**
**220g (8oz) fresh cockles, thoroughly cleaned**
**400g (14oz) fresh clams, thoroughly cleaned**
**50g (2oz) wakame seaweed, soaked for 10 minutes, then drained**
**a handful of flat-leaf parsley, roughly chopped**
**4 teaspoons lemon juice**

**For the Jerusalem artichokes:**
**450g (1lb) Jerusalem artichokes, peeled and sliced into quarters**
**500ml ($2^1/_4$ cups) water**
**30g (2 tablespoons) unsalted butter**
**a squeeze of lemon juice**
**5 pinches of sea salt**
**a pinch of freshly ground black pepper**

Put all the ingredients for the Jerusalem artichokes in a medium saucepan and bring to the boil. Reduce the heat and simmer (there should be bubbles just breaking the surface) for 10 minutes, until the artichokes are just cooked; they should be soft but still retain their texture.

While the artichokes are cooking, cook the shallot and crushed garlic in the butter in a medium saucepan over a medium heat for 2 minutes, until softened. Turn up the heat to full, add the white wine, cockles and clams and cover with a lid. Cook for 2–3 minutes, until the shells just open, then add the remaining ingredients and taste. Adjust the seasoning if required.

To serve, drain the Jerusalem artichokes and arrange them in the centre of 4 deep plates. Spoon the fricassée of cockles and clams around them.

**Variations**

You could replace the cockles or clams with fresh mussels. Clams or mussels cooked in this way would be delicious served in half their shell with a little garlic and parsley butter, sprinkled with breadcrumbs and toasted under a hot grill (broiler).

# Roasted Duck Breasts with Butternut Squash, Braised Chestnuts and Plum Sauce

**Fresh chestnuts are best for this dish, but peeling them at home can be tricky and time consuming. You can now buy vacuum-packed or frozen peeled chestnuts, which make a good alternative.**
**The sauce can be made 24 hours in advance; the chestnuts can be cooked 6 hours in advance and reheated.**

**Serves 4**

**4 organic or free-range duck breasts (half breasts) on the bone, weighing about 220g (8oz) each, skin scored**
**4 pinches of sea salt**
**a pinch of freshly ground black pepper**

For the plum sauce:

**300ml (1 1/4 cups) red wine, preferably Cabernet Sauvignon**
**1/2 cinnamon stick**
**1 slice of orange**
**1 bay leaf**
**75g (3oz) best-quality Agen prunes, pitted**
**2 teaspoons Demerara (light brown) sugar**
**120ml (1/2 cup) brown chicken stock**
**15g (1/2oz) raw duck foie gras, optional**
**3 pinches of sea salt**
**a pinch of freshly ground black pepper**

For the braised chestnuts:

**30g (2 tablespoons unsalted butter**
**1 celery stick, cut into slices 1cm (1/2 inch) thick**
**1 Braeburn apple, skin on, cored and cut into 2cm (3/4-inch) dice**
**200g (7oz) chestnuts, peeled**
**200ml (7oz) water or light chicken stock**
**3 pinches of sea salt**
**a pinch of freshly ground white pepper**
**4 pinches of caster (superfine) sugar**
**a squeeze of lemon juice**

For the roast butternut squash:

**1 tablespoon groundnut (peanut) oil, or other unscented oil**
**20g (4 teaspoons) unsalted butter**
**500g (18oz) butternut squash, peeled, deseeded and cut across into four 1.5cm (3/4-inch) slices**
**300g (10oz) parsnips, peeled and cut lengthways into quarters**
**4 pinches of sea salt**
**a pinch of freshly ground black pepper**

First make the sauce. Boil the red wine, cinnamon stick, orange slice and bay leaf together until the wine has reduced by half. Remove from the heat, add the prunes and leave to marinate for 2 hours. Remove the cinnamon, orange slice and bay leaf from the mixture. In a medium pan, soften the Demerara sugar on the stove, then add the reduced red wine, marinated prunes and the chicken stock and bring to the boil. Remove from the heat and blend for 1 minute in a liquidizer (blender). Add the raw foie gras, if using, and continue to blend for 30 seconds. Taste and correct the seasoning, if necessary, with the sea salt and black pepper.

For the braised chestnuts, melt the butter in a small saucepan on a medium heat and sweat the celery, apple and chestnuts in it for 4 minutes. Pour in the water or stock, bring to the boil and season with the salt, pepper, sugar and lemon juice. Cover with a lid and cook on a low heat (with bubbles just breaking the surface) for 20 minutes, until soft and melting.

Season the duck breasts with the salt and pepper. Place them skin-side down in a large frying pan (skillet) over a medium heat and cook for 10 minutes, pouring off the excess fat every 2 minutes, until the skin is golden brown and crisp. Turn the duck on to the flesh side and sear for 1 minute to lock the juices inside during cooking. Turn back on to the skin side and place in an oven preheated to 180°C/350°F/Gas Mark 4. Cook for 4 minutes, then remove from the oven and leave to rest for 4 minutes.

While the skin of the duck is rendering, cook the butternut squash. Heat the groundnut oil and butter in a large ovenproof frying pan on a medium heat, add the butternut squash slices and parsnips and season with the salt and pepper. Cook for 8 minutes on each side, until coloured, then transfer the pan to the oven to finish cooking for 4 minutes.

To serve, put a slice of butternut squash in the centre of each plate and top with the duck breasts. Rest the parsnips against the duck and scatter the chestnuts, apple and celery around the outside. Spoon the hot sauce generously around the plate.

## Gâteau à la Crème Fraîche et au Sucre

**This is a rich and immensely satisfying dessert that is well worth the effort; the proof is in the proving!**

**Serves 4**

**15g (1/2oz) fresh yeast**
**2 tablespoons warm water**
**2 large (extra-large) eggs**
**125g (1 stick) unsalted butter, melted and cooled**
**50g (4 tablespoons) caster (superfine) sugar**
**250g (1 3/4 cups) plain (all-purpose) flour**
**2 pinches of salt**
**1 egg yolk, lightly beaten, to glaze**

For the cream filling:

**3 egg yolks**
**30g (2 1/2 tablespoons) caster (superfine) sugar**
**grated zest of 1 lemon**
**130ml (1/2 cup) crème fraîche**
**10g (2 teaspoons) unsalted butter, cut into small pieces**
**20g (1 3/4 tablespoons) caster (superfine) sugar**

In a small bowl, mix the fresh yeast with the warm water. Place the eggs, melted butter, yeast mixture, sugar, flour and salt in an electric mixer and mix for 5 minutes on low speed. Increase the speed to medium and beat the mixture for 5 minutes. Transfer the dough to a large bowl and cover with cling film (plastic wrap). Leave to prove in a warm place for 2 hours (the temperature needs to be about 30°C/86°F; an airing cupboard is ideal).

Lightly flour a work surface and your hands. Bring the dough together with the palms of your hands to form a ball, flatten it slightly and, with a rolling pin, roll it out into a 30cm (12-inch) circle. Fold the dough over the rolling pin and gently place it on a 30 x 42cm (12- x 17-inch) baking tray. Fold the edge of the dough in on itself and press down to seal, creating a 3cm (1 1/4-inch) rim (be sure to create a tight seal or, as the gâteau cooks in the oven, it may unfold). Be careful not to stretch the dough. Leave in a warm place for 45 minutes.

Meanwhile, make the filling. In a large mixing bowl, mix the egg yolks, 10g (1 tablespoon) of the sugar and the lemon zest together, then gradually mix in the cream. Set aside.

Brush the rim of the dough with the egg yolk and prick the base evenly with a fork to help it rise and cook evenly. Pour the cream mixture over the dough and sprinkle with half the remaining sugar and the diced butter. Place in an oven preheated to 190°C/375°F/Gas Mark 5 and bake for 20–25 minutes.

To serve, remove from the oven and sprinkle the remaining sugar on top.

four

# HESTON BLUMENTHAL

## Fat Duck

Heston Blumenthal has been described as a culinary alchemist for his innovative style of cuisine. His work researches the molecular compounds of dishes to enable a greater understanding of flavour. This original and scientific approach has teamed him with fellow chefs, scientists and psychologists throughout the world. His restaurant, the Fat Duck, in Bray, Berkshire, opened in 1995 and was awarded its third Michelin star in 2004. Heston Blumenthal is currently working with the effects that sound creates on the texture of food and on the palate.

**What are your favourite foods/tastes/flavours?**

I find this really difficult to answer as I am discovering new foods/tastes and flavour combinations all the time. Some of the flavours that rekindle childhood memories certainly have as strong an effect on me as anything else.

**What are your favourite utensils?**

My knives.

**What is your most useful piece of kitchen equipment?**

A great team, motivated, enthusiastic and eager to ask questions.

**What is your favourite season?**

Winter.

**What is your favourite mealtime?**

For me, Sunday lunch is the most important meal of the week. It is the one time that we are guaranteed to spend together around the table. My wife cooks the most delicious lunch and the kids provide the best entertainment. I often get told off for calling it Sunday lunch when, due to my job, we do not actually eat until about 7. It should therefore be called Sunday dinner!

**How do you decide what to cook?**

This decision can come from all angles. Often though, it is an ingredient of such beautiful quality that I need look no further for inspiration.

**What inspires you?**

Learning something new or finding an ingredient of outstanding quality. This knowledge can be anything from the way we register flavour to something pulled from the gastronomic archives.

**What is your favourite drink?**

Tea.

**What are your likes and dislikes?**

I dislike not having a 48-hour day and I like spending time with my family.

**How can you inspire others to enjoy great food and cooking?**

I can only hope by my enthusiasm, energy, and also by passing on my experiences, especially to my children.

**How and why did you become a chef?**

During my first trip to France as a teenager on a family holiday, some twenty years ago, I was exposed to gastronomy in Provence, at l'Oustau de Baumanière.

**What are your top ten ingredients?**

This list changes daily. We are currently working on new dishes, and the discovery of new ingredients and how we can combine them is fascinating. I am a firm believer in context, though. Muscadet tastes better in the Loire Valley with fresh oysters; butterscotch Angel Delight tasted incredible when I was about eight years old; and spit-roast chicken seemed fit for a king at a family picnic.

**What are your kitchen secrets?**
That would be telling!

**What are your top tips?**
Always use an oven thermometer, especially in a domestic oven.

**Do you ever eat junk food?**
I am not sure what exactly constitutes junk food but I do like tomato ketchup (catsup) from a certain producer.

**How do you feel about cooking for children?**
It can be one of the most rewarding experiences, not only for the enjoyment but because we have a duty, especially as parents, to introduce our children to as many flavours as possible. I feel so passionate about it that I wrote an entire book on the subject!

**Can you give one piece of advice for the domestic cook?**
This might seem like a simple piece of advice but it is essential to take some time to read and visualize a recipe thoroughly before you start cooking. This way, the chances of things going wrong are significantly reduced.

* Pea and Ham Soup
* Oxtail and Kidney Pudding
* Trifle

## Pea and Ham Soup

**Serves 6**

**50g ($3^1/_2$ tablespoons) butter**
**200g (2 cups) shallots, sliced**
**75g (3oz) pancetta, chopped**
**1 garlic clove, crushed**
**500g ($3^1/_3$ cups) frozen peas, defrosted**
**salt and freshly ground black pepper**

For the ham hock stock:

**1 small onion, cut in half**
**1 large carrot, cut in half**
**1 celery stick, cut in half**
**1 large leek (white part only), cut in half**
**1 garlic clove, crushed**
**1 bay leaf**
**4–6 sprigs of thyme**
**4 black peppercorns**
**1 ham hock**
**2 litres (2 quarts) water**

To garnish:

**2 smoked bacon rashers (slices), cut into 1cm ($^1/_2$-inch) dice**
**180g ($1^1/_4$ cups) frozen peas**

Combine all the ingredients for the ham hock stock in a large, heavy-based pan and bring to the boil over a medium heat. Skim any scum from the surface, reduce the heat and simmer gently for $2^1/_2$ hours, until the ham hock is cooked. Remove from the heat and leave to cool, then strain through a fine sieve, reserving the ham hock. Set aside.

To make the soup, heat the butter in a large pan, add the shallots, pancetta and garlic and sweat for 10–15 minutes, until the shallots are tender. Add the ham stock, bring to the boil and skim any scum from the top. Add the peas and return to the boil, then purée in a liquidizer (blender). Pass through a fine sieve into a clean pan, bring to the boil and correct the seasoning.

Shortly before serving, fry the diced smoked bacon in a hot pan until crisp. Flake the meat from the reserved ham hock. Cook the peas in boiling salted water until tender, then drain. Divide the peas and ham between 6 soup bowls, pour the soup on top, then scatter over the bacon and drizzle over a little of the rendered bacon fat.

**Opposite: Oxtail and Kidney Pudding**

# Oxtail and Kidney Pudding

**Serves 6**

**2.5kg (5$^1/_2$-lb) oxtail**
**flour for dusting**
**150g ($^3/_4$ cup) dripping or lard**
**100ml (7 tablespoons) brandy**
**250ml (1 cup) red wine**
**175g (1$^3/_4$ cups) leeks, sliced**
**75g celery ($^2/_3$ cup), sliced**
**175g carrots (generous 1 cup), sliced**
**300g (3 cups) onions, sliced**
**$^1/_2$ star anise**
**200g (2$^3/_4$ cups) mushrooms, sliced**
**4 tablespoons olive oil**
**a little caster (superfine) sugar**
**250g (9oz) tomatoes, halved**
**1 bay leaf**
**6 sprigs of thyme**
**8 black peppercorns**
**1 litre (1 quart) beef stock**
**1 litre (1 quart) chicken stock**
**salt and freshly ground black pepper**

For the kidneys:

**2 ox kidneys**
**2 sprigs of thyme**
**2 black peppercorns**
**1 bay leaf**

For the suet pastry:

**1kg (heaped 7 cups) self-raising (self-rising) flour**
**15g (1 tablespoon) salt**
**500g (18oz) suet**
**600ml (2$^1/_2$ cups) water**
**1 egg, lightly beaten, to glaze**

Season the oxtail with salt and pepper and dust with flour. Heat half the dripping or lard in a large frying pan (skillet), add the oxtail and cook until well browned all over (you will probably have to do this in batches). Remove from the pan, pour in the brandy and red wine and bring to the boil, stirring to deglaze the pan. Remove from the heat and set aside.

Heat the remaining dripping or lard in a large pan, add the leeks, celery and carrots and fry until well coloured. Remove from the pan with a slotted spoon and set aside. Add the onions and star anise to the pan and fry until tender and almost caramelized, then remove and set aside. Finally, add the mushrooms and fry until well coloured. Set aside with the other vegetables.

Heat the oil and a sprinkling of sugar in a large frying pan over a fairly high heat, then add the tomatoes, cut-side down, and cook until caramelized. Deglaze with a splash of water and remove from the heat.

Put the oxtail, vegetables and tomatoes in a large casserole, add the bay leaf, thyme, peppercorns and beef and chicken stocks and bring to the boil. Cover the pan and transfer to an oven preheated to 160°C/325°F/Gas Mark 3. Bake for 4 hours, until the oxtail is very tender. Leave to cool, then strain the mixture, reserving the sauce. Pick the meat off the bones in as large pieces as possible and set aside.

Trim the ox kidneys and remove any sinew. Place in a pan with enough cold water to cover and bring to the boil. Drain and refresh in cold water, then return to the pan with the thyme sprigs, peppercorns and bay leaf. Cover with cold water again, bring to the boil and simmer for about 2 hours, until tender. Leave to cool, then drain and dice the kidneys.

To make the suet pastry, sift the flour and salt into a bowl and stir in the suet. Add the water a little at a time until the dough comes together; do not overwork the dough. Cover and leave to rest for at least 20 minutes.

To assemble the puddings, take six 300ml (1$^1/_4$-cup) pudding basins (ovenproof bowls), or use one 1.7 litre (3$^3/_4$-cup) basin, and butter them 3 times, freezing them briefly each time. Divide the pastry into 6 balls and roll out each one into a circle 5mm ($^1/_4$ inch) thick. Cut away a quarter wedge from each circle to use for the lid, then use the rest of the pastry to line the pudding basins. Roll out the pastry for the lids to the same thickness. Put the cooked oxtail and kidney in the basins, then fill them up with the reserved sauce, so it comes just below the rim. Brush the lip of the pastry with the beaten egg, then place the lids on top and seal. Double wrap each basin in cling film (plastic wrap) and steam for 2 hours. Let them rest overnight, then reheat in a steamer before serving.

# Trifle

**Serves 6**

**12 sponge fingers (ladyfingers)**
**360g (generous 1 cup) redcurrant jelly**
**30g (2 tablespoons) amaretti biscuits, crushed**

For the custard:

**110g (1/2 cup) caster (superfine) sugar**
**6 egg yolks**
**375ml (1 1/2 cups plus 2 tablespoons) double (heavy) cream**
**375ml (1 1/2 cups plus 2 tablespoons) whole milk**
**1 vanilla pod (vanilla bean), split lengthways in half**

For the syllabub:

**zest of 1/2 lemon**
**55g (1/4 cup) caster (superfine) sugar**
**125ml (1/2 cup) (hard) cider**
**1 tablespoon brandy**
**1 tablespoon Bristol Cream sherry**
**360ml (1 1/2 cups) double (heavy) cream**
**5 1/2 tablespoons Amontillado sherry**

For the green tea mix:

**1 teaspoon green tea, or 1 tea bag**
**3 1/2 tablespoons Amontillado sherry**
**10g (2 teaspoons) caster (superfine) sugar**
**1 teaspoon lime juice**

First make the custard. Beat the sugar and egg yolks together in a large bowl. Heat the cream, milk and vanilla pod together until they just start to boil. Remove from the heat and pour gently over the egg yolk mixture, whisking constantly. Pour back into the pan and cook, stirring constantly with a wooden spoon, until the custard is thick enough to coat the back of the spoon. Do not let it boil. Pour through a fine sieve into a bowl and place this bowl in a large bowl of ice so the custard cools down quickly. Stir frequently as it cools, so it doesn't form a skin.

To make the syllabub, mix together the lemon zest, sugar, cider, brandy and Bristol Cream sherry and leave to macerate for 30 minutes. Strain through a fine sieve into a large bowl. Add the double cream and Amontillado sherry and whip together until the mixture just holds its shape, being careful not to overwhip it.

For the green tea mixture, let the green tea infuse in a cup of boiling water for 5 minutes, then strain. Pour 3 1/2 tablespoons of the green tea into a bowl and mix in the sherry, sugar and lime juice.

To assemble the trifle, soak the sponge fingers in the green tea mixture, then place them in 6 individual glass bowls or one large one. Spread the redcurrant jelly over the soaked sponge fingers, then pour the custard on top and chill until set. Place the syllabub on top of the set custard. Sprinkle over the crushed amaretti biscuits and serve immediately.

# five

# DANIEL BOULUD

**Daniel**

Daniel Boulud was raised on his family's farm near Lyons, surrounded by the wonders of produce fresh from the fields and his grandmother's inspiring home cooking. He trained under some of France's most respected chefs, including Roger Vergé, Georges Blanc and Michel Guérard, and eventually moved to the United States in 1981. As chef of Le Cirque, Boulud made it one of the United States' most acclaimed restaurants. In 1993 he opened Daniel, a world-class restaurant frequently honoured for its contemporary, seasonal French cuisine.

**What are your favourite foods/tastes/flavours?**
Potatoes.
Great charcuterie.

**What is/are your favourite utensil/s?**
Mortar and pestle.

**What is the most essential piece of kitchen design and equipment?**
Kitchen lighting is so important and so often ignored. It should be designed to cover the practical needs of your work spaces but also be gentle in its aesthetic and comfort level.

**What is your favourite season?**
Every season for a different reason.

**What is your favourite breakfast/lunch/tea/dinner?**
Breakfast: granola.
Lunch: a great salad and fresh fish.
Dinner: the sky's the limit.

**How do you decide what to cook?**
Every dish starts with the season and the best possible ingredients available in that time and place.

**What inspires you?**
Cooking for people who love great food. I love to be moved by them to push the outer limits and take their senses to a level they never expected to reach. Yet at other times simply making people happy and comfortable in the restaurant is more than enough inspiration.

**Is it people, places, books, tastes?**
Great art, great music, great personalities, generous spirits.

**What is your favourite drink?**
Rhône wine.

**What are your likes and dislikes?**
I hate bananas.

**How can you inspire others to enjoy great food and cooking?**
Enjoy good food with some one you love and who shares your love of good things.

**How did you become a chef?**
By learning from great mentors and then passing their lessons and inspiration along to the talented young cooks I work with today.

**How do you feel about cooking for kids?**
It's so important to introduce them to and inspire them with good, healthy, fresh foods at an early age. Cooking with them is a great way to sensitise them to nutrition and fresh food.

**Can you give one piece of advice for the domestic cook?**
Work with what you find in season locally.

* Artichoke and Radicchio Clafoutis
* Lamb Stew with Rosemary and Orange
* Ruby Grapefruit and Pomegranate Sabayon

# Artichoke and Radicchio Clafoutis

**Serves 6**

**2 medium (large) eggs, at room temperature**
**3 medium (large) egg whites, at room temperature**
**4 teaspoons sugar**
**125ml (1/2 cup) double (heavy) cream**
**1 firmly packed teaspoon fresh yeast**
**35g (1/4 cup) plain (all-purpose) flour**
**7 tablespoons extra virgin olive oil**
**juice of 2 lemons**
**20 baby artichokes**
**50g (2oz) pancetta or bacon, cut into 5mm dice (optional)**
**8 mushrooms, cut into slices 5mm (1/4-inch) thick**
**1 large shallot, finely diced**
**50g (2oz) rocket (arugula)**
**1 small head of radicchio, about 350g (12oz), trimmed and leaves separated**
**salt and freshly ground black pepper**

In a bowl, whisk together the eggs, egg whites and sugar, then set aside. Gently heat the cream in a saucepan until it is barely warm. Remove from the heat and add the yeast, stirring until smooth. Stir the cream into the egg mixture and whisk in the flour, followed by 2 tablespoons of the olive oil. Cover with cling film (plastic wrap) and chill for 1 hour.

Combine the juice of 1 lemon with 500ml (2 cups) water in a large bowl. Trim the artichoke stems and snap off the outer leaves until the remaining leaves are half yellow and half green. Cut off the remaining green parts and discard. Slice the artichokes lengthways in half and drop into the lemon water.

Warm 1 tablespoon of the oil in a medium frying pan (skillet) over a high heat. When the pan is hot but not smoking, add the pancetta, if using, and cook, stirring frequently, for 1 minute. Drain the artichokes and add them to the pan with the juice of 1/2 lemon. Reduce the heat to medium and season with salt and pepper. Cover and cook, stirring occasionally, for 10–12 minutes until the artichokes are tender. Transfer to a plate.

Add 1 tablespoon of olive oil to the pan, then add the mushrooms and shallot and season with salt and pepper. Cook for 3 minutes, tossing frequently. Add the rocket and a quarter of the radicchio leaves, season again and cook, tossing constantly, for about 2 minutes, just until the rocket and radicchio have wilted. Transfer the vegetables to a plate lined with kitchen paper towels and leave to cool, then chop coarsely. Stir the mushroom mixture into the clafoutis batter and adjust the seasoning. Pour half the batter into a lightly oiled 15cm (6-inch) round cake tin (pan), about 5cm (2 inches) deep, and sprinkle the artichoke and pancetta mixture on top. Cover with the remaining batter – the tin should be about three-quarters full. Bake in the centre of an oven preheated to 150°C/300°F/Gas Mark 2 for 35–40 minutes, until a knife inserted in the middle comes out clean.

Meanwhile, whisk together the remaining lemon juice and the remaining 3 tablespoons of olive oil. Toss the remaining radicchio with this vinaigrette and season to taste with salt and pepper.

To serve, unmould the clafoutis, re-invert it right side up on to a plate and cut it into 6 wedges. Serve hot, accompanied by the radicchio salad.

# Lamb Stew with Rosemary and Orange

**Serves 6**

**4–6 tablespoons extra virgin olive oil**
**1.8kg (4lb) shoulder of lamb, boned and cut into 2.5cm (1-inch) chunks**
**1 large onion, cut into wedges 1cm (1/2-inch) thick**
**4 small carrots, cut into slices 1cm (1/2-inch) thick**
**2 large turnips, peeled and cut into 1cm (1/2-inch) cubes, or 16 baby turnips, peeled and trimmed**
**1 large celeriac (celery root), peeled and cut into 1cm (1/2-inch) cubes**
**1 fennel bulb, trimmed and cut into 6 wedges**
**3 garlic cloves, coarsely chopped**
**1 teaspoon finely chopped rosemary**
**1 cinnamon stick**
**35g (1/4 cup) plain (all-purpose) flour**
**2 tablespoons tomato purée (paste)**
**1 teaspoon finely chopped flat-leaf parsley**
**juice of 1 orange**
**125ml (1/2 cup) dry white wine**
**1.2–1.5 litres (5–6 cups) water or unsalted chicken stock**
**4 plum tomatoes, peeled, deseeded and cut into 1cm dice**
**1/2 teaspoon finely grated orange zest**
**salt and freshly ground black pepper**

Warm 2 tablespoons of the olive oil in a large casserole (Dutch oven) over a high heat. Season the lamb with salt and pepper, then add to the pan and sear on all sides until golden brown. Transfer the lamb to a plate. Add 2 tablespoons of the oil to the pot and reduce the heat to medium-high. Add the onion, carrots, turnips, celeriac, fennel, garlic, rosemary and cinnamon stick. Season with salt and pepper and cook, stirring, for 10–12 minutes, until the vegetables soften. Return the lamb to the pan and cook, stirring, for 6–8 minutes, adding more olive oil if needed.

Sprinkle the flour on top and continue to cook, stirring, for 5 minutes. Stir in the tomato purée and parsley. Add the orange juice and wine and cook until the liquid has reduced by half. Add enough water or stock to almost cover the lamb and vegetables and bring to the boil. Add the tomatoes and orange zest, cover the casserole and transfer to an oven preheated to 150°C/300°F/Gas Mark 2. Cook for 1–1 1/4 hours, until the lamb is fork-tender. Serve immediately.

# Ruby Grapefruit and Pomegranate Sabayon

**Serves 6**

**6 large ruby-red grapefruit**
**750ml (3 cups) pomegranate juice (available at Middle Eastern shops), or about 5 pomegranates, peeled, seeds removed from membranes and reserved**
**150g ($^3/_4$ cup) caster (superfine or granulated) sugar**
**1 tablespoon grated fresh ginger**

For the sabayon:

**5 medium (large) egg yolks**
**1$^1/_2$ tablespoons caster (superfine or granulated) sugar**
**1$^1/_2$ tablespoons white wine**
**1$^1/_2$ tablespoons grenadine**
**1$^1/_2$ tablespoons water**
**1 tablespoon grated fresh ginger**

With a knife, cut away the skin of the grapefruit, removing every trace of white, cottony pith and exposing the moist, glistening fruit. Then cut between the membranes to release the grapefruit segments. Remove the pips (seeds) from the segments.

If you are not using ready-made pomegranate juice, place the pomegranate seeds in a blender or food processor and process, scraping down the sides of the container as needed, until the seeds are broken down and have yielded their juice. Strain, discarding whatever solids remain; you should have 750ml (3 cups) juice. Pour the pomegranate juice into a saucepan, add the sugar and ginger and bring to the boil. Add the grapefruit segments, bring the mixture back to a simmer, then remove from the heat. Set aside to cool. This can be made a day ahead and stored in the fridge.

Place all the ingredients for the sabayon in a heatproof bowl and set it over a pan of simmering water, making sure the water isn't touching the base of the bowl. Cook, whisking constantly, until the mixture is warm to the touch and has thickened. Remove the bowl from the heat and whisk with an electric mixer on medium-high speed for 4–5 minutes, until the sabayon is cool to the touch.

Drain the grapefruit segments, saving the syrup, pat them dry and divide them between 6 gratin dishes or ovenproof dinner plates, arranging them in a pinwheel pattern. Spoon some of the sabayon into the centre of each dish. Place the dishes under a hot grill (broiler) to brown the sabayon evenly. Drizzle a little of the pomegranate syrup around the grapefruit and serve immediately.

six

# STEVEN DOHERTY

## The First Floor Café

Steven Doherty began his culinary career at the Savoy Hotel in London in 1976. Two years later he moved to Le Gavroche, where he rose up the ranks to become head chef, the position he held when it won its three Michelin stars. In 1990 Steven became group executive chef for Roux Restaurants Ltd. He then moved to the Punch Bowl at Crosthwaite, in 1990, which was subsequently voted Lake District Pub of the Year. In 2003 Steven set up the First Floor Café in the Lakeland Ltd store in Windermere and is a consultant for café operations in their new stores.

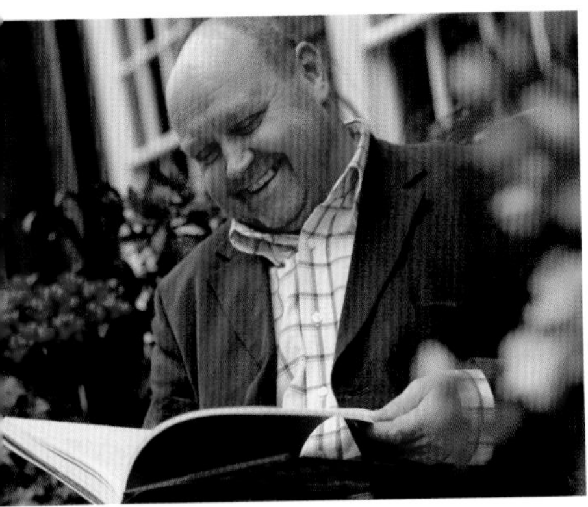

**What are your favourite foods/flavours?**
Great Chinese, wonderful cheese and bread, pizza from a wood-fired oven, salads with fabulous olive oil, anything chargrilled.

**What are your favourite utensils?**
Aquatronic scales, kitchen timers.

**What is your most useful piece of kitchen equipment?**
A combi-oven.

**What is your favourite season?**
Winter.

**What is your favourite meal?**
Breakfast: bacon and eggs.
Lunch: salad niçoise with fresh tuna.
Dinner: steamed sea bass, ginger and spring onion (scallion).

**How do you decide what to cook?**
Seasons, time.

**What inspires you?**
New ideas, classic themes, books and tastes.

**What is your favourite drink?**
Good champagne.

**What are your likes and dislikes?**
I dislike bad manners and bad restaurants.

**How can you inspire others to enjoy great food and cooking?**
Keep it simple; buy the best; be seasonal; cook with what you know.

**How did you become a chef?**
I was inspired by Graham Kerr, the Galloping Gourmet.

**What are your top ten ingredients?**
Extra virgin olive oil, sourdough bread, free-range eggs, fresh ginger, Kikkoman soy sauce, sea bass, seasonal salad items, pistachios, French purple peaches, grass-fed Cumbrian beef.

**What are your kitchen secrets?**
The seven Ps! Proper planning and preparation prevent a p... poor performance!

**What are your top tips?**
We all have different tastes – follow whatever style inspires you and stay with it.

**Do you have any favourite junk food?**
A hamburger with melted cheese.

**How do you feel about cooking for children?**
I do everyday simple stuff, cooked well.

**Can you give one piece of advice for the domestic cook?**
Cook what YOU like and understand.

* French Bean, Roquefort, Walnut and Chive Salad with a Walnut Oil Dressing, Warm Beetroot and Crème Fraîche
* Seared Tuna Steaks on a Spiced Sweet Potato Mash with Ginger and Spring Onion Dressing
* Honey, Whisky and Drambuie Crème Brûlée



# French Bean, Roquefort, Walnut and Chive Salad with a Walnut Oil Dressing, Warm Beetroot and Crème Fraîche

**Serves 4**

**2 large cooked beetroot (beets)**
**100g ($3^1/2$oz) green beans**
**100g (generous $^3/4$ cup) walnut halves**
**2 tablespoons chopped chives**
**100g ($3^1/2$oz) Roquefort cheese**
**200ml (7oz) crème fraîche**

For the dressing:

**$3^1/2$ tablespoons white wine vinegar**
**2 teaspoons Dijon mustard**
**150ml ($^2/3$ cup) walnut oil**
**salt and freshly ground white pepper**

Wrap the beetroot in foil and warm them in an oven preheated to 190°C/375°F/Gas Mark 5 for 15 minutes. Cut each beetroot into 8 segments.

Blanch the green beans in boiling salted water for 1 minute, then drain and refresh in iced water. Drain again thoroughly. Make the dressing by whisking together the vinegar, mustard, salt and pepper. Gradually whisk in the walnut oil, then taste for seasoning.

Mix together the green beans, beetroot, walnuts and chopped chives. Add the dressing and arrange the salad in a bowl. Crumble the cheese over the salad and drizzle the crème fraîche over the top.

# Seared Tuna Steaks on a Spiced Sweet Potato Mash with Ginger and Spring Onion Dressing

**Serves 4**

**4 x 125g (4-oz) fresh tuna steaks**
**plain (all-purpose) flour for dusting**
**$3^1/2$ tablespoons sunflower oil**
**salt and freshly ground black pepper**

For the spiced sweet potato mash:

**2 teaspoons sunflower oil**
**500g (3 cups) orange-fleshed sweet potatoes, peeled and diced**
**1 small onion, chopped**
**1 teaspoon ground cumin**
**1 teaspoon ground coriander**
**2 teaspoons grated fresh ginger**
**1 chilli, deseeded and finely chopped**
**2 garlic cloves, crushed**
**225ml (1 cup) coconut milk**
**3 tablespoons roughly chopped coriander (cilantro), plus extra to garnish**

For the dressing:

**2 teaspoons grated fresh ginger**
**4 spring onions (scallions), sliced**
**150ml ($^2/3$ cup) light soy sauce**

For the mash, heat the sunflower oil in a heavy-based saucepan, add the sweet potatoes, onion, cumin and ground coriander and sweat for 5 minutes, until softened but not browned. Stir in the ginger, chilli, garlic and coconut milk, season lightly with a pinch of salt and bring to the boil. Cover the pan and simmer over a low heat for 15 minutes, until the sweet potatoes are tender. Mash the mixture, mix well with a whisk and keep warm.

For the dressing, mix together all the ingredients in a bowl. Dust the tuna lightly with flour and season with salt and pepper. Heat the sunflower oil in a non-stick frying pan (skillet) until nearly smoking. Add the tuna immediately and cook for 1 minute on each side. Remove the fish from the pan and place on a tray lined with kitchen paper towels to drain.

To serve, mix the fresh coriander into the mash, place a spoonful of mash on each plate and put the fish on top. Spoon the dressing around and garnish with coriander.

# Honey, Whisky and Drambuie Crème Brûlée

**If you glaze the brûlées with a blowtorch, it is best to hold the moulds in a cloth in case the hot caramel runs down the side. The glazing process will take 1–2 minutes, so don't rush it and burn them.**

**Serves 4**

**110g (1/3 cup) clear Acacia honey**
**9 egg yolks**
**125g (generous 1/2 cup) caster (superfine) sugar**
**2 tablespoons whisky**
**5 1/2 tablespoons Drambuie**
**600ml (2 1/2 cups) double (heavy) cream**

Warm the honey in a microwave for a few seconds. Whisk together the egg yolks, 75g (6 1/4) tablespoons of the sugar, the whisky and Drambuie, then add the warm honey. Bring the cream to the boil, then remove from the heat and whisk in the egg mixture. Strain through a fine sieve into a jug.

Place 4 ramekins on a shallow baking tray and pour the mixture into them. Half fill the baking tray with warm water, then place in an oven preheated to 150°C/300°F/Gas Mark 2 and cook for 20–30 minutes. The mixture should set and not wobble. Remove from the oven and leave to cool.

To serve, sprinkle the brûlées with the remaining sugar and glaze with a blowtorch or by putting them under a hot grill (broiler).

# seven

# ALAIN DUCASSE

## Essex House

**Alain Ducasse was brought up amongst pullets, ducks and geese near Castelsarrazin in France. In twenty-five years, he has developed considerable expertise in the art of good living and eating, which he expresses in his diverse activities. He is the creator of restaurants on four continents, an innkeeper and an instructor. Alain Ducasse drives his business in the spirit of sharing a passion – a state of permanent marvel that allows him to embrace the world's diversity and all its cultural richness.**

Cooking is a matter of truth. Because the raw material is of the utmost importance and the material does not lie. Red mullet from the Mediterranean Sea possesses a special iodized flavour; American beef and its Japanese counterpart are two distinct taste experiences. Take tomatoes – nothing could seem more banal. But believe me, when they come straight from the vegetable garden to your plate, full of the Provençal sun, they taste just like a gift from the gods! A chef must be very humble to deal with the truth of the ingredients. He or she must find them, respect them and let them express their own genius.

Cooking is discovery. Cooking is as old as humanity and as diverse as the soils, climates and cultures of the world. I am obsessed by the idea that we might lose an ancestral way of cooking. To make my own modest contribution to our collective memory, I asked a team of historians to investigate the archives of Mediterranean cooking. They worked for months gathering together all the centuries-old methods of fishing, cultivating, preserving and preparing food. With the help of my cooks, we resuscitated the recipes and adapted them to modern tastes in order to give them a new life. I have the same burning passion when it comes to discovering the diversity of contemporary cooking manners. I remember some 'fried ravioli' I ate in the street in Tokyo, from the most humble pedlar you can imagine. They were just right – I can't say it better. Cooking is diverse and I want it to remain diverse. And I love discovering this diversity throughout the vast world.

Cooking is sharing. When I create a new restaurant, my first thoughts are about its atmosphere. Everything contributes to it: light and sound, colours and materials, decoration and table settings – and, most importantly, the staff. The look and feel of the place are as important as what is on the plate. Moreover, both must be in tune and reinforce each other. This means I can offer what my guests are expecting: a total eating experience. And most of the time, these eating experiences are shared experiences. A couple goes to a restaurant to share a privileged moment of intimacy; friends dine out for entertainment; business lunches are a smart opportunity to turn a formal relationship into a relaxed dialogue. I want my restaurants to live up to all the expectations people might have when they meet. More than that, I want my restaurants to embellish and exalt those shared moments and turn them into unforgettable memories.

In a nutshell, cooking is life. Grounded on a biological need, cooking transcends it. Based on raw materials from the earth and the waters, cooking sublimates them. There is a lot of generosity in the alchemical process of cooking. The marvel of a delicious dish, the harmony of a well thought-out meal, the delicate match of a wine with the flavour of food, are genuine gifts made to others. I cannot imagine a chef preparing a food he does not like himself. Love of food is the most precious ingredient a chef can utilize in his recipes. And, everywhere in the world, the best foods always have the inimitable taste of love.

* Riviera Salad, like a Niçoise
* Roast Veal with Vegetables in Garlic and Shallot Butter
* Brioche French Toast with Sautéed Seasonal Fruits

## Riviera Salad, like a Niçoise

**Serves 4**

**1/2 medium seedless (hothouse) cucumber, peeled and cut into 1cm (1/2-inch) dice**
**1 red (bell) pepper, roasted, peeled, deseeded and cut into 5mm (1/4-inch) strips**
**a sprig of thyme**
**1 garlic clove, lightly crushed**
**8 tablespoons extra virgin olive oil**
**12 slices of baguette, toasted**
**1/2 garlic clove**
**4 quail's eggs, boiled for 5 minutes, then shelled and halved lengthways**
**8 Niçoise olives, a thick slice cut off each and the remainder reserved for another use**
**4 small purple artichokes**
**500ml (2 1/4 cups) groundnut (peanut) oil**
**1 celery heart, trimmed, sliced paper thin and set aside in cold water**
**100g (3 1/2oz) mixed green salad leaves (mesclun)**
**4 tomatoes, skinned, deseeded and quartered**
**lemon juice**
**8 small spring onions (scallions), white parts only, sliced paper thin**
**8 anchovy fillets packed in oil**
**100g (3 1/2oz) white tuna packed in oil**
**8 basil leaves, cut into thin ribbons**
**8 small red radishes, sliced paper thin**
**fine sea salt and freshly ground black pepper**

For the tapenade:

**200g (1 1/2 cups) Niçoise olives, pitted**
**1 tablespoon capers, drained and coarsely chopped**
**1/4 teaspoon lemon juice**
**1/2 garlic clove**
**1 tablespoon sherry vinegar**
**4 tablespoons extra virgin olive oil**
**a pinch of fine sea salt**

For the vinaigrette:

**1 tablespoon sherry vinegar**
**4 tablespoons extra virgin olive oil**

Place the diced cucumber in a colander and sprinkle with 1 tablespoon of salt; set aside for about 10 minutes so that the cucumber gives off its water. Wipe off as much salt as you can with a kitchen cloth or paper towels and set the cucumber aside.

In a small bowl, combine the roasted pepper with the thyme, garlic clove and 1 tablespoon of the olive oil, then set aside. To make the tapenade, put the olives in a blender or mini food processor with the capers, lemon juice, garlic, sherry vinegar, olive oil, salt and some pepper to taste and blend to a thick paste. Transfer to a small bowl and set aside.

To make the vinaigrette, put the vinegar in a small bowl with a pinch of salt and some pepper. Add the olive oil and stir vigorously with a fork to blend. Set aside.

Rub the baguette slices lightly on one side with the half garlic clove, then spread with a thin layer of the tapenade; reserve a little tapenade for the dressing. Garnish 8 of the slices with half a quail's egg, then place a slice of olive on top of each egg. Set all the slices aside on a plate.

Trim and halve the artichokes, then slice them paper thin. Heat the groundnut oil in a large, deep pan over a medium-high heat. When the oil is very hot (190°C/375°F), carefully put in half the artichoke slices. Fry for about 2 minutes, until the artichokes are light golden brown, then remove with a slotted spoon and place on several layers of kitchen paper towels. Season immediately with a pinch of salt. Combine the remaining artichoke slices with 1 tablespoon of the vinaigrette and toss to coat.

In a small bowl, toss the cucumber with 1 tablespoon of the vinaigrette. Drain the celery heart and pat dry, then toss it with another tablespoon of vinaigrette, reserving the remaining vinaigrette for another use.

To assemble the salad, arrange the ingredients on 4 serving plates in the following order: first the mesclun, then the red pepper, tomatoes, cucumber, raw artichoke slices, celery heart, spring onions, anchovy fillets, tuna and basil leaves. Scatter the radishes and fried artichokes on top and sprinkle with a few drops of lemon juice. Arrange 3 tapenade toasts on the side of each plate, 2 with quail's eggs, 1 plain. In a small bowl, stir together the remaining 7 tablespoons of olive oil and the remaining tapenade, then transfer to a sauceboat. Serve the salad immediately, passing the sauceboat at the table.

# Roast Veal with Vegetables in Garlic and Shallot Butter

**Serves 4**

**1 x 800g ($1^{3}/_{4}$-lb) boneless veal rump**
**2 tablespoons olive oil**
**150g (5oz) meaty veal scraps, ask your butcher for these**
**25g (2 tablespoons) unsalted butter**
**4 tablespoons chicken stock**
**fine sea salt and freshly ground pepper**

For the vegetables:

**3 tablespoons olive oil**
**6 pearl onions, outer layer peeled off**
**10–12 small new potatoes, about 300g (10oz), scrubbed and cut in half**
**4 carrots, peeled and cut on the diagonal into slices 5mm ($^{1}/_{4}$ inch) thick**
**8 very slim young leeks, cut into 4cm ($1^{3}/_{4}$-inch) pieces**

For the garlic and shallot butter:

**140g ($1^{1}/_{4}$ sticks) unsalted butter**
**15g (2 tablespoons) ground almonds**
**1 slice, about 25g (1oz), Parma ham or other cured ham, cut into very small dice**
**1 small garlic clove, finely chopped**
**1 small shallot, finely chopped**
**3 tablespoons finely chopped flat-leaf parsley**

First make the garlic and shallot butter. In a small bowl, combine all the ingredients, then season with salt and pepper. Shape into a log, wrap in cling film (plastic wrap) and set aside. You won't need all the butter but it keeps well in the fridge or freezer.

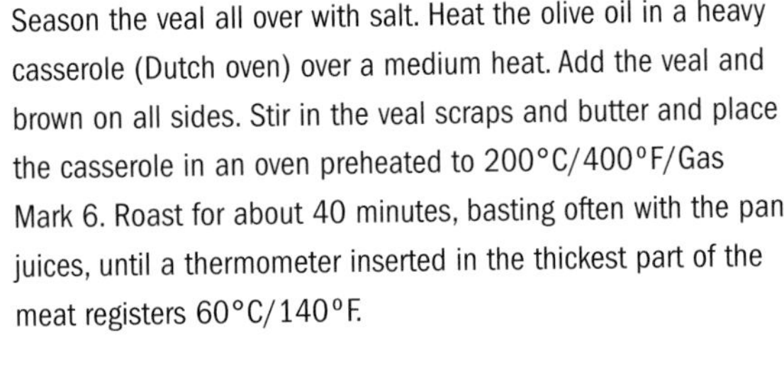

Season the veal all over with salt. Heat the olive oil in a heavy casserole (Dutch oven) over a medium heat. Add the veal and brown on all sides. Stir in the veal scraps and butter and place the casserole in an oven preheated to 200°C/400°F/Gas Mark 6. Roast for about 40 minutes, basting often with the pan juices, until a thermometer inserted in the thickest part of the meat registers 60°C/140°F.

Meanwhile, prepare the vegetables. Heat the olive oil in a pan over a medium heat. Add the onions and potatoes and cook, stirring often, for about 8 minutes, until lightly browned. Add the carrots, reduce the heat to low and cook, stirring frequently, for 5 minutes. Add the leeks and cook, stirring often, for about 10 minutes, until all the vegetables are tender when pierced with the tip of a small, sharp knife. Remove from the heat and cover to keep warm.

Remove the veal from the oven and transfer to a wire rack set over a platter. Cover loosely with aluminum foil and leave to rest for 15 minutes. Meanwhile, set the casserole in which the veal was cooked over a medium heat and heat until the juices begin to bubble. Add 2 tablespoons of the chicken stock and stir and scrape up the browned bits stuck to the bottom and sides of the pan. Repeat with the remaining 2 tablespoons of stock. Strain this jus though a fine sieve into a bowl and set aside. To finish the vegetables, return the pan to a low heat, add 2 tablespoons of the garlic and shallot butter and half the veal jus and toss to melt the butter and coat the vegetables well (save the remaining jus for another use). Season the vegetables with salt to taste.

Arrange the vegetables on a warmed serving platter and place the veal roast on top. Serve immediately, slicing the veal and serving it with the vegetables.

# Brioche French Toast with Sautéed Seasonal Fruits

**Serves 4**

**2 large (extra-large) eggs**
**1 large (extra-large) egg yolk**
**175g ($^3/_4$ cup) plus 2 tablespoons granulated sugar**
**$^1/_2$ vanilla pod (vanilla bean), or $^1/_2$ teaspoon vanilla extract**
**250ml (1 cup) milk**
**4 slices of brioche, cut 2cm ($^3/_4$ inch) thick**
**40–50g (scant $^1/_2$ cup) icing (confectioners') sugar**
**50–75g ($^1/_2$–$^3/_4$ stick) unsalted butter**
**rich vanilla ice cream, to serve (optional)**

For the sautéed fruit:

**40g ($^1/_3$ cup) (dried) currants**
**11 (2 tablespoons) dark rum**
**65g (4 tablespoons) unsalted butter**
**50g ($^1/_4$ cup) granulated sugar**
**2 dessert apples, such as Reinette, peeled, cored and quartered**
**1 pear, such as Bartlett, peeled, quartered and cored**
**$^1/_2$ small pineapple, peeled, cored and cut into rings 1cm ($^1/_2$ inch) thick**
**$^1/_2$ quince, peeled, cored and cut into 4**
**1 pomegranate, seeds scooped out**
**juice of $^1/_2$ orange**
**juice of $^1/_2$ lemon**

First prepare the fruit. In a small bowl, soak the currants in the rum to soften. Melt the butter in a large frying pan (skillet) over a medium heat. Add the sugar and cook, stirring, until it begins to dissolve. Add the apples, pear, pineapple, quince and pomegranate seeds and stir to coat them with the butter and sugar. Cook for 7–10 minutes, until softened. Stir in the currants and rum, plus the orange and lemon juice, and simmer until the liquid is reduced by half. Remove from the heat and set aside.

For the French toast, beat together the eggs, egg yolk and sugar. With a sharp knife, slit open the vanilla pod and scrape the seeds into the egg mixture, or add the vanilla extract. Add the milk and stir until blended. Put each slice of brioche in the egg mixture and leave for about 2 minutes, until thoroughly soaked. Then remove with a fish slice (pancake turner) and place on a platter. Sift some of the icing sugar through a fine sieve over the top of each slice to cover evenly.

Melt 50g ($3^1/_2$) tablespoons of the butter in a large frying pan (skillet) over a medium heat. Add the brioche slices, sugared-side down, and cook for about 5 minutes, until lightly browned underneath. Sift more icing sugar over the top, then turn and brown the other side, adding more butter if necessary. Remove from the heat and place each slice in a shallow serving bowl. Spoon the fruit over the French toast and top with vanilla ice cream, if you wish. Serve immediately.

# eight

# ANTON EDELMANN

## Allium

After twenty-one years at London's Savoy Hotel, Anton Edelmann joined leading catering and support services provider, Sodexho, in 2003 as the first principal chef for Directors Table, its fine-dining division for business and industry clients in London. Anton is in charge of planning the menu and developing a signature menu range for city clients; training and motivating the team of chefs; running master classes for clients and staff; and developing and managing the restaurant, Allium, in Dolphin Square, London. Last year the Anton Edelmann Culinary Academy was launched at Allium to develop and enhance the skills of Sodexho's chefs.

**What are your favourite foods/tastes/flavours?**
Fish, slow-braised meats, passion fruit, fresh ripe tomatoes.

**What are your favourite utensils?**
A stick blender, a garlic peeler and Japanese knives.

**What is your most useful piece of kitchen equipment?**
A steamer and a simmering plate.

**What are your favourite seasons?**
Spring and summer.

**How do you decide what to cook?**
What's in season and what I see in the shops and at market stalls.

**What inspires you?**
Looking at food and eating it.

**What is your favourite drink?**
Red wine.

**What are your likes and dislikes?**
I dislike lettuce out of a bag and unripe tomatoes.

**How can you inspire others to enjoy great food and cooking?**
By cooking and eating with them.

**How did you become a chef?**
I started in my uncle's hotel in the school holidays, at the age of ten.

**What are your top ten ingredients?**
Tomatoes, fish, pasta, potatoes, asparagus, goose liver, scallops, olive oil, herbs and spices, horseradish.

**What are your kitchen secrets?**
Always plan well and buy quality produce.

**What are your top tips?**
Keep it simple.

**Do you have any favourite junk food?**
Home-cut chips (french fries).

**How do you feel about cooking for children?**
Great.

**Can you give one piece of advice for the domestic cook?**
Don't be afraid of food, it won't bite. Always take a lot of time over it, perhaps with a glass of red wine.

* Fish Cakes on Tomato Carpaccio
* Black Forest Onion and Smoked Bacon Tart
* Riesling-marinated Berries with Elderflower Sorbet

# Fish Cakes on Tomato Carpaccio

**I have used many different recipes for fish cakes over the years but I always come back to this one. It's light, as there are no potatoes in it, and very tasty.**

**Serves 4**

**100g (3½oz) salmon fillet, skinned and pin bones removed**
**100g (3½oz) whiting fillet, skinned and pin bones removed**
**100g (3½oz) cod fillet, skinned and pin bones removed**
**25g (1oz) gherkins, finely chopped**
**25g (1oz) spring onions (scallions), finely chopped**
**1 fresh chilli, deseeded and finely chopped**
**¼ teaspoon very finely chopped fresh ginger**
**3 tablespoons mayonnaise**
**4 slices of white bread, without crusts, made into crumbs**
**4 vine-ripened tomatoes**
**a little olive oil**
**salt and freshly ground black pepper**
**a handful each of rocket (arugula) and frisée lettuce, to serve**

**For the tomato crisps (crisps):**
**1 tomato, very thinly sliced**
**olive oil for brushing**
**chopped thyme**

**For the lemon dressing:**
**2 tablespoons olive oil**
**1½ teaspoons lemon juice**

First make the tomato crisps (chips). Place the tomato slices on a baking tray lined with lightly oiled baking parchment paper. Sprinkle with thyme and some salt and pepper, then turn the slices over and repeat. Place in an oven preheated to 110°C/225°F/Gas Mark ¼ and leave until the tomato slices are dry and crisp – this can take several hours, depending on the moisture content of the tomatoes. Remove from the oven and leave to cool. (The tomato crisps can be made a day in advance and stored in an airtight container.)

To make the fish cakes, put all the fish in a steamer and steam for about 3 minutes. Cover with cling film (plastic wrap) and leave to cool. Flake the fish and mix with the gherkins, spring onions, chilli, ginger, mayonnaise and 2 tablespoons of the breadcrumbs. Season with salt and pepper. Put the remaining breadcrumbs in a dish, then put in the fish mixture and shape it with a palette knife (metal spatula) into 4 cylinders, about 4cm (1¾ inches) high and 6cm (2¼ inches) wide. Make sure they are well coated with breadcrumbs. Chill the fish cakes for 30 minutes to firm them up.

Mix together the ingredients for the lemon dressing, season with salt and pepper and set aside.

Slice the tomatoes very thinly, then arrange them, slightly overlapping, on 4 serving plates. Season with salt and pepper and drizzle with olive oil.

To cook the fish cakes, heat a little oil in an ovenproof non-stick frying pan (skillet) and fry the fish cakes until golden brown on both sides. Transfer the pan to an oven preheated to 220°C/425°F/Gas Mark 7 and cook for about 6 minutes, until the fish cakes are heated through.

To serve, put the fish cakes on top of the tomatoes. Toss the rocket and frisée in the lemon dressing, place it on top of the fish cakes, and arrange the tomato crisps on top.

# Black Forest Onion and Smoked Bacon Tart

**This is my mother's recipe and we always drink new wine with it in the Black Forest. It takes a little time to prepare but it's really worth the effort, as the strong flavour of the bacon works extremely well with the onions.**
**Any young and fruity white wine goes well with this tart.**

**Serves 4**

**250g (1 3/4 cups) strong (bread) white flour**
**90g (2/3 cup) wholemeal (whole-wheat) flour**
**15g (1/2oz) fresh yeast**
**1 teaspoon sugar**
**200ml (7oz) water**
**2 teaspoons caraway seeds**
**5 tablespoons crème fraîche**
**3/4 teaspoon salt**
**1kg (6 cups) onions, finely chopped**
**10g (2 teaspoons) butter**
**1 egg, beaten**
**200g (7oz) smoked streaky bacon rashers (slices)**
**salt and freshly ground black pepper**

Mix the flours in a large bowl and make a well in the centre. Crumble in the yeast, then add the sugar and 4 tablespoons of the water. Mix with a little of the surrounding flour until it has a spongy texture. Cover the bowl with a cloth and leave in a warm place for about 30 minutes, until the 'sponge' has doubled in size.

Add the caraway seeds, 4 teaspoons of the crème fraîche, the salt and the remaining water. Mix with a spoon, bringing in the flour from the sides to form a smooth dough. Cover the bowl with a cloth and leave in a warm place for 30 minutes or until doubled in size.

Meanwhile, sweat the onions in the butter over a low heat until very soft but not coloured. Allow to cool slightly, then mix in the beaten egg and half the remaining crème fraîche. Season to taste with salt and pepper.

Roll out the dough on a lightly floured surface to a thickness of 5mm (1/4 inch). Grease a tart tin or baking sheet and line with the dough. Brush lightly with a little water and then spread the onion mixture over the top. Cover with the remaining crème fraîche and arrange the bacon rashers over the top.

Bake in an oven preheated to 220°C/425°F/Gas Mark 7 for 40–50 minutes, until the base is crisp and brown and the topping is golden. Serve hot, cut into slices.

# Riesling-marinated Berries with Elderflower Sorbet

**This is a very quick and easy recipe. Light and refreshing, the sorbet works wonderfully well with any seasonal berries and fruits. However, if you don't feel like making the sorbet, any good-quality bought sorbet or ice cream will do. The longer you infuse the mint the better!**

**Serves 4**

**juice of 3 limes**
**150ml ($^2/_3$ cup) Riesling wine**
**4 tablespoons crème de cassis**
**50g (scant $^1/_2$ cup) icing (confectioners') sugar**
**2 teaspoons chopped mint**
**350g (12 oz) mixed summer berries, such as raspberries, strawberries, blackberries, blueberries and loganberries**
**4 mint sprigs, to decorate**

For the elderflower sorbet:
**150g ($^3/_4$ cup) caster (superfine) sugar**
**350ml ($1^1/_2$ cups) water**
**350ml ($1^1/_2$ cups) elderflower syrup**

To make the elderflower sorbet, put the sugar in a pan with the water and dissolve over a low heat, then bring to the boil. Remove from the heat, add the elderflower syrup and leave to cool completely. Churn in an ice-cream maker. If you don't have an ice-cream maker, pour the mixture into a large freezer-proof bowl, cover and freeze until almost set, then transfer to a food processor and whiz to break down the ice crystals. Return the mixture to the bowl, cover and freeze again for 3 hours, until almost set. Repeat the process once more to obtain a fine-textured sorbet. Cover and freeze for another 2 hours. Just before serving, mash the sorbet well with a fork.

To make the marinade, mix together the lime juice, Riesling and crème de cassis. Stir in the icing sugar and whisk to mix thoroughly. Stir in the chopped mint, cover and chill for at least 1 hour. Strain through a fine sieve.

Rinse the berries and dry them carefully. Divide them between 4 deep serving dishes, such as small soup plates. Spoon the lime marinade over the berries.

Shape the sorbet into quenelles by dipping a dessertspoon in hot water and scraping it across the surface of the sorbet, rolling it into the spoon to make a neat shape. Place a quenelle of sorbet on top of the berries, decorate with a sprig of mint and serve.

# nine

# MARK EDWARDS

## Nobu London

**Classically trained chef Mark Edwards spent his early career in some of Europe's most renowned establishments before moving to New York. Here he acquired his passion for Asian food, after which he spent time working in the Far East. In 1994 he landed the job of head chef at Vong London, and three years later he teamed up with Nobu Matsuhisa to open Nobu London. Mark is now executive chef for the Nobu group.**

**What are your favourite foods/tastes/flavours?**
I like most things but prefer clean, simple flavours.

**What are your favourite utensils?**
Chopsticks and a good pepper mill.

**What is the most useful piece of kitchen design and equipment?**
A good, well-lit and well-ventilated area with adequate space to work on.

**What is your favourite season?**
I love what all of them have to offer.

**What is your favourite mealtime?**
It has to be dinner.

**How do you decide what to cook?**
Usually what I see at the market makes me decide.

**What inspires you?**
Life!

**What is your favourite drink?**
Gin and tonic.

**What are your likes and dislikes?**
I like fresh, healthy-looking ingredients and hate old, badly handled ones.

**How can you inspire others to enjoy great food and cooking?**
Cooking for people and cooking with people is usually the best way to inspire.

**How did you become a chef?**
Good question! It just seemed to happen naturally.

**What are your top ten ingredients?**
Whatever is best at that particular time or place.

**What are your kitchen secrets?**
I don't keep secrets in the kitchen. My staff need to know what I know when cooking the same dish.

**What are your top tips?**
If you don't succeed at first, try again!

**Do you ever eat junk food?**
I avoid junk food as much as possible.

**How do you feel about cooking for children?**
It brings more of a fun element into cooking, especially if you can do it together.

**Can you give one piece of advice for the domestic cook?**
Simple is always best.

* Broad Beans Edamame Style
* Cold Inaniwa Noodles with Grilled Chicken
* Roasted Pineapple Soup with Coconut Ice Cream

## Broad Beans Edamame Style

**This is an excellent way of eating fresh broad beans when in season, and also makes a change from the traditional Japanese style of eating edamame, or soy beans, at the beginning of a meal.**

**Serves 4**

**400g (2$^1/_4$ cups) shelled young broad (fava) beans**
**Maldon sea salt**

Bring a pan of water to a rolling boil and add the beans. Simmer for about 1–2 minutes, checking that the beans are only just cooked. Quickly drain the beans and shake off excess water, then toss with enough salt to season them. Serve immediately.

# Cold Inaniwa Noodles with Grilled Chicken

**This dish is good served with grilled asparagus. Inaniwa noodles look a little like flat spaghetti and are available from Japanese stores and some Asian shops.**

**Serves 4**

**300g (10oz) Japanese inaniwa noodles**
**4 chicken breasts (breast halves), skin on, or use skinless ones if you prefer**
**2 1/2 tablespoons chopped chives**
**salt and freshly ground black pepper**
**frisée lettuce, to serve**

**For the dressing:**
**3 1/2 tablespoons lemon juice**
**3 1/2 tablespoons rice vinegar**
**3 tablespoons soy sauce**
**1 teaspoon red chilli paste**
**2 teaspoons garlic purée**
**3 1/2 tablespoons tomato passata (strained puréed tomatoes)**
**150ml (2/3 cup) grapeseed oil**

First make the dressing. Mix together the lemon juice, vinegar, soy sauce, chilli paste, garlic purée, passata and some black pepper. Whisk in the grapeseed oil and set aside.

Bring a large pan of water to the boil, add the noodles and cook for 3–5 minutes, until just tender. Drain well, refresh under cold running water and drain again.

Season the chicken breasts and cook them on a ridged griddle pan for 10–15 minutes, until cooked through. Keep warm.

Wash the noodles again and shake off excess water. Place in a bowl and toss gently with the dressing. Arrange the frisée lettuce on 4 serving plates, place the noodles on top and sprinkle with the chopped chives. Slice the hot chicken breasts, place on top of the noodles and serve.

# Roasted Pineapple Soup with Coconut Ice Cream

**Serves 4**

**1 pineapple**
**1.5 litres (6 cups) water**
**200g (1 cup) muscovado sugar**
**juice and pared zest of 2 limes**
**$^1/_2$ red chilli**
**20g (4 teaspoons) fresh ginger, roughly chopped**
**2 lemongrass sticks, roughly broken up**
**2 vanilla pods (vanilla beans)**
**coconut ice cream, to serve**

**For the pineapple confit:**
**1 pineapple, peeled, cored and diced**
**250g ($1^1/_4$ cups) caster (superfine) sugar**
**500ml ($2^1/_4$ cups) water**

Roast the pineapple whole, with the skin on, in an oven preheated to 220°C/425°F/Gas Mark 7 for 45 minutes, until caramelized on the outside. Remove from the oven and leave to cool. Cut off the skin and roughly chop the flesh into 2cm ($^3/_4$-inch) chunks. Place in a large pan with the water, sugar, lime juice and zest, chilli, ginger and lemongrass. Split the vanilla pods lengthways in half, scrape out the seeds and set aside. Put the empty pods into the pan. Bring to the boil, then reduce the heat and simmer gently for 1 hour. Remove the ginger, lemongrass, chilli and lime zest.

Pour the pineapple chunks and liquid into a blender and process until smooth, then strain through a fine sieve. Mix in the vanilla seeds and set aside.

To make the pineapple confit, put the diced pineapple in a pan with the sugar and water and bring to the boil. Simmer for 5 minutes or until the pineapple is tender, then set aside.

To serve, place a little of the pineapple confit in soup bowls. Gently heat the soup but don't let it boil. Ladle it into the bowls, scoop some coconut ice cream into the centre and serve immediately.

# ten

# RICHARD EKKEBUS

## Landmark Mandarin Oriental

**Richard Ekkebus began his career in his native country, the Netherlands, then worked with some of the greatest chefs in France. After seven years as executive chef at the Royal Palm Hotel in Mauritius, he moved to the legendary Sandy Lane in Barbados, where he was 'utterly seduced' by the wide-ranging culinary traditions of the Caribbean. Now executive chef at the Landmark Mandarin Oriental, Hong Kong, Richard applies his passion and vast knowledge to a menu that reflects his exceptional flair and culinary skill.**

**What are your favourite foods/tastes/flavours?**
I love Asian and oriental food. At a very early age, I was initiated into cuisines such as Chinese, Indonesian, Thai and Japanese. It was a treat to travel through the kitchens of faraway countries. My taste for travelling and my passion for cooking probably date back to those years. I am still attracted to the simplicity, contrasting flavours and variety of textures of these cuisines.

**What are your favourite utensils?**
My Nenohi knives, made from the highest-grade Nenox high-carbon, stain-resistant steel. Probably the finest Western-style chef's knives available, they are heavy and therefore almost do the job for you. Also good, heavy-bottomed saucepans, made of copper and stainless steel. Bourgeat makes these cooking pots fantastically.

**What is the most useful piece of kitchen design and equipment?**
The flow is without any doubt the most important part of kitchen design; without a good flow a kitchen simply doesn't work. Both the Paco Jet and the Thermo Mixer have become very important parts of my kitchen.

**What is your favourite season?**
Summer, because of the abundance of fruit and vegetables but also because of the sun. I have been working in tropical climates for the past nine years; you can see that the sun makes people feel happy.

**What is your favourite mealtime?**
I force myself to have breakfast and therefore skip it most of the time. The best meal is lunch, with a siesta in the afternoon.

**How do you decide what to cook?**
It depends on my mood.

**What inspires you?**
Mainly products and travel, but inspiration can come from anywhere – books, people, colleagues etc.

**What is your favourite drink?**
That depends on the occasion. After work, an ice-cold beer (I am, after all, a Dutchman). On my day off, a rum punch made by my wife, Fiona. I also enjoy great wines and champagne.

**What are your likes and dislikes?**
I like a job well done. I dislike sloppiness.

**How can you inspire others to enjoy great food and cooking?**
By being enthusiastic every day about what I am doing. I am naturally spontaneous about my job and how much I enjoy it.

**How did you become a chef?**
My grandparents were restaurateurs and my grandmother was the chef. I grow up in an environment where food was important, not just a way of filling your stomach. I went to study after high school and thought about becoming an engineer. At weekends I made some pocket money in some fine restaurants; it took me just a couple of weeks to

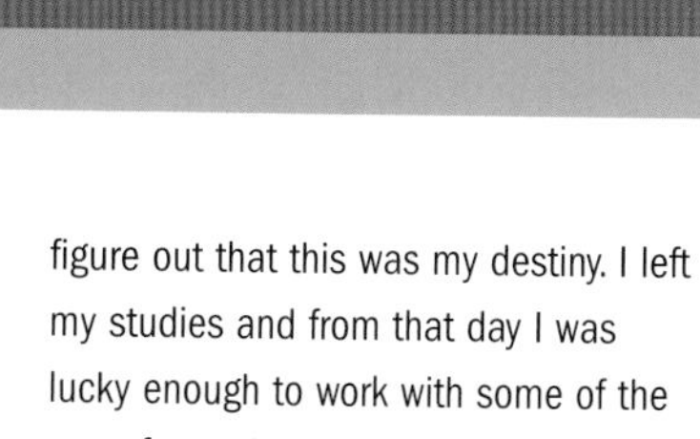

figure out that this was my destiny. I left my studies and from that day I was lucky enough to work with some of the most fantastic chefs in Holland, Belgium and France.

**What are your top ten ingredients?**

1 Sea salt – sel gris de Guerande and fleur de sel. Without salt, there are no expressive flavours. When used in the right amount, it will boost any flavour.
2 Vegetables – artichokes, beans (both dried and fresh), Asian vegetables in general, various cucurbitaceous, Japanese pumpkins, butternut squash ...
3 Spices – dried and fresh chillies, sumac, cumin, black pepper, coriander (cilantro), cassia, cinnamon, the list is long.
4 Crustaceans – I love Australian West Coast lobsters and marrons but any live crustacean will do.
5 Fish – any kind, as long as it is line caught and has bulging eyes, bright red gills and firm flesh covered with viscous liquid.
6 Shellfish – oysters from Gillardeau in France, clams, scallops, just about anything in a shell.
7 Oils – extra virgin olive oil, almond oil, untoasted sesame oil.
8 Meat – in particular lamb from my native region, Zeeland in Holland, or from Mont-Saint-Michel in France, which has a naturally mild, salty flavour as the lambs graze near the seashore, where the grass is slightly salted by the seawater. Also, milk-fed veal (*veau sous la mère*) and well-marbled beef, such as Wagyu or Kobe.
9 Fruit – especially citrus fruits, such as pomelo, lime and blood oranges, but also mangoes, tamarind and Mauritian wild guavas.
10 Chocolate – epecially bitter chocolate; in the Caribbean and South America we have the best of the best.

**What are your kitchen secrets?**

None. I was brought up in kitchen environments where you needed to fight hard to get your hand on the chef's signature recipe. The chef would do certain preparations only behind closed doors or during our break. There is much more transparency these days, and young chefs can find all the answers on the internet or in magazines and books. I therefore think that the evolution of chefs is much faster now. It is all there, you just need to grab it!

**What are your top tips?**

It has been repeated so often: buy quality and buy in season.

**Do you have any favourite junk food?**

I am Dutch, so in season we eat new herring, called Matjes, in a piece of paper in the street. I love street food, in particular in countries such as Vietnam and Thailand.

**How do you feel about cooking for children?**

My children, Mathis and Emma, have not been brought up on so-called kids' food, they have always eaten everything. Both of them love to go to great restaurants, and they always accompany us. They make their own choice from the menu (the adult one). They love food that is well prepared, and they have a fantastic nose for what is good and what isn't!

**Can you give one piece of advice for the domestic cook?**

Get yourself the best tools and ingredients you can afford. Do not hesitate to ask for advice from professionals. Read the recipe before starting to cook. But most importantly, enjoy what you do; your guests will notice the difference.

* Heirloom Tomatoes and Watermelon with Picodon Goat's Cheese and Cubebs Dressing
* Farm-raised Chicken with Curry Leaves, Plantain Mousseline and Butternut Squash and Curry Emulsion
* My Revisited Lime Tart

## Heirloom Tomatoes and Watermelon with Picodon Goat's Cheese and Cubebs Dressing

**Serves 4**

**1 tablespoon aged sherry vinegar**
**5 tablespoons extra virgin olive oil**
**4 Heirloom tomatoes, or large, vine-ripened tomatoes, skinned and core removed**
**1/4 watermelon, seedless if possible**
**20g (about 20 leaves) mint**
**1 1/2 Picodon goat's cheeses**
**fleur de sel or coarse sea salt**
**freshly ground cubebs or black pepper**

Put the vinegar in a bowl and whisk in some salt and cubebs or black pepper according to taste. Add the olive oil in a thin stream and whisk until the mixture is emulsified.

Cut the tomatoes horizontally into slices 8mm (3/8 inch) thick, discarding the bottom slice of each tomato. Cut the watermelon the same way and then trim the slices of watermelon to the same round shape as the tomatoes; you will need equal quantities of watermelon and tomato slices. Sprinkle each slice with salt, cubebs or black pepper and a few drops of the dressing.

On individual plates, reassemble the tomatoes, putting a slice of watermelon and a mint leaf between each layer. Spear with a small skewer. Crumble the goat's cheese over the tomato and watermelon, then sprinkle with a little of the dressing.

# Farm-raised Chicken with Curry Leaves, Plantain Mousseline and Butternut Squash and Curry Emulsion

**Serves 4**

**6 garlic cloves, unpeeled**
**200ml (7oz) skimmed (skim) milk**
**4 large, corn-fed chicken breasts (breast halves), skin on**
**$^1/_2$ teaspoon garam masala**
**12 small fresh curry leaves**
**a pinch of ground ginger**
**2 tablespoons olive oil**
**salt and freshly ground white pepper**

For the butternut squash and curry emulsion:
**2 tablespoons olive oil**
**150g (scant 1 cup) butternut squash, peeled, deseeded and diced**
**25g ($2^1/_2$ cups) onion, chopped**
**1 tablespoon finely chopped fresh ginger**
**$^1/_2$ tablespoon Madras curry powder**
**$^1/_2$ teaspoon ground turmeric**
**1.5 litres (6 cups) chicken stock**
**100g (7 tablespoons) butter, cut into small cubes**

For the plantain mousseline:
**400g (14oz) half-ripe plantains, peeled**
**150g (5oz) ripe plantains, peeled**
**200g (7oz) potatoes, peeled**
**200ml (7oz) full-cream milk**
**90g (6 tablespoons) butter, cut into small cubes and kept ice cold**

For the vegetables:
**300g (10oz) runner beans, trimmed**
**20g (2 tablespoons) butter**
**200g ($1^1/_3$ cups) butternut squash, peeled and cut into very small dice**
**$3^1/_2$ tablespoons chicken stock**

Blanch the garlic cloves 3 times in boiling water, changing the water each time. Put them in a saucepan, cover with the skimmed milk and cook for about 20–30 minutes, until the garlic is mellow and tender. Leave to cool, then peel the garlic and purée in a blender. Pass through a fine sieve.

Lift the skin away from the chicken breasts, rub the garlic purée and garam masala over the flesh and insert 3 small curry leaves under the skin of each breast. Make sure you do not rip the skin. Sprinkle the chicken on all sides with the ground ginger and some salt and pepper. Pack the breasts 2 at a time in zip-lock bags, or wrap them in cling film (plastic wrap). Remove as much air from the bags as possible, then seal. Heat a large saucepan or deep roasting tin (pan) of water to 80°C/178°F, place the sealed chicken breasts in the pan and leave for 15–18 minutes, using a thermometer to check that the temperature of the water remains constant. (Poaching the wrapped-up chicken like this captures all the flavours and keeps the flesh fantastically moist.) Cool the chicken breasts down rapidly in a large bowl filled with ice cubes and water. Place this in the refrigerator for 1 hour.

For the emulsion, heat the olive oil in a saucepan, add the squash, onion and ginger and cook for 7–8 minutes, until lightly caramelized. Add the curry powder and turmeric and sweat for 2 minutes. Add the chicken stock, bring to the boil and simmer for 15–20 minutes. Mix with a handheld blender until smooth. Add the butter and mix vigorously, then check the seasoning and pass through a fine sieve. Keep warm.

To make the plantain mousseline, put the plantains and potatoes in a pan and cover with cold salted water. Bring to the boil, cook over a medium heat for about 25 minutes, until tender, then drain. In a separate pan, heat the milk to boiling point, then remove from the heat. Pass the potatoes and plantains through a vegetable mill or a sieve into a heavy-based saucepan. Put the pan on a low heat to steam the vegetables dry, then gradually incorporate three-quarters of the milk, mixing vigorously. Now mix in the butter in small amounts to give a smooth mixture. Season with salt to taste. Only add the remaining milk if the mousseline is too dry. Keep warm and covered till needed.

For the vegetables, blanch the runner beans in a large pan of boiling salted water, then drain and cool down rapidly in iced water. Melt the butter in a small saucepan, add the diced butternut squash and cook for 3–4 minutes, until very lightly caramelized. Add the blanched beans and the chicken stock and leave to simmer until nicely glazed. Keep warm.

Heat the olive oil in a large, heavy-based non-stick frying pan (skillet) over a medium heat. Unwrap the chicken breasts, put them in the pan skin-side down and cook over a low heat for 8–10 minutes, until the skin is golden brown and crisp, basting it every minute with the olive oil to prevent it drying out. Drain on kitchen paper towels and cut each breast into 5 slices. Arrange a 'nest' of the runner beans in the centre of 4 serving plates and fill up with the plantain mousseline. Sprinkle the butternut squash dice on top of the beans. Mix the emulsion with the handheld blender until frothy and spoon it around the runner beans. Place the crispy chicken on top and serve.

# My Revisited Lime Tart

**Serves 4**

For the lime peel preserve:

**4 limes**
**450ml (2 cups) water**
**60g (5 tablespoons) caster (superfine or granulated) sugar**

For the lime sorbet:

**165g (3/4 cup) plus 2 tablespoons granulated sugar**
**450ml (2 cups) water**
**3g (1/2 teaspoon) green apple pectin, optional**
**50g (4 tablespoons) liquid glucose**
**265ml (1 cup plus 3 tablespooons) lime juice**
**grated zest of 1 lime**

For the lemon custard:

**5 eggs**
**80g (6 1/2 tablespoons) granulated sugar**
**50ml (3 1/2 tablespoons) single (light) cream**
**100ml (7 tablespoons) lemon juice**

For the caramelized rice crispies:

**50g (3 1/2 tablespoons) granulated sugar**
**40ml (2 1/2 tablespoons) water**
**100g (3 3/4 cups) rice crispies**

For the lime foam:

**31 (2 tablespoons) lime juice**
**50g (1/4 cup) granulated sugar**
**125ml (1/2 cup) full-fat milk**
**125ml (1/2 cup) whipping cream**

For the lime peel preserve, wash and peel the limes. Remove the bitter white film from inside the peel with a small sharp knife, then slice the peel into fine strips. Bring 200ml (7oz) of the water to the boil in a small pan and plunge in the peel. Blanch for 10 seconds, then strain. Put the remaining 250ml (1 cup) water in a pan with the sugar and bring to the boil. Add the peel and simmer over a low heat for 30 minutes, until tender. Remove from the heat.

To make the lime sorbet, put the sugar, water and apple pectin, if using, in a saucepan and bring to the boil. Add the glucose and let it dissolve, then remove from the heat. Put the pan in a bowl filled with ice and leave to cool. Stir in the lime juice and pass the mixture through a fine sieve. Freeze in an ice-cream machine, adding the grated lime zest when the sorbet is almost frozen.

For the lemon custard, beat the eggs and sugar together in a bowl, then mix in the cream, followed by the lemon juice. Place the bowl over a pan of gently simmering water, making sure the water does not touch the base of the bowl. Cook for 15-20 minutes, whisking vigorously, until the custard thickens. Strain through a fine sieve and leave to cool. Store in the fridge.

Next make the caramelized rice crispies. Put the sugar and water in a pan and bring to the boil. Add the rice crispies and mix until they are all coated thinly with the syrup. Sprinkle them over a baking tray lined with baking parchment and place in an oven preheated to 180°C/350°F/Gas Mark 4. Leave for 5-10 minutes, until lightly caramelized. Remove from the oven and leave to cool, stirring them occasionally to prevent them sticking to each other. You can keep them for 1 week in an airtight container.

Finally, make the lime foam. Put the lime juice in a small pan and bring to the boil. Stir in the sugar, milk and cream and cook until it reaches 70°C/158°F on a sugar (candy) thermometer. Remove from the heat, pour into a bowl and place in a larger bowl full of ice. Leave to cool. Just before serving, whiz the mixture with a hand blender until frothy.

To assemble the dessert, put 6 tablespoons of the lemon custard in each of 4 whisky tumblers. Cover with 3 tablespoons of caramelized rice crispies and a tablespoon of preserved lime peel. Top with a big scoop of lime sorbet and then completely cover with the frothy lime foam. Serve immediately.

# eleven

# CHRIS GALVIN

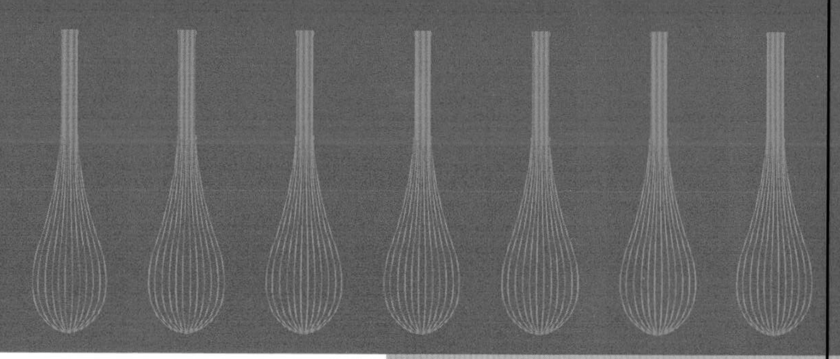

## The Wolseley

Chris Galvin began his career as a chef at the Ritz Hotel in London. He then worked at Inigo Jones, before moving to New York as head chef at Menage à Trois with Antony Worrall Thompson. On his return to London, he worked at L'Escargot and the Lanesborough Hotel, then joined the Conran Group and gained a Michelin star at Orrery, where he became chef-patron. He was promoted to chef-director for Conran Restaurants and joined the Wolseley café-restaurant in Piccadilly, in London, as executive chef in 2003.

**What are your favourite foods/tastes/flavours?**
The first arrival of any ingredient as it comes into season.

**What is your favourite utensil?**
A 20cm/8-inch cook's knife.

**What is your most useful piece of kitchen design and equipment?**
Good lighting, efficient work flow and a good-quality stove.

**What is your favourite season?**
Autumn.

**What is your favourite mealtime?**
Probably dinner, though all the others come a very close second!

**How do you decide what to cook?**
Ideally it's dictated by what's best available.

**What inspires you?**
Visiting markets and suppliers. Also, like most chefs, I love reading.

**What is your favourite drink?**
Probably white Burgundy, Meursault or Montrachet.

**What are your likes and dislikes?**
I like making customers happy, and passing on knowledge. I dislike lack of respect for ingredients.

**How can you inspire others to enjoy great food and cooking?**
By sharing knowledge and experiences and encouraging people to explore all things gastronomic.

**How did you become a chef?**
I remember being absolutely absorbed by food and restaurants from my early teens. This turned into a consuming passion that has never left me.

**What are your top ten ingredients?**
Poulet de Bresse, Pyrenees lamb, turbot, ceps (porcini), potatoes, tomatoes, artichokes, eggs, olive oil, parsley.

**What are your kitchen secrets?**
Always imagine you are cooking for a king/queen or someone you love!

**What are your top tips?**
Only use the very best available ingredients and keep your knives razor sharp.

**Do you have any favourite junk food?**
I can't think of any.

**How do you feel about cooking for children?**
I have four children so I understand the importance of cooking for children. I feel if we spent more time around a table with them and restaurants made it easier, the world might be a better place in the future. Children have to form social eating habits at some point, and from

my experience the earlier the better. It's amazing how quickly they adapt if you take the time to eat out with them and show them how pleasurable it can be.

**Can you give one piece of advice for the domestic cook?**

Always allow enough time to prepare a special meal – this can mean half a day. It takes me ages to cook something like this, so you are not alone. Also, when reading a recipe, close your eyes and cook the dish from start to finish in your head. You will be amazed at the way your cooking starts to flow, without constantly having to refer to the recipe.

* Soupe au Pistou
* Roast Shoulder of Lamb with Anchovies and Rosemary, Served with Pommes Dauphinoises and Mesclun Salad
* Croustade of Apples with Calvados Crème Fraîche

## Soupe au Pistou

**Serves 4**

**100ml (7 tablespoons) olive oil, preferably Provençal**
**1 onion, chopped**
**450g (1lb) French (green) beans, sliced 1.5cm/3/4-inch thick**
**450g (1lb) small broad (fava) beans**
**200g (1 1/3 cups) shelled peas**
**4 new carrots, sliced**
**2 courgettes (zucchini), sliced**
**100g (2/3 cup) Charlotte potatoes, peeled and cut into 1cm/1/2-inch dice**
**2 litres (2 quarts) Vichy water**
**50g (2oz) dried noodles or tagliatelle, broken into 2cm (3/4-inch) pieces**
**2 tomatoes, skinned, deseeded and diced**
**50g (1/3 cup) Gruyère cheese, finely grated**
**salt and freshly ground black pepper**

**For the pistou:**
**8 garlic cloves, peeled**
**8 stems of basil**
**2 teaspoons pine nuts**
**250ml (1 cup) extra virgin olive oil, preferably Provençal**

First make the pistou. Pound the garlic to a purée in a pestle and mortar, then add the basil leaves and pine nuts and pound with the garlic. Slowly work in the olive oil to form a sauce, then season with a little salt.

For the soup, heat the olive oil in a large pan, add the onion and cook gently until softened. Add the remaining vegetables, cover and sweat gently for a few minutes, without letting them colour. Add the water and bring to the boil. Simmer for about 8 minutes, until the vegetables are cooked. Add the noodles and cook for 4–5 minutes, until tender. Season to taste.

Remove from the heat, drop in the tomatoes and stir in the pistou. Divide between 4 bowls and sprinkle with the Gruyère.

# Roast Shoulder of Lamb with Anchovies and Rosemary, Served with Pommes Dauphinoises and Mesclun Salad

**Try to buy the very best-quality lamb you can. Shoulder is a cheaper cut that is worth the trouble of sourcing, as it delivers an amazing flavour. Ask your butcher to remove as much sinew as possible.**

**Serves 4**

**1 shoulder of lamb, boned, sinew removed, then rolled and tied (ask your butcher to do this)**
**2 garlic cloves, cut into thin slivers**
**leaves from a sprig of rosemary**
**15g (1/2oz) good-quality canned anchovies, such as Ortiz**
**20g (4 teaspoons) duck fat, melted**
**sea salt and freshly ground black pepper**

For the lamb stock:

**2 tablespoons olive oil**
**1kg (2 1/4lb) bones from the shoulder, chopped into 5cm/2-inch pieces (ask your butcher to do this)**
**1 carrot, roughly chopped**
**1 onion, roughly chopped**
**1 celery stick, roughly chopped**
**1 teaspoon tomato purée (paste)**
**a sprig of thyme**

For the lamb jus:

**20g (generous 1 tablespoon) shallot, sliced**
**150ml (2/3 cup) red wine, preferably Languedoc style**
**3 good sprigs of thyme**

For the Pommes Dauphinoises:

**1 garlic clove, peeled**
**50g (3 1/2 tablespooons) softened butter**
**200g (7oz) floury potatoes, peeled and cut into slices 3–4mm (about 1/8 inch) thick**
**50g (1/3 cup) Gruyère cheese, grated**
**500ml (2 1/4 cups) double (heavy) cream**
**250ml (1 cup) plus 2 tablespoons milk**
**a pinch of grated nutmeg**
**salt and freshly ground white pepper**

For the Mesclun Salad:

**250g (9oz) mixed young salad leaves**
**a few drops of lemon juice**
**2 tablespoons extra virgin olive oil**
**25g (2 tablespoons) mixed tarragon, chervil, parsley and chives, roughly chopped**
**salt and freshly ground black pepper**

**For the lamb**

First prepare the lamb stock. Heat the olive oil in a large, heavy pan until very hot and add the bones. Cook until coloured, then add the carrot and let that colour, too. Add the onion, celery and tomato purée, stirring to cook a little. Add the thyme and enough water to cover and bring to the boil. Skim any scum from the top and simmer for 1 1/2 hours, then strain through a sieve and set aside.

Make about 10 incisions in the shoulder of lamb, 1cm (1/2 inch) deep, and insert the garlic, rosemary leaves and anchovies into them, pushing them in until they are just showing on the surface. Rub the surface with the duck fat and place in a hot roasting tin (pan) just large enough to hold the lamb. Season with salt and pepper. Place in an oven preheated to 230°C/450°F/Gas Mark 8 and roast for 15 minutes, turning the meat every 5 minutes to sear and start to caramelize all over. Turn the oven down to 180°C/350°F/Gas Mark 4 and roast for 1 hour, basting every 15 minutes. Remove from the oven and transfer to a serving plate. Cover with foil and leave to rest for at least 15 minutes.

Meanwhile, make the jus. Put the roasting tin on the hob (stovetop), add the shallot and cook for a minute or two over a moderate heat. Swill the wine around the tin, stirring with a wooden spoon to scrape up any bits of meat. Allow to bubble and reduce by about half, then add the thyme and 250ml (1 cup) of the lamb stock. Bring to the boil and skim any froth from the surface, then simmer until reduced to about 100ml (7 tablespoons); it should be just thick enough to coat the back of a spoon. Pass though a sieve and adjust the seasoning if necessary.

Carve the lamb into slices and divide between 4 serving plates. Spoon the potatoes (see below) on to the plates and pour a little of the jus around. Accompany with the salad (see below).

**For the Pommes Dauphinoises**

Rub the inside of a thick roasting dish with the garlic clove, then smear it with the soft butter. Layer the potatoes in the dish, seasoning as you go with salt, pepper and nutmeg and sprinkling a little cheese throughout (reserve some cheese for the top). Put the cream and milk in a pan and bring to the boil, then pour them over the potatoes; they should come just to the top of the potatoes. Place in an oven preheated to 180°C/350°F/Gas Mark 4 for 50 minutes, until the potatoes are tender, then turn up the oven to 200°C/400°F/Gas Mark 6 and cook for 10 minutes longer, to colour the top.

**For the Mesclun Salad**

Place the mixed leaves in a salad bowl. Whisk the lemon juice and olive oil together and season to taste. Sprinkle this dressing over the mixed leaves and toss with the herbs just before serving.

# Croustade of Apples with Calvados Crème Fraîche

**Serves 4**

**100g ($^1/_2$ cup) caster (superfine) sugar**
**75g ($^3/_4$ stick) chilled unsalted butter**
**6 Braeburn apples, peeled, cored and sliced into eighths**
**4 drops of lemon juice**
**300g (10oz) puff pastry**
**120ml ($^1/_2$ cup) Calvados crème fraiche (see Note below)**

Heat the sugar and butter in a large, heavy-based frying pan (skillet) by swirling them over a moderate heat until the sugar has dissolved and the butter melted. Continue to cook until the mixture turns into an amber caramel. Please take care, as it will reach a very high temperature. As the caramel turns golden, drop the apples into it and gently turn them over to coat. Add the lemon juice and cook for 2–3 minutes, until the apples are almost cooked but still firm in the middle. Remove the apples from the pan with a slotted spoon and set aside. Pour the remaining caramel into four 10cm (4-inch) rösti pans, one large ovenproof frying pan or a cake tin (pan) and leave to cool. Arrange the apples in the pans, round-side down, packing them in as tightly as possible. The base of the pans should be completely covered.

Roll out the puff pastry on a lightly floured surface until it is 4mm (about $^1/_4$ inch) thick and cut out four 12cm (5-inch) circles. Prick them with a fork to stop them rising too high, then cover the apples with them, tucking down the edges with the aid of a small palette knife (metal spatula) or fork. Bake in an oven preheated to 240°C/475°F/Gas Mark 8 for 12–16 minutes, until the pastry is golden. Remove from the oven and leave to settle for 3–4 minutes. Cover each pan with a serving plate, so that the tart can be inverted on to the plate by quickly turning it over and lifting off the pan. If it sticks, try heating the pan to loosen the caramel, then try again. Please remember the caramel is very hot, so take care when attempting this.
To serve, simply scoop out a ball of the crème fraîche and place in the middle of each tart, then pour any remaining caramel around the edge.

**Note**

Calvados crème fraîche can be found in some shops or can easily be made at home by mixing a capful of Calvados with 125ml ($^1/_2$ cup) thick crème fraîche. Spoon the mixture into some clean muslin (cheesecloth) and leave hanging overnight, with a dish underneath to catch residue moisture. The next day you will be able to form a scoop or quenelle of the crème fraîche without it being runny.

# twelve

# ROSE GRAY & RUTH ROGERS

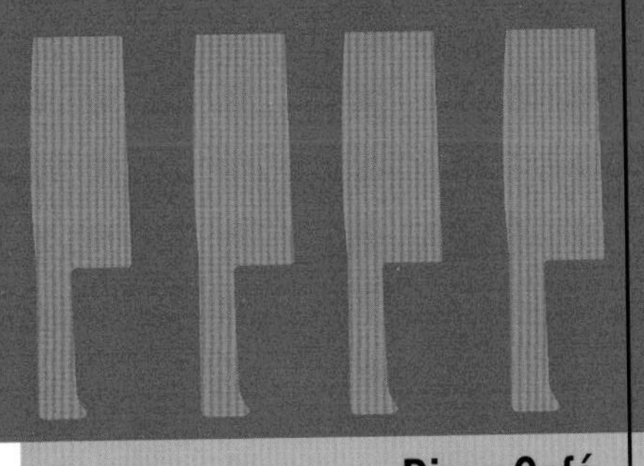

## River Café

Rose Gray and Ruth Rogers opened the River Café in 1987, bringing to London the flavours of Italian home cooking with an emphasis on the finest ingredients, an all-Italian wine list, and a modern, open dining atmosphere. The River Café has since earned a Michelin star and appears in *Restaurant* magazine's list of the top 50 restaurants in the world. Ruth and Rose have written six cookbooks and presented a 12-part series for Channel 4, 'The Italian Kitchen'.

**What are your favourite foods/flavours?**
Lemon, anchovies, chilli, olive oil.

**What are your favourite utensils?**
Mezzeluna and pestle and mortar.

**What is your most useful piece of kitchen equipment?**
Stainless steel surfaces, thick-bottomed stainless steel pans.

**What is your favourite season?**
Autumn.

**What is your favourite mealtime?**
Lunch – time to digest.

**How do you decide what to cook?**
What looks great in the market, what is seasonal.

**What inspires you?**
Italian food and culture.

**What is your favourite drink?**
Chianti Classico.

**What are your likes and dislikes?**
Likes – all good food, great restaurants.
Dislikes – fast food, bad restaurants.

**How can you inspire others to enjoy great food and cooking?**
By example – see our books.

**How did you become chefs?**
See our books.

**What are your top ten ingredients?**
Peeled plum tomatoes, basil, garlic, extra virgin olive oil, porcini mushrooms, fennel seeds, cavolo nero, artichokes, langoustines, polenta bramata.

**What are your kitchen secrets?**
Keep it simple.

**What are your top tips?**
Always buy the best-quality ingredients.

**Do you ever eat junk food?**
Dark chocolate, if you can call that junk!

**How do you feel about cooking for children?**
Love it.

**Can you give one piece of advice for the domestic cook?**
Be confident, read cookbooks.

* Asparagus with Anchovy Butter
* Sea Bass with Potatoes
* Dark Chocolate Truffle Cake

# Asparagus with Anchovy Butter

**Choose asparagus with tightly closed tips and firm stalks.**

**Serves 4**

**6 anchovy fillets**
**juice of $^{1}/_{2}$ lemon**
**150g ($1^{1}/_{4}$ sticks) unsalted butter, softened**
**800g ($1^{3}/_{4}$lb) asparagus**
**extra virgin olive oil**
**50g (2oz) Parmesan cheese**
**salt and freshly ground black pepper**

Rinse, dry and roughly chop the anchovies. In a bowl, mix them with the lemon juice and some black pepper, then use a fork to mix in the butter.

Cook the asparagus in boiling salted water until tender. Drain and season to taste. Drizzle with olive oil and place on warm plates. Spoon over the anchovy butter and scatter with Parmesan shavings.

# Sea Bass with Potatoes

**Serves 4**

**800g ($1^3/4$lb) waxy potatoes, peeled**
**extra virgin olive oil**
**1 x 2kg ($4^1/2$lb) sea bass**
**50g ($^1/3$ cup) black olives, pitted**
**50g ($3^1/2$ tablespoons) capers, rinsed**
**2 tablespoons thyme leaves**
**150ml ($^2/3$ cup) dry white wine**
**salt and freshly ground black pepper**

For the Salsa Verde:
**a large bunch of flat-leaf parsley**
**a bunch of basil**
**a handful of mint leaves**
**3 garlic cloves, peeled**
**100g (7 tablespoons) salted capers, rinsed**
**100g ($3^1/2$oz) salted anchovy fillets, rinsed**
**2 tablespoons red wine vinegar**
**5 tablespoons extra virgin olive oil**
**1 tablespoon Dijon mustard**
**sea salt and freshly ground black pepper**

Cook the potatoes in boiling salted water until just tender. Drain and cut them lengthways into 5cm (2-inch) slices.

Line a baking tray with baking parchment paper, drizzle with olive oil and cover with the potatoes. Place the fish on top and scatter over the olives, capers and thyme. Push some inside the fish and season.

Put in an oven preheated to 200°C/400°F/Gas Mark 6 and cook for 5 minutes. Pour over the wine and a little more oil, return to the oven and bake for about 20 minutes, until the fish is cooked.

Remove the fillet from each side of the bass and divide into 4. Serve the fish with the potatoes, olives and capers, the cooking juices poured over and salsa verde (see below).

**For the salsa verde**
If using a food processor, pulse-chop the parsley, basil, mint, garlic, capers and anchovies until roughly blended. Transfer to a large bowl and add the vinegar. Slowly pour in the olive oil, stirring constantly, and finally add the mustard. Check the seasoning.

This sauce may also be prepared by hand, on a board, preferably using a mezzaluna.

# Dark Chocolate Truffle Cake

**This dark chocolate truffle cake can be made the day before, so long as you keep it covered in the fridge. Serve as a dessert with crème fraîche. Choose the best chocolate you can find, with 70 per cent cocoa solids. The taste of the cake reflects the flavour of the chocolate. Good brands to look for are Green and Black's organic, Valrhona and Amedei.**

**Serves 4**

**225g (8 oz) chocolate, with 70 per cent cocoa solids**
**300ml ($1^1/4$ cups) double (heavy) cream**
**2 tablespoons unsweetened cocoa powder**

Break the chocolate into pieces and melt in a bowl placed over a pan of simmering water, making sure the water doesn't touch the base of the bowl. Warm the cream, then stir it into the warm chocolate. Place a 15cm (6-inch) cake ring on a flat plate. Pour the mixture into the ring and leave in the fridge for 1 hour to set.

To remove the ring, soak a dishcloth in very hot water and wrap it around the ring for 2 minutes to melt the edges of the cake slightly, making it easy to turn out. Shake the cocoa powder over the top.

# ANGELA HARTNETT

thirteen

## Angela Hartnett at The Connaught

Coming from an Italian–Irish background, Angela has always had a love of food. After completing a History degree, she worked in Cambridge for a couple of years, with a brief stint in Barbados. From there she went to work for Gordon Ramsay, starting as a chef de partie at his first restaurant, Aubergine. There followed ten years working with him in various restaurants, including a stint as executive chef at his restaurant in Dubai. Back in London, she was appointed head chef at the Connaught, where she won her first Michelin star, becoming one of a handful of women to have this honour in the UK.

**What are your favourite foods/flavours?**
Italian food, then Japanese.

**What are your favourite utensils?**
A metal spoon I have had for years, since the days of working for Gordon [Ramsay]. My grandmother's coffee machine – an original you have to turn upside down to work.

**What is your most useful piece of kitchen equipment?**
An ice-cream machine. I just love the idea of all those frozen flavours. Italians make the best ice cream.

**What is your favourite season?**
Summer for all the soft fruits, autumn for the white truffles from Italy, plus you can start to make lovely hot soups.

**What is your favourite mealtime?**
Breakfast.

**How do you decide what to cook?**
I talk to my head chef, see what's in season and what's available and just go for it.

**What inspires you?**
I love to eat. I'm also inspired by places, going abroad, and eating out in different restaurants.

**What is your favourite drink?**
Black coffee first thing in the morning, or pink champagne.

**What are your likes and dislikes?**
I dislike coriander and coconut. I love everything else.

**How can you inspire others to enjoy great food and cooking?**
By showing them, letting them enjoy the flavours, and making them understand it is not so difficult.

**How did you become a chef?**
I always wanted to run a restaurant and was lucky to work with chefs who were prepared to let me learn.

**What are your top ten ingredients?**
Olive oil, basil, tomatoes, fresh pasta, flat-leaf parsley, garlic, rosemary, vanilla, white truffles, pumpkin.

**What are your kitchen secrets?**
No secrets, just buy the best ingredients you can afford.

**Do you have any favourite junk food?**
Kentucky Fried Chicken.

**How do you feel about cooking for children?**
I love to cook for children, especially my nephews, Finn and Billy.

**Can you give one piece of advice for the domestic cook?**
Keep your knives sharp.

My passage
to India

* Pumpkin Tortelli with Amaretti Biscuits
* Braised Halibut on Red and Yellow Pepper Confit
* Roasted Figs in Red Wine Served with Zabaglione

## Pumpkin Tortelli with Amaretti Biscuits

**For me, cooking is about the family sitting around the table, talking and laughing. That's how I was brought up, and we are all a product of our environment.**
**I have chosen these dishes because they illustrate the above. Nothing is complicated, and all the cooking has done is transform the raw ingredients into a meal.**

**Serves 4**

**1kg (2 1/4lb) pumpkin**
**4 tablespoons olive oil**
**20g (4 teaspoons) butter**
**1 large onion, thinly sliced**
**50g (1 cup) fresh breadcrumbs**
**50g (2oz) Parmesan cheese, freshly grated, plus extra to serve**
**30g (2 tablespoons) amaretti biscuits, crushed, plus extra to serve**
**1 egg, beaten with 1 tablespoon water, for the egg wash**
**sea salt and freshly ground black pepper**

For the pasta dough:

**550g (3 2/3 cups) strong (bread) white flour**
**a pinch of salt**
**2 tablespoons olive oil**
**4 eggs**
**6 egg yolks**

For the sage emulsion:

**200g (1 3/4 sticks) butter**
**200ml (7oz) vegetable stock**
**6–8 sage leaves, shredded**

Cut the pumpkin into pieces, season with salt and wrap in foil. Roast in an oven preheated to 200°C/400°F/Gas Mark 6 until tender. Meanwhile, heat the olive oil and butter in a pan, add the onion and cook gently until very soft but not coloured.

When the pumpkin is done, remove the skin and put the flesh in a food processor with the onion. Process until smooth, then leave in a sieve or a piece of muslin (cheesecloth) overnight to drain off any excess liquid. Mix with the breadcrumbs, Parmesan and amaretti biscuits. Season to taste with salt and pepper, adjusting the amount of amaretti or Parmesan, if liked. The mixture should be firm enough to hold together but not too dry.

To make the pasta dough, put the flour, salt and olive oil in a food processor and blitz well. Whisk the eggs and yolks together and slowly pour half of them into the flour mixture, blitzing all the time. Add enough of the remaining egg to give a mixture like large breadcrumbs (you may not need all the egg). When you can press the mixture together with your fingers to form a dough, it's ready. Turn out on to a board and knead by hand until smooth and elastic. Wrap in cling film (plastic wrap) and leave to rest in the fridge for 1–2 hours.

Cut the dough into 8 pieces and shape them into balls. Keep each one wrapped in cling film until ready to roll out. Using a hand-cranked pasta machine, roll a pasta ball into a long, thin sheet, about 80 x 13cm (32 x 5 1/4 inches). Trim the edges to neaten, then, with a long edge nearest you, place rounded teaspoonfuls of the filling in a single line along one third of the pasta, spacing them about 1cm (1/2 inch) apart. Brush between the heaps of filling with the egg wash and lightly brush the other two-thirds of the dough, too. Carefully fold the pumpkin-topped third of the pasta over to enclose the filling, pressing between the filling with your fingers to seal it and expel any air pockets. Fold the other third of the pasta over the top and press between the filling again, then cut out the tortelli with a fluted pasta cutter. Repeat with the remaining pasta sheets and filling.

If you are not going to serve the tortelli immediately, blanch them in boiling water for 30 seconds, then drain, refresh in iced

water and drain again. Leave in the fridge, drizzled with a little olive oil to prevent them sticking.

For the sage emulsion, gently melt the butter in a large pan and skim off the white froth from the top. Add the vegetable stock and bring to the boil, then whiz with a handheld blender to emulsify. Add the sage.

Cook the tortelli in a large pan of boiling water for 2 minutes or until they rise to the surface. Remove from the pan and add to the sage emulsion. Serve immediately, finished with freshly grated Parmesan and a sprinkling of crushed amaretti biscuits.

# Braised Halibut on Red and Yellow Pepper Confit

**This is very good served with roasted artichokes and sautéed new potatoes.**

**Serves 4**

**4 x 125g (4-oz) pieces of halibut fillet**
**1 tablespoon olive oil**
**1 tablespoon chopped chervil**
**500ml (2 1/4 cups) good-quality chicken stock, boiled until reduced by half**
**10g (2 teaspooons) butter**
**150ml (2/3 cup) vinaigrette (made using 5 parts olive oil to 1 part white wine vinegar)**
**1 fennel bulb, finely shredded**
**salt and freshly ground black pepper**
**sprigs of dill, to serve**

For the red and yellow pepper confit:
**3 red (bell) peppers**
**3 yellow (bell) peppers**
**1/2 head of garlic**
**3 sprigs of thyme**
**3 sprigs of rosemary**
**4 tablespoons olive oil**
**6 large basil leaves, shredded**

First prepare the pepper confit. Put the peppers on a baking tray, scatter with the garlic, thyme and rosemary and then bake in an oven preheated to 200°C/400°F/Gas Mark 6 until the skin starts to blister. Remove from the oven, place the peppers in a bowl and cover tightly with cling film (plastic wrap). This enables the skin to be removed easily. Peel the skin off the peppers, cut the flesh into strips and sauté lightly in the olive oil with the basil for 2–3 minutes. Season to taste and remove from the heat.

Season the halibut with salt and pepper. Heat the olive oil in a large, non-stick frying pan (skillet), add the halibut skin-side down and cook over a medium-high heat until coloured underneath. Turn the fish over, sprinkle with the chervil and cover with the reduced chicken stock (this keeps the fish lovely and moist and ensures it cooks quickly). Add the butter and cook for about 4 minutes, until the fish is done. Remove from the pan.

To serve, divide the pepper confit between 4 plates and place the fish on top. Drizzle with some of the vinaigrette. Toss the shredded fennel with a little vinaigrette and place on top of the fish, then garnish with the dill.

# Roasted Figs in Red Wine Served with Zabaglione

**Serves 4**

**8–12 figs per person, depending on size**
**500g ($2^1/_2$ cups) caster (superfine) sugar**
**1 litre (1 quart) water**
**375ml ($1^1/_2$ cups) red wine**

For the zabaglione:
**4 egg yolks**
**60g (5 tablespoons) caster sugar**
**10g (2 teaspoons) muscovado sugar**
**240g (generous 1 cup) Moscato wine, or other sweet dessert wine**

Peel the figs, taking care not to damage the shape. Put the sugar, water and wine in a heavy-based pan and place over a low heat, stirring occasionally, until the sugar has dissolved. Bring to the boil, then reduce the heat and add the figs. Cover the mixture with a piece of baking parchment paper and poach the figs for 8–10 minutes, until tender. Drain well, reserving the liquid. If not serving immediately, let the figs cool and then store them in a container in the fridge.

To make the zabaglione, put all the ingredients in a large bowl set over a pan of simmering water, making sure the water does not touch the base of the bowl. Whisk with a balloon whisk or a handheld electric beater until the mixture is thick and fluffy and has at least doubled in size. Serve immediately with the figs, warming them through in the cooking liquor if necessary. To make the dish even richer, you could boil the fig cooking liquid until thick and syrupy and serve it on the side.

# SHAUN HILL

Shaun Hill started his career at Robert Carrier's groundbreaking London restaurant in the late 1960s. He spent nine years as head chef at Gidleigh Park in Devon and ten years as chef-patron of Merchant House in Ludlow, Shropshire, England.

**What is your favourite utensil?**
A carving fork that has one long stem before a curved prong is ideal for carving, holding food steady, and generally poking at things – or people.

**What is your most useful piece of kitchen equipment?**
A liquidiser (blender). This will centrifuge broth into sauce, emulsifying ingredients with olive oil to give a smooth, creamy consistency. Food processors are handy but do nothing that a sharp knife and more time won't achieve.

**What is your favourite season?**
Autumn, when game – the last truly seasonal food – becomes available, along with the best selection of fruit and vegetables. More importantly, the cooling weather makes you feel hungrier. No surprise that Harvest Festival happens in autumn.

**What inspires you?**
The produce and the possibilities.

**What is your favourite drink?**
Red Burgundy, Claret, Riesling, how do you choose? I keep experimenting in case a final decision dawns.

**What are your likes and dislikes?**
I really dislike the pomposity and pretension that can surround food and cookery. I am also wary of food created by chefs who are driven by craft skills rather than pleasure. I like good company and booze to go with the meal.

**What are your kitchen secrets?**
Take care over basics, such as the timing of your cooking and the sequence in which you make things. No amount of elaborate garnish will help an incorrectly seasoned or clumsily cooked dish.

**Can you give one piece of advice for the domestic cook?**
Work to the advantages of home cooking rather than trying to imitate restaurant meals. A restaurant will have a brigade of chefs preparing stocks or chopped peeled tomatoes all afternoon and will, as they do not join you at the table, be able to complete lots of last-minute touches that may be awkward at home. On the other hand, at home you may safely ask people to eat when the food is ready and will not expect everyone to be eating something different. Whole roast duck or chicken, for instance, takes longer to cook than a restaurant diner will be prepared to wait, so will always be a better home dish.

UM!
Please do not hesi
Would you please
With best wishes.
917 613 4165
Salutes parents
Bathes daily
STANDARD TER
FE
AUTUMN TERM
SPRING TERM
SUMMER TER
HE
EMBER 2004 (12wks)
H 2005 (10wks)
(10 wks)

* Spiced Quail
* Fish Stew with Garlic, Saffron and Chilli
* Rhubarb Tart with Ginger Custard

# Spiced Quail

**This dish looks complex and packed with different ingredients but in fact it is very straightforward. A couple of points to watch: quail, like all poultry, are easier to negotiate if the wishbones are removed before cooking. And a liquidizer is best for making the sauce. A food processor cannot be substituted here.**

**Serves 4**

**4 large quail**

For the marinade:

**1/2 small red (bell) pepper**
**1/2 small chilli**
**1 large garlic clove**
**1 tablespoon mint**
**1 teaspoon ground cumin**
**1 teaspoon saffron threads**
**2 tablespoons olive oil**
**salt and freshly ground black pepper**

For the sauce:

**4 tablespoons water or chicken stock**
**4 tablespoons olive oil**
**2 tablespoons sesame oil, not toasted**
**4 tablespoons pine nuts**
**4 tablespoons flat-leaf parsley**
**a few drops of Tabasco sauce**
**a few drops of lemon juice**
**a few drops of soy sauce**

For the salad:

**4 small handfuls of mixed salad leaves**
**1 teaspoon olive oil**
**a few drops of lemon juice**
**a few pomegranate seeds and toasted pine nuts, optional**

First make the marinade. Finely chop the red pepper, chilli, garlic and mint, then crush them to a pulp with the cumin and saffron, using the flat of your knife blade and a little salt, or a pestle and mortar. Work in the olive oil, then massage the result into the skin of the quail. Leave for a few hours, preferably overnight.

Put the quail in a roasting tin (pan) and roast in an oven preheated to 200°C/400°F/Gas Mark 6. The time taken will vary according to the size of the birds but should be around 20 minutes.

For the sauce, place all the ingredients in a liquidiser (blender) and blend until smooth. If it is too thick, add a little water or lemon juice; if too thin, add a little more oil. Your aim is the consistency and texture of thick cream. (You won't need all the sauce for this recipe but it keeps well in the fridge or freezer.)

When the quails are done, dress the salad leaves with the oil, lemon juice and a little salt and place them in a pile on 4 plates. Garnish with a few pomegranate seeds and toasted pine nuts, if liked. Put the hot quail on a tablespoonful of the sauce next to the salad. Place the roasting tin on the hob (stovetop) and add a tablespoon of water, stirring and scraping the base of the tin to deglaze it. Strain a few drops of this on to each quail and serve.

# Fish Stew with Garlic, Saffron and Chilli

**This dish is a regular vehicle for tidying the remains of whatever fish was on Saturday's menu. It is as time sensitive as any soufflé, as I don't like overcooked fish (I hate traditional bouillabaisse-type jobs, as the fish is almost always cooked to death in order to make the liquor taste better), but it can be put together fairly swiftly from the sort of things that are always in my kitchen.**

**This stew is meant to be warm and spicy rather than vindaloo. The method is based on bourride, in that it is thickened with garlic mayonnaise, but the result is sharper and more citric.**

**The fish used can, of course, vary according to what suits and what is available. I tend to boil scraped new potatoes in the liquor and serve them in the stew. No other vegetables, though, just a salad with the cheese course that always follows.**

**Serves 4**

**1 tablespoon sunflower oil**
**2 shallots, chopped**
**1/4 red (bell) pepper, chopped**
**1 tablespoon chopped celery**
**1 teaspoon saffron threads**
**1 bird's eye chilli, chopped**
**grated zest of 1/2 orange**
**1 garlic clove, peeled**
**500ml (2 1/4 cups) chicken stock**
**150g (5oz) halibut fillet**
**150g (5oz) red mullet fillet**
**100g (3 1/2oz) white scallop meat**
**50g (2oz) cooked prawns or shrimps**

**For the garlic mayonnaise:**

**2 egg yolks**
**1 garlic clove, finely chopped**
**1 tablespoon Dijon mustard**
**1 tablespoon lemon juice**
**3 1/2 tablespoons sunflower oil**
**3 1/2 tablespoons olive oil**
**salt and freshly ground black pepper**

First make the garlic mayonnaise. Whisk together the egg yolks, garlic, mustard and lemon juice, then whisk in the oils, a drop at a time at first, adding them a little faster as the emulsion thickens. Season to taste and set aside.

Heat the sunflower oil in a large pan, add the shallots, red pepper and celery and sweat until softened. Add the saffron, chilli, garlic and orange zest, then the stock. Bring to the boil and simmer for a few moments. Add the fish in the order in which it takes to cook – in this case the halibut, followed by the red mullet and then at the last moment the scallops and prawns or shrimps.

Take the pan off the heat and strain all the liquid into a liquidiser (blender), along with the bits and pieces of vegetable and orange. Blend with the mayonnaise, adding the mayonnaise a spoonful at a time and stopping when the soup begins to thicken. Pour the liquor back on to the fish and warm through gently. Serve with warm crusty bread.

# Rhubarb Tart with Ginger Custard

**Serves 4**

**600g (1$^1$/4lb) rhubarb, cut into 3cm (1$^1$/4-inch) lengths**
**2 eggs, plus 4 egg yolks**
**100g ($^1$/2 cup) caster (superfine) sugar**
**150ml ($^2$/3 cup) double (heavy) cream**

For the pastry:

**200g (1$^3$/4 sticks) unsalted butter**
**90g (7$^1$/2 tablespoons) caster (superfine) sugar**
**2 eggs**
**475g (3$^1$/3 cups) plain (all-purpose) flour**

For the ginger custard:

**5 medium (large) egg yolks**
**50g (4 tablespoons) caster (superfine) sugar**
**275ml (1 cup plus 3 tablespoons) whole milk**
**40g (3 tablespoons) crystallized ginger, chopped**

To make the pastry, beat together the butter and sugar until pale. Beat in 1 egg, then beat in 100g ($^2$/3 cup) of the flour and the remaining egg. Fold in the remaining flour to give a smooth dough. Cover the pastry with cling film (plastic wrap) and leave to rest in a cool place for an hour.

Roll out the pastry and use to line a 26cm (10$^1$/2-inch) tart tin (pan). Prick with a fork a couple of times and bake blind for 15 minutes in an oven preheated to 200°C/400°F/Gas Mark 6 (if the pastry bubbles up, gently tamp it down with a cloth or a piece of paper).

Place the rhubarb in the cooked pastry case. Whisk the eggs and egg yolks with the sugar and cream and pour this over the rhubarb. Return the tart to the oven and bake for 40 minutes, until just set.

Meanwhile, make the custard. Whisk the egg yolks and sugar together in a bowl. Heat the milk and ginger to boiling point, then whisk into the egg and sugar mixture. Return this custard to the saucepan and cook very gently for about 10 minutes, stirring constantly, until it starts to thicken – don't let it boil. Serve with the rhubarb tart.

# HYWEL JONES

## Lucknam Park

London life, Michelin star – Hywel Jones had it all. This talented chef's career got off to a flying start and he eventually earned his star at Foliage in the Mandarin Oriental Hyde Park Hotel. Fast forward to Lucknam Park in Wiltshire, where Hywel's sensitive creativity is taking the menu to new heights. Perfect combinations, new dishes, superb Welsh produce where possible, are all part of Hywel's innovative repertoire.

**What are your favourite foods/tastes/flavours?**
I pretty much like all types of food as long as they are done well. I am especially fond of my mother's lamb stew.

**What is your favourite utensil?**
A Thermomix.

**What is your most useful piece of kitchen equipment?**
Fridges.

**What is your favourite season?**
Each season brings with it some goodies but it would have to be spring. As well as all the food that starts then, it brings a bit of sunshine that gets you thinking about the summer.

**What is your favourite meal?**
Breakfast: poached haddock.
Lunch: roast chicken baguette.
Dinner: anything cooked by someone else.

**How do you decide what to cook?**
Pretty much all of what I cook is dictated by what is in season or is particularly good quality.

**What inspires you?**
I take inspiration from all kinds of things, as most people do. I find people like Matthew Pinsent tremendously inspirational. His absolute will to win makes you think about how committed you are.

**What is your favourite drink?**
Stella Artois by the bucket full! Or Brains SA, as they sponsor Wales.

**What are your likes and dislikes?**
Likes – watching Wales beat England at rugby.
Dislikes – watching England beat Wales at rugby.

**How can you inspire others to enjoy great food and cooking?**
For people to enjoy good food, they need to appreciate it. To appreciate food you need to go back to grassroots level and look at what goes into producing it. Too many people pick things up off supermarket shelves without the slightest idea of how much time, effort and work has gone into it. For example, the guy I buy my smoked salmon from goes to Scotland every two weeks to handpick his salmon. He refuses to vacuum pack his produce, as he believes it affects the quality. When you see his passion for what he does, it makes you appreciate the end results even more.

**How did you become a chef?**
I used to enjoy cookery lessons at school and it stemmed from there.

**What are your top ten ingredients?**
Fresh crabmeat, beetroot (beets), rosemary, salt, salt-marsh lamb, Pant Mawr cheese, raspberries, English asparagus, spring peas, morels.

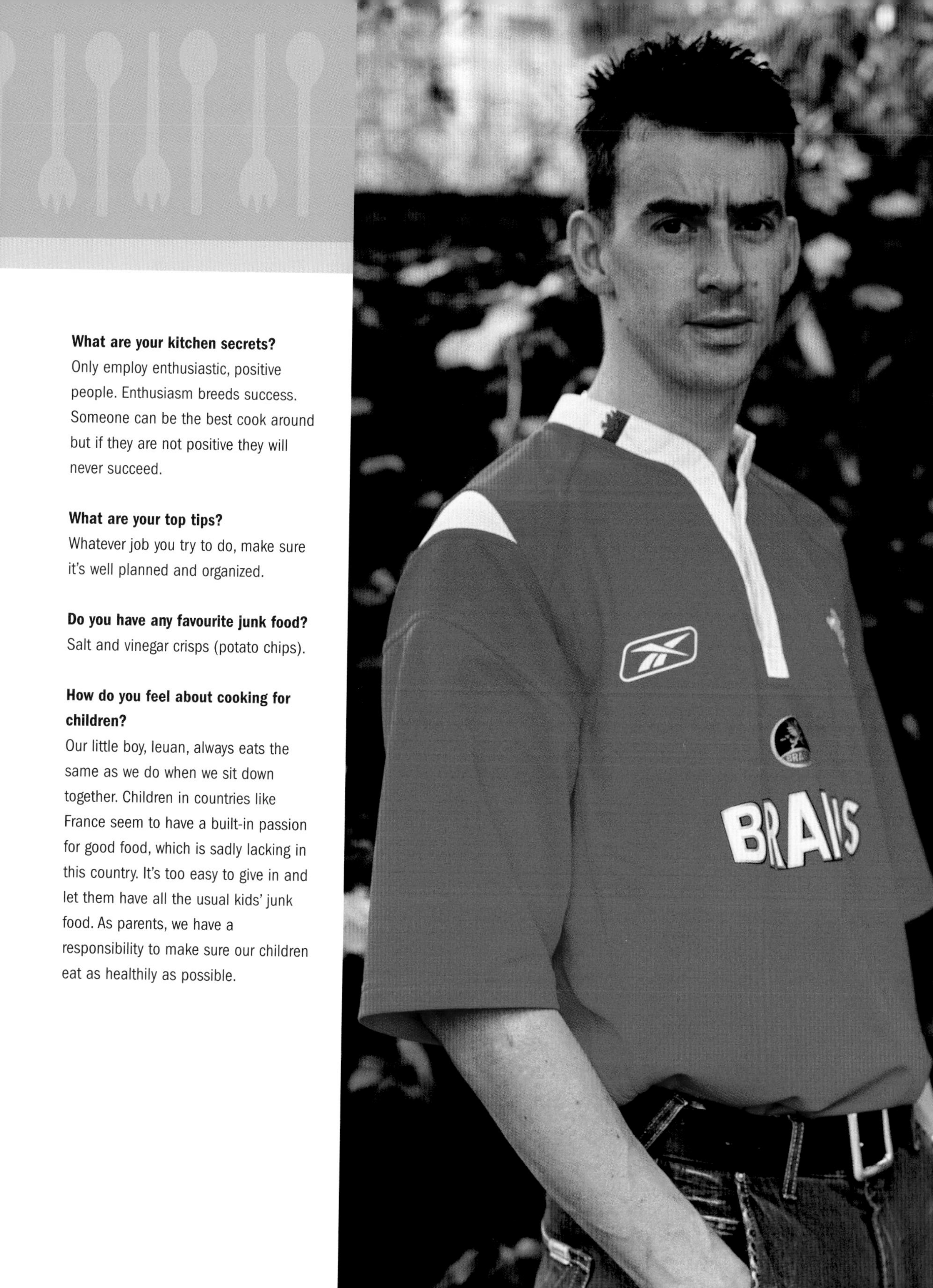

**What are your kitchen secrets?**
Only employ enthusiastic, positive people. Enthusiasm breeds success. Someone can be the best cook around but if they are not positive they will never succeed.

**What are your top tips?**
Whatever job you try to do, make sure it's well planned and organized.

**Do you have any favourite junk food?**
Salt and vinegar crisps (potato chips).

**How do you feel about cooking for children?**
Our little boy, Ieuan, always eats the same as we do when we sit down together. Children in countries like France seem to have a built-in passion for good food, which is sadly lacking in this country. It's too easy to give in and let them have all the usual kids' junk food. As parents, we have a responsibility to make sure our children eat as healthily as possible.

* Warm Organic Salmon with Crab Croquettes and Beetroot and Vanilla Dressing
* Cassoulet Toulouse
* Lavender Sablés with Honey Crème Fraîche and Raspberries

## Warm Organic Salmon with Crab Croquettes and Beetroot and Vanilla Dressing

**Serves 6**

**1 frisée lettuce**
**2 tablespoons chopped chives**
**600g (1 1/4 lb) organic salmon fillet, skinned**
**olive oil**
**lemon juice**
**sea salt and freshly ground black pepper**

For the beetroot and vanilla dressing:

**1 large beetroot (beet), peeled and cut into 1cm (1/2-inch) dice**
**olive oil for drizzling**
**1 vanilla pod (vanilla bean), slit open lengthways**
**a few drops of balsamic vinegar**

For the crab croquettes:

**300g (10oz) fresh white crabmeat**
**1 tablespoon mayonnaise**
**a few sprigs of coriander (cilantro)**
**cayenne pepper**
**lemon juice**
**1 egg, beaten**
**100g (2 cups) fresh breadcrumbs**
**oil for deep-frying**

First make the dressing. Place the diced beetroot on a piece of aluminium foil, drizzle with a little olive oil and scrape the seeds from the vanilla pod on to it. Sprinkle a few grains of sea salt on top. Wrap up in the foil and bake in an oven preheated to 160°C/325°F/Gas Mark 3 for 1 1/2 hours or until soft. Open the foil and blend the contents in a food processor to make a dressing. If it is too thick, add about a tablespoon of water; it should be the consistency of double (heavy) cream. Season with the balsamic vinegar and set aside.

Using a clean kitchen cloth, squeeze any excess moisture from the crabmeat. Place the crab in a mixing bowl and stir in the mayonnaise. Tear the coriander leaves into the mixture and season with cayenne pepper and lemon juice to taste. Divide into 6 and shape into cylinders about 1.5cm (3/4-inch) thick. Coat in the beaten egg, then in the breadcrumbs, and reshape if necessary. Place in the fridge.

Finely pick the yellow heart of the frisée lettuce, discarding the dark outer leaves. Wash and dry thoroughly and mix with the chopped chives.

Slice the salmon thinly, removing any dark flesh, and arrange neatly in a single layer in the centre of 6 lightly oiled serving plates. Brush the salmon with olive oil and season with salt and pepper. Place under a hot grill (broiler) for a few seconds, until it starts to change colour, then remove from the heat and season with lemon juice. Dress the frisée salad with a little olive oil and place in the centre of the salmon.

Deep-fry the croquettes in hot oil for about 1 minute, until golden brown. Drain on kitchen paper towels, then place them on the salad. Drizzle the beetroot dressing around and serve.

# Cassoulet Toulouse

**My first job was in a restaurant called Le Cassoulet, working for Gilbert Viader. We always had cassoulet on the menu and once a week all the staff sat down to eat a large pot of it. It was one of the first dishes I learned to cook and it still tastes fabulous.**

**Serves 6**

- **500g (2½ cups) dried haricot (navy or great northern) or cannellini beans, soaked in cold water for 24 hours**
- **2 large onions, 1 peeled and studded with a clove, 1 finely diced**
- **1 large carrot**
- **4 garlic cloves, crushed**
- **1 bouquet garni, made up of 2 sprigs each of thyme and parsley and 2 bay leaves**
- **80g (3oz) pork back fat, finely chopped**
- **80g (3oz) pork rind, cut into 1cm (½-inch) squares, blanched in boiling water, then refreshed in cold water**
- **50g (2oz) duck fat**
- **480g (17oz) pork neck fillet (tenderloin), cut into cubes**
- **1 large tablespoon tomato purée (paste)**
- **480g (17oz) Toulouse sausage ring**
- **100g (2 cups) fresh breadcrumbs**
- **sea salt and freshly ground black pepper**

For the confit duck legs:

- **6 small duck legs**
- **1 bouquet garni**
- **duck fat to cover**
- **sea salt and freshly ground black pepper**

First prepare the confit duck legs. Put the duck legs in a dish in a single layer and season heavily with salt and pepper. Refrigerate for 24 hours. Wash the seasoning off the duck legs and pat dry. Put them in a heavy-based pan with the bouquet garni, cover with duck fat, then cover the pan and simmer very gently for about 1½ hours, until the meat is tender enough to come away from the bone. Remove from the heat and set to one side.

Drain the beans, cover with plenty of fresh water and bring to the boil. At the same time, bring 2 litres (2 quarts) of water to the boil in a large casserole with the studded onion, the whole carrot, crushed garlic, bouquet garni, back fat and pork rind. When both pans have come to the boil, skim the froth off the pan of beans, then carefully decant the beans into the pan with the vegetables and pork. Simmer very gently for 2–2½ hours, until the beans are almost tender.

Meanwhile, cook the diced onion in half the duck fat until softened. Add the diced pork neck fillet and the tomato purée and cook over a gentle heat for about 20 minutes, turning constantly.

In a separate pan, fry the sausage ring in the remaining duck fat until golden brown on one side only.

Once the beans are ready, stir in the diced pork and onion mixture. Season heavily with sea salt and black pepper. Put the sausage ring on top, coloured-side down, then cover and place in an oven preheated to 160°C/325°F/Gas Mark 3. Cook for 1 hour, then add the confit duck legs and sprinkle with the breadcrumbs. Cook, uncovered, for 1 hour longer, until everything is tender and the crumbs are browned.

# Lavender Sablés with Honey Crème Fraîche and Raspberries

**Lucknam Park is surrounded by lavender, which I use in lots of different ways – for example, in jams, ice cream and even with potatoes. But these sablé biscuits are the business. The recipe below makes more than you need but they keep well in an airtight tin.**

**Serves 6**

**250g (2¼ sticks) unsalted butter**
**150g (1¼ cups) icing (confectioners') sugar**
**375g (2½ cups) plain (all-purpose) flour**
**3 eggs**
**1 tablespoon fresh lavender petals**
**1 tablespoon organic honey**
**400ml (1¾ cups) crème fraîche**
**2 punnets of raspberries**
**icing (confectioners') sugar for dusting**

Cream the butter and sugar together until light and fluffy. Fold in the flour, eggs and lavender and form into a dough. Do not overwork. Chill for 2 hours, or even overnight if convenient.

Roll out the dough on a lightly floured surface until it is 3mm (⅛ inch) thick and cut into rounds with a 7cm (2¾-inch) cutter. Place on greased baking sheets and leave to rest in the fridge for 1 hour. Bake in an oven preheated to 160°C/325°F/Gas Mark 3 for about 5 minutes, until golden. Remove from the oven and leave to cool.

Add the honey to the crème fraîche and whisk thoroughly. The mixture will initially turn liquid but will then re-thicken.
To serve, put a sablé on each serving plate, spoon the cream mixture on to it and top with another sablé. Sprinkle the raspberries around and dust with icing sugar.

# sixteen

# THOMAS KELLER

## The French Laundry

Widely regarded as one of America's finest chefs, Thomas Keller worked in ten Michelin-starred restaurants in France before returning to the US in 1984. He gained national recognition at La Reserve, Restaurant Raphael and his own Rakel, all in New York City, before becoming chef-proprietor of the world-renowned French Laundry restaurant in Napa Valley, California. His third restaurant, Per Se, opened in New York's Time Warner Center in early 2004 and received a coveted four-star rating from *The New York Times*. Keller is the author of the acclaimed *The French Laundry Cookbook* and *Bouchon*.

**What are your favourite foods/tastes/flavours?**
Sushi, salty, fat.

**What is your favourite utensil?**
A palette knife.

**What is the most useful piece of kitchen equipment and design?**
No one piece is more important than another. All are important, and what is essential is the integration of all the elements you need.

**What is your favourite season?**
Autumn.

**What is your favourite meal?**
Oatmeal for breakfast.

**How do you decide what to cook?**
My decision about what to cook is based on food I find inspiring and food that is in season. The decision is directed by a flash of inspiration.

**What inspires you?**
Everything.

**What are your likes and dislikes?**
I have no tolerance for bad food, unsanitary conditions, chaos and confusion. I like consistency, quality, standards and searching for new standards.

**What is your favourite drink?**
Red wine.

**How can you inspire others to enjoy great food and cooking?**
By giving them an example of the difference between great food and cooking and mediocre food and cooking. Being exposed to this difference first hand is paramount in understanding great cooking.

**How did you become a chef?**
Purely by accident; my Mom hired me because she felt sorry for me.

**What are your top ten ingredients?**
Top ingredients cannot be limited to ten. Everything that is available has the potential to be revered. It is important to avoid isolating ingredients, because seasons change and quality varies. If your focus is quality, your top ingredients are the best ingredients available to you at a given moment.

**What are your kitchen secrets?**
To have no secret.

**What are your top tips?**
Cooking is about being aware. Ultimate awareness creates more opportunity for inspiration. Inspiration leads to interpretation, which in turn leads to evolution.

**What is your favourite junk food?**
In-N-Out burger is my favourite fast food. Reese's or Snickers are favourite junk foods.

**How do you feel about cooking for children?**

I love it. Children are easy and predictable – once you know what they want, you can please them.

**Can you give one piece of advice for the domestic cook?**

Create relationships with your local food suppliers. This will ensure the continued availability of increasingly better products.

* Olive Oil and Sherry Vinegar Cured Sardines with a Bitter Orange Coulis and Pickled Bermuda Onions
* American Pot Roast *en Cocotte* with Winter Vegetables and Wholegrain Mustard Sauce
* Shortbread Millefeuille with Fresh Berries and Cream

## Olive Oil and Sherry Vinegar Cured Sardines with a Bitter Orange Coulis and Pickled Bermuda Onions

**Serves 4**

**4 very fresh sardines, filleted**
**250ml (1 cup) sherry vinegar**
**500ml (2 cups) extra virgin olive oil**
**5 peppercorns**
**3 sprigs of thyme**
**1 garlic clove, peeled**

For the bitter orange coulis:
**175g (6oz) navel orange zest, including about 25 per cent pith, about 4 medium to 6 large oranges**
**400g (2 cups) granulated sugar**
**orange juice**
**white wine vinegar**
**orange-infused extra virgin olive oil**

For the pickled Bermuda onions:
**30g (1/4 cup) red onions, sliced**
**4 tablespoons water**
**4 tablespoons red wine vinegar**
**50g (1/4 cup) caster (superfine) sugar**

To serve:
**a handful of mixed salad leaves, tossed in best-quality extra virgin olive oil and a little aged sherry vinegar**
**salt and freshly ground black pepper**

Put the sardines in a shallow dish, pour the sherry vinegar over them and leave for 15 minutes. Remove the sardines, pat dry and then leave to marinate in the olive oil with the aromatics for up to 1 week.

For the bitter orange coulis, blanch the orange zest 6 times, as follows:

- the second time in 500ml (2 cups) water and 50g (3 1/2 tablespoons) sugar for 6 minutes;
- the third time in 500ml (2 cups) water and 50g (3 1/2 tablespoons) sugar for 6 minutes;
- the fourth time in 500ml (2 cups) water and 75g (1/3 cup) sugar for 6 minutes;
- the fifth time in 500ml (2 cups) water and 75g (1/3 cup) sugar for 10 minutes;
- the sixth time in 750ml (3 1/3) cups water and 125g (1/2 cup plus 2 tablespoons) sugar for 20 minutes.

Then purée the blanched zest in a blender or food processor and strain through a fine sieve. Thin the purée with a mixture of half orange juice and half water until it is the consistency of processed yoghurt, then add white wine vinegar and orange-infused extra virgin olive oil to taste.

To prepare the pickled onions, blanch the onions in boiling water for 1 minute, then drain well. Put the water, vinegar and sugar in a small pan and bring to the boil, stirring to dissolve the sugar. Remove from the heat and add the blanched onions. Leave to cool – the onions will keep in their pickling liquid for 1 week.

To serve, lightly grill the sardines on a ridged griddle pan over a medium heat. Remove from the grill and drain off excess oil on kitchen paper towels. Place 2 fillets in the centre of each serving plate and garnish with the onions, salad leaves and bitter orange coulis.

# American Pot Roast *en Cocotte* with Winter Vegetables and Wholegrain Mustard Sauce

**Serves 4**

**1kg ($2^{1}/_{4}$lb) trimmed forerib of beef off the bone (boneless beef rib roast), ask your butcher for the trimmings and bones to use for the sauce**
**125ml ($^{1}/_{2}$ cup) canola oil**
**3 large carrots, cut into batons**
**16 baby turnips, peeled**
**1 head of celeriac (celery root), peeled and cut into 1cm ($^{1}/_{2}$-inch) cubes**
**16 small new potatoes, peeled**
**16 baby leeks, trimmed**
**salt and freshly ground black pepper**

For the wholegrain mustard sauce:

**4 tablespoons vegetable oil**
**300g (10oz) beef bones, cut up small – ask your butcher to do this**
**350g (12oz) lean, meaty trimmings from the beef**
**150g (1 cup) carrots, cut into 5mm ($^{1}/_{4}$-inch) dice**
**120g ($^{1}/_{2}$ cup) vine-ripened tomatoes, cut into 5mm ($^{1}/_{4}$-inch) dice**
**120g ($^{3}/_{4}$ cup) white onions, cut into 5mm ($^{1}/_{4}$-inch) dice**
**75g ($^{3}/_{4}$ cup) leek tops, cut into 5mm ($^{1}/_{4}$-inch) dice**
**1 tablespoon wholegrain mustard**
**1 tablespoon crème fraîche**
**1 tablespoon butter**

First make the base for the mustard sauce. Pour the oil into a large, heavy-based pan and place over a moderate heat. When hot, add the beef bones and cook until well browned. Add the beef trimmings and brown thoroughly. Add the vegetables and cook until caramelised. Deglaze by pouring in 100ml (scant $^{1}/_{2}$ cup) water and stirring to scrape up all the sediment from the base of the pan. Simmer until the liquid has almost completely evaporated and has reduce to a glaze. Repeat this process twice, using 150ml ($^{2}/_{3}$ cup) water each time. Repeat one last time, using 1 litre (1 quart) water and simmering until reduced to about 200ml (7oz). Strain through a fine sieve and leave to cool.

Season the beef and let it come to room temperature for 30 minutes. Heat the oil in a large casserole (Dutch oven), add the beef and brown on all sides. Remove the meat from the pan and drain off half the oil. Add all the vegetables except the leeks and reduce the heat to moderate. Season the vegetables with salt and pepper and cook until they begin to brown lightly around the edges. Return the beef to the casserole, cover and place in an oven preheated to 200°C/400°F/Gas Mark 6. Cook for 12 minutes, then remove the lid and cook for a further 10 minutes, which should give medium-rare meat. Remove from the oven and leave to rest for 20–30 minutes.

Bring the sauce base to a simmer and whisk in the mustard, crème fraîche and butter. Strain through a fine sieve and keep warm. Cook the leeks in boiling salted water until tender, then drain.

To serve, arrange the roast vegetables in the centre of 4 plates. Cut 12 slices of beef and arrange on top of the vegetables. Garnish the beef with the leeks and spoon the sauce around.

# Shortbread Millefeuille with Fresh Berries and Cream

**Serves 4**

For the vanilla shortbread:

**60g ($^1/_2$ cup) plain (cake) flour**
**100g ($^3/_4$ cup) strong (all-purpose) white flour**
**60g ($^1/_2$ cup) icing (confectioners') sugar**
**1/2 vanilla pod (vanilla bean)**
**140g ($1^1/_4$ sticks) butter, chilled and diced**

For the vanilla Chiboust:

**40g ($^1/_4$ cup) plain (all-purpose) flour**
**3 egg yolks**
**240g ($1^1/_4$ cups) caster (superfine) sugar**
**250ml (1 cup) milk**
**$^1/_2$ vanilla pod (vanilla bean)**
**30g (2 tablespoons) butter**
**3 egg whites**

For the sauce anglaise:

**6 egg yolks**
**140g ($1^1/_4$ cups) caster (superfine) sugar**
**500ml ($2^1/_4$ cups) double (heavy) cream**
**1 vanilla pod (vanilla bean)**

To serve:

**225g (8oz) raspberries**
**225g (8oz) blueberries**

To make the vanilla shortbread, sift all the dry ingredients into a mixing bowl. Using a sharp knife, slit the vanilla pod in half lengthways and scrape the seeds into the bowl. Add the diced butter and rub it into the dry ingredients until the mixture forms a dough. Wrap in cling film (plastic wrap) and leave in the fridge to rest for at least 2 hours.

Shortly before you want to roll out the shortbread, take the dough out of the fridge and leave at room temperature until pliable. Roll out on a lightly floured work surface to 3mm ($^1/_8$ inch) thick, place on a baking sheet (cookie sheet) and chill again. When firm, cut into 6 x 2.5cm ($2^1/_2$- x 1-inch) rectangles. Bake in an oven preheated to 160°C/325°F/Gas Mark 3 until golden, about 8 minutes in a convection oven, 15 minutes in a conventional oven. Leave to cool, then store in an airtight container.

Next make the Chiboust. Using a whisk, combine the flour, egg yolks and 30g ($2^1/_2$ tablespoons) of the sugar in a bowl. Put the milk and another 30g ($2^1/_2$) tablespoons sugar in a small saucepan. Using a sharp knife, slit the vanilla pod open lengthways and scrape the seeds into the pan. Bring the mixture to the boil, then remove from the heat and pour a little of the hot liquid on to the egg yolk mixture. Pour this mixture back into the pan and mix well. Strain into a clean pan and cook gently, stirring, until thickened. Remove from the heat and stir in the butter. Transfer this pastry cream to a bowl and then place in an ice bath to cool.

Put the remaining sugar in a small, heavy-based pan with $1^1/_2$ tablespoons of water and heat gently until the sugar has dissolved. Raise the heat and cook without stirring until the mixture reaches 120°C/248°F on a sugar (candy) thermometer. Immediately place the pan in an ice bath to stop the cooking, then remove. In a free-standing electric mixer, whisk the egg whites until they form medium peaks, then pour in the sugar syrup down the side of the bowl, whisking constantly. Continue to whisk until you have a thick, velvety meringue and the mixture is cool. Fold this meringue into the cooled pastry cream and place in the fridge.

Finally make the sauce anglaise. Whisk the egg yolks with half the sugar in a bowl. Put the cream and the remaining sugar in a heavy-based pan, then slit open the vanilla pod and scrape the seeds into the pan. Bring the mixture to the boil, remove from the heat and pour a little of the hot cream on to the egg yolk mixture. Mix well, then pour back into the pan and cook gently over a low heat, stirring constantly, until the sauce has thickened enough to coat the back of the spoon (do not let it boil). Strain through a fine sieve into a clean bowl. Place in an ice bath to cool, then transfer to the fridge.

To serve, place a rectangle of shortbread in the centre of each serving plate and spread a spoonful of the Chiboust over it. Arrange some raspberries and blueberries on top of the Chiboust, then place another rectangle of shortbread on top of the berries. Cover with Chiboust and berries once more, then top with a final rectangle of shortbread. Pour the crème anglaise around the plate and serve.

**Opposite: top, American Pot Roast *en Cocotte* with Winter Vegetables and Wholegrain Mustard Sauce; bottom, Shortbread Millefeuille with Fresh Berries and Cream**

seventeen

# GRAY KUNZ

## Café Gray

Gray Kunz is chef/owner of Café Gray, a modern European restaurant located in the Time Warner Center in New York City. He established himself as one of the premier chefs in New York while at Lespinasse, his four-star restaurant in the St Regis Hotel. Café Gray offers elegant, brasserie-style food, rooted in the Viennese tradition, reflected through the prism of 'Kunzian Cuisine', an inspired synthesis of seasonal ingredients, Eastern flavours and spices, and European culinary tradition. Gray Kunz is the author of *The Elements of Taste* (Little Brown, 2001).

**What are your favourite foods/tastes/flavours?**
Simple, home-cooked meals, strong/bold flavours.

**What is your favourite utensil?**
The Gray Kunz spoon.

**What is your most useful piece of kitchen equipment?**
A stove.

**What is your favourite season?**
Spring and autumn.

**What is your favourite meal?**
Breakfast: porridge.
Lunch: Sunday lunch.
Dinner: spaghetti with tomato sauce.

**How do you decide what to cook?**
Whatever is left over in the refrigerator.

**What inspires you?**
People and markets.

**What is your favourite drink?**
Sparkling water.

**What are your likes and dislikes?**
Likes: simple, clean and tasty approaches.
Dislikes: cuisines with no foundation.

**How can you inspire others to enjoy great food and cooking?**
By being a great teacher.

**How did you become a chef?**
It just evolved.

**What are your top ten ingredients?**
Fish, braised veal breasts, kaffir lime, lemongrass, spices, acidity, chocolate, chervil, ginger, steak.

**What are your kitchen secrets?**
Ask my son.

**What are your top tips?**
Stay positive.

**Do you have any favourite junk food?**
A Twix.

**How do you feel about cooking for children?**
Essential.

**Can you give one piece of advice for the domestic cook?**
Stay simple while being adventurous.
Surround yourself with the proper tools.

* Pasta Fiori with Tomato Concasse, Rosemary and Thyme
* Plancha-seared Redfish with Watercress and Ginger Broth
* Pear Soup with Vanilla Ice Cream and Almond Tuiles

## Pasta Fiori with Tomato Concasse, Rosemary and Thyme

**Serves 4**

For the pasta:

**a pinch of saffron threads**
**450g (3¼ cups) plain (all-purpose) flour**
**80g (½ cup) semolina**
**2 eggs**
**a pinch of fine sea salt**

For the tomato concasse:

**4 tablespoons extra virgin olive oil**
**90g (½ cup) shallots, diced**
**25g (2 tablespoons) garlic, chopped**
**6 tablespoons white wine**
**5 sprigs of rosemary**
**5 sprigs of thyme**
**1.4kg (3lb) Roma tomatoes, skinned, deseeded and diced**
**sugar to taste**
**cayenne pepper to taste**
**15g (¼ cup) parsley, finely chopped**
**15g (1 tablespoon) butter**
**15g (1 tablespoon) Parmesan cheese, freshly grated**
**salt and pepper**

For the beurre fondue:

**120ml (½ cup) chicken stock**
**115g (1 stick) butter, diced**
**salt and pepper**

For the sauce:

**½ tablespoon finely diced shallot**
**1 garlic clove, sliced**
**a pinch of rosemary**
**a pinch of thyme**
**2 tablespoons extra virgin olive oil**
**150ml (⅔ cup) chicken stock**
**2 tablespoons lemon juice**
**a pinch of salt**
**a pinch of sugar**
**a pinch of cayenne pepper**
**30g (2 tablespoons) butter**

For the garnish:

**5 sprigs of lemon thyme**
**10 basil leaves**
**10 opal basil leaves**
**Parmesan shavings (optional)**

To make the pasta, infuse the saffron in 4 tablespoons of warm water. Then sift the flour into the bowl of a food mixer and add the semolina, eggs, salt and saffron infusion. Mix with a dough hook until the dough comes away from the side of the bowl and forms a ball. Remove and knead until firm. Wrap the dough in cling film (plastic wrap) and chill for at least 2 hours. This will make more pasta dough than needed but the extra can be frozen for later use.

Roll out the dough on a pasta machine to number 6 and then cut it into 10cm (4-inch) rounds. You will need 2 per person, with a hole cut in the middle of half of them.

For the tomato concasse, heat the oil in a saucepan, add the shallots and garlic and sweat until tender. Add the white wine and simmer until reduced. Tie the rosemary and thyme in a bouquet and add to the pan with the tomatoes. Simmer until the mixture is thick and has reduced by three-quarters. Season with salt, pepper, sugar and cayenne. This will again make more than needed but the rest can be frozen for later use. Stir in the parsley, butter and Parmesan just before serving.

For the beurre fondue, put the chicken stock in a sauté pan and simmer until reduced by half. Whisk the butter piece by piece into the chicken stock to emulsify. Season to taste.

For the sauce, sweat the shallot, garlic, rosemary and thyme in the oil, then add the chicken stock and simmer until reduced by a third. Season with lemon juice, salt, sugar and cayenne, then whisk in the butter.

Cook the pasta in boiling salted water until tender, then drain well. Mix the pasta with the beurre fondue until coated. To serve, place a sheet of pasta (without hole) in 4 serving bowls. Spoon the tomato fondue into a mound in the centre of the pasta and cover with the second sheet (with hole). Pour the sauce around the pasta and garnish with the lemon thyme, basil and opal basil, plus Parmesan shavings, if liked.

# Plancha-seared Redfish with Watercress and Ginger Broth

Serves 4

4 x 175g (6-oz) red bass fillets, or substitute halibut if necessary
oil
40g (2$^{1}/_{2}$ tablespoons) butter
salt and pepper

For the pea purée:
240g (1$^{2}/_{3}$ cups) frozen peas
150ml ($^{2}/_{3}$ cup) chicken stock

For the vegetables:
150g (5oz) sugarsnap peas
300g (10oz) pea shoots
a pinch of salt
a pinch of sugar
a pinch of pepper
a pinch of cornflour (cornstarch)
55g (4 tablespoons) butter
50g ($^{1}/_{3}$) red (bell) pepper, cut into tiny dice, about 2mm ($^{1}/_{8}$ inch)

For the watercress and ginger broth:
15g (1 tablespoon) butter, plus extra to serve
30g (2 tablespoons) shallots, finely chopped
55g (2oz) fresh ginger, thinly sliced
1 garlic clove, crushed
a pinch of salt
a pinch of sugar
240g (2 cups) watercress, chopped

For the garnish:
30g (1oz) young ginger, cut into rounds
watercress leaves

Put the peas and chicken stock in a blender and process to a smooth, thick purée.

Next prepare the vegetables. Remove the peas from inside the sugarsnaps and cook in boiling salted water for 1 minute. Drain and quickly place in a bowl of iced water. Pick the pea shoots from their stems and toss them in a bowl with the salt, sugar, pepper and cornflour. Place a saucepan over a medium heat, add 30g (2 tablespoons) of the butter and the pea shoots and cook until wilted. Add the sugarsnap peas and pea purée to bind. Finish with 15g (1 tablespoon) of the butter. In a separate pan, heat the red pepper in the remaining butter to warm through.

For the watercress broth, heat the butter in a large pan, add the shallots, 40g (1$^{1}/_{2}$oz) of the ginger and the garlic and sweat until softened. Season with the salt and sugar. Add the chopped watercress leaves and stems and sweat until wilted, then add enough water just to cover and bring to a simmer. Cover and cook for 20 minutes. Remove from the heat and add the remaining ginger. Blend with a hand blender to break up, being careful not to purée it. Strain through a fine sieve lined with muslin (cheesecloth).

Score the skin side of the fish. Brush the fish with oil and season with salt, then sear it skin-side down on a plancha or in a hot pan with a little oil. Just before you are ready to turn the fish, put the butter on the plancha or in the pan. Wait until it becomes frothy and starts to go brown, then turn the fish and baste with the butter. Season with salt and pepper.

To serve, put the pea shoots and pea purée in the centre of 4 shallow bowls, then place the watercress leaves and rounds of ginger around the edge. Place the seared fish on top of the peas, skin-side up. Reheat the broth in a small saucepan, add a knob of butter and whiz with a hand blender. Spoon the broth around the fish and top the fish with the finely diced red pepper.

# Pear Soup with Vanilla Ice Cream and Almond Tuiles

**Serves 4**

**10 pears, preferably Bosc**
**1 Tahitian vanilla pod (vanilla bean), split**
**225g (1 cup plus 2 tablespoons) caster (superfine or granulated) sugar**
**1.5 litres (6 cups) water**
**juice of $^{1}/_{2}$ lemon**
**Poire Williams liqueur, to taste**
**a pinch of salt**
**port**
**vanilla ice cream, to serve**

For the almond tuiles:
**150g ($1^{1}/_{4}$ sticks) butter**
**150g ($^{3}/_{4}$ cup) caster (superfine) sugar**
**2 tablespoons liquid glucose**
**3 tablespoons plain (all-purpose) flour**
**3 tablespoons ground almonds (finely ground blanched almonds)**

First make the tuiles. Cream the butter and sugar together, then add the glucose. Combine the flour and almonds and add to the tuile mixture. Make teaspoon-sized balls of the batter and place on a silpat mat or a baking sheet lined with parchment paper, ensuring that each has room to spread. Bake in an oven preheated to 190°C/375°F/Gas Mark 5 for about 3–5 minutes, until golden. While they are still warm, lift the tuiles off the baking sheet and place over a rolling pin to make a 'U' shape. If they become firm, they can be warmed in the oven again to make them easier to shape.

Peel 2 of the pears. Using a parisienne cutter, make about 40 small balls of pear flesh, reserving the waste. Split the remaining pears through the cores. In a stockpot, combine the split pears with the waste from the first 2 pears. Add the vanilla pod, sugar, water and lemon juice and bring to the boil. Simmer until the liquid is reduced by a quarter. Strain the liquid into a bowl, then cool this 'soup' by placing it in a larger bowl filled with ice. When it is cold, adjust the flavour with sugar, lemon juice, Poire Williams and a pinch of salt.

Put half the parisienne pears in a pan, cover with a small amount of the soup and bring to the boil. Simmer until translucent, then set aside for garnish. Cool the soup and return it to the large batch. Put the remaining parisienne pears in a pan, cover with port and simmer until translucent. Remove with a slotted spoon and simmer the cooking liquid until reduced and syrupy.

To serve, place 5 parisienne pears of each colour in the centre of each bowl and stand an almond tuile on top of them. Spoon the soup into the bowl. Place a scoop of vanilla ice cream in the tuile and drizzle with the port reduction.

# eighteen

# NIGELLA LAWSON

**Nigella Lawson is the author of five bestselling books: *How to Eat* ('the most valuable culinary guide published this decade', *Daily Telegraph)*; *How to Be a Domestic Goddess* (Illustrated Book of the Year in the British Book Awards, 2001); *Nigella Bites* (winner of a W. H. Smith Award, 2001); and most recently, *Forever Summer* and *Feast*. Together with her successful Channel 4 television series, these have made her a household name around the world. She was *Vogue*'s food writer for several years and is now a contributor to the *New York Times*.**

I am afraid I am rather an imposter here: I am not a professional chef, but just a home cook. I never am, strictly speaking, 'on duty', so haven't got any secret 'off-duty' recipes up my sleeve. But having got that admission out of the way, I do feel that my lack of training or expertise makes my time easier in these pages. All my recipes are direct accounts of what I cook at home and, although I love cooking and often find it a great excuse to put off things I need to do but enjoy less – my accounts, filing, arguing with my children over their homework, or slaving over a hot word processor – I never have the time or the patience for fiddly work.

As for what I cook and when, on the whole I think it's best to let greed or, more decorously, appetite decree the menu. The weather, both meteorological and emotional, informs this choice obviously. When it's dull and Novemberish out, or dank and doleful within, I want to feast on pumpkin – garishly, ridiculously, orange and satisfyingly seasonal. I want to wade into a thick, aromatic stew, something that salves the soul and warms the body. And I feel really at home, relaxed and happy, if the smell of baking emanates welcomingly, easefully, from the oven.

One of the things I unaccountably remember from science lessons at school is that matter can be neither created nor destroyed. Risking the irritation of the physicists among you, I feel that that has imprecise but real application in cooking. Recipes don't come from nothing. The food exists already, the ingredients are there. And even if you feel that you are putting things together in some new way, you're probably not. That's not a bad thing: novelty can be dangerous in the kitchen. I feel lucky that I don't, from the warmth and cosiness of my own kitchen, have to be innovative or original.

Besides, I've always felt that whatever is true out of the kitchen is true in the kitchen: it's all about balance. Luckily, this is easier to find in the kitchen than in life at large. Striving for originality or effect is a recipe for disaster. Cooking has, I'm afraid, slightly been turned into some sort of Higher Discipline, but really it's just about trying to put things together harmoniously. The pumpkin, feta and radicchio salad here is the autumnal baby of the watermelon and feta salad I did in *Forever Summer*. I loved, in that, the contrast between the sweet and juicy melon and the crumbly, saline feta. This recipe illustrates the virtues of unoriginality well. For all that the pairing of watermelon and feta cheese sounds outlandish and novel, it is in fact a traditional Middle Eastern culinary partnership. It makes sense: when it's hot you want sugar, hydration and salt; the sheep's cheese and watermelon are on hand, made or grown nearby, to provide all these in a savoury and refreshing package.

The autumn after I'd started making that salad, I wanted to make a slightly more cold-weather version. Thus the dense sweetness of the pumpkin stands in for the summery watermelon. In place of leafy parsley and fresh mint, I

substituted radicchio, the slight bitterness of this lettuce providing another counterpoint to both sweet and salt. And the red leaves seem to make this look so mellow and autumnal. You could toss in some black olives, as I suggested in the watermelon version, but they seemed somehow in the wrong register to me as I assembled this autumnal salad for the first time. The pine nuts, sweet and waxy and toasted until their flavour really comes out, felt right, and I continue with them.

Both summer and more wintry versions of this salad are dressed with red onion, cut into fine half-moons and steeped in lime juice. You could use lemon or good wine vinegar, but you mustn't leave out their acid bath. What this steeping does is remove the acrid after-breath you can get from eating raw onions. As a bonus, the acid also bleaches the maroon-edged onion a luminescent puce pink. It may sound ludicrous to say how much joy I get from a little bowl of sliced onions, so beautiful are they, steeped and pinked, but, as I always tell my children, you are going to have a much nicer life if you can get pleasure out of small things like this.

As for this salad and how to serve it: it is presented here as a starter but I must be honest and say I rarely eat in that kind of formal, three-course way. While it's true that the intensity and vibrancy of the radicchio and pumpkin, dotted with crumbling white, provide contrast – that balance, that harmony – to the brown, gloopy depths of the stew (I love a stew, but no one can make great aesthetic claims on its behalf), and so would partner each other well as part of one big dinner, I think it makes much more sense to make the salad the lunch, in its entirety, for the day you're having the stew for dinner (or vice versa).

Whatever: the salad's a cinch to make. There's hardly any cooking involved: the pumpkin can be roasted a day ahead, and the pine nuts simply need to be shaken about in a dry pan over the heat. Then you just assemble it by hand. To be good, food doesn't need to be complicated, and in fact it is mostly all the better for being simple. I think people are often put off cooking because they think it involves some arcane art, some beyond-reach dexterity. Present them with this sort of food and even the most fretfully unconfident can see that it is something they could do. They're right: they could. But all my food is like that. I don't try to make my recipes patronisingly easy-peasy, it's just that I don't have the expertise or ability (or temperament) to do recipes that are complicated myself. It's that straightforward. Let's just call it making a virtue out of necessity.

A stew is the ultimate home food: it's not pretty, but it tastes good, feeds plenty and you make it in advance. A stew is always better a day or two after it's made, and this stew really needs time to sit to allow the meat to get really tender and the flavours to mellow. If I were ever to claim an instance of 'off-duty' cooking, I suppose it would be this: for even though all my recipes are for the food that emanates from my kitchen in the normal run of things, I have become accustomed to steering myself away – in my books – from ingredients that may be difficult to source. When I cook this stew at home for myself, I like to use shin of beef on the bone, just sliced like beef osso buco. The bones and their marrow intensify the taste and bolster the texture, and I love the way they clank around in the pan as you brown them.

But even if you don't want to use the heavy, meaty discs, this stew is gorgeous enough made with regular chunks of stewing steak. I just use more carrots, and cut them slightly bigger, when using the big, bone-in pieces rather than the diced meat. But whichever way you make the stew, you end up with a big panful of the stuff, and few things make me as happy as a bout of large-panned, army-style catering. I'm not expecting you to want to feed enormous numbers of people necessarily, but I've never seen the point of cooking small amounts of stew. I have a slight addiction to those disposable, see-through, lidded microwave trays – like little transparent boxes – and each contains two generous ladlefuls of stew, to be frozen and reheated as an easy, comforting dinner for two any time midweek.

And if the stew looks like school dinner, it doesn't taste remotely like it. The bitterness of the Guinness and orange mellows after a day or two's steeping once cooked, and the allspice and carrots – and the meat, too, come to think of it – offer a sweet counterpoint.

Of course, you could serve mashed potatoes alongside, but I don't. I like this with a bowlful of short, stubby pasta, dressed in a little cream, a ladleful or so of the thick, meaty sauce, a good cupful of grated Parmesan and some nutmeg. I've eaten some wonderful winter meals in the north of Italy (and Switzerland), where heavy meat casseroles were accompanied by cream-bound spaetzle and other fat, robust and chewy noodles. You know it makes sense. Or I hope you do.

As for pudding, well, I'm not sure you really need one. Most often, I just make my favourite fruit salad of all time: a juicy, jewelled salad of mango, blueberries, pomegranate seeds and the juice of a lime. To get the pomegranate seeds out without having a nervous breakdown, first chunk out the mango into a bowl, catching any juices as you go, then tumble in the blueberries. Cut a pomegranate – or more than one if you want a vast bowlful – in half and hold one half, cut-side down, over the bowl. Get a wooden spoon and start thwacking the pomegranate. Nothing much will happen at first but, after a few blows, seeds will begin falling and then raining down on to the salad. Pick any large bits of bitter yellow membrane out with your fingers. Then mix with your hands and squeeze in the lime juice and any red, fragrant pomegranate juice you can get from the emptied husks of fruit.

But I do like a spot of baking – the simplest, least fancy sort – at the weekend, and there is something about having a cake on hand to offer with a cup of tea or coffee as you slump, sofa-bound, later. The orange in this banana bread echoes the flavouring of the stew, without reminding you too emphatically of it. No one ever feels bad eating banana bread and I'm always happy to make it, as I never seem to have a kitchen without some bananas going threateningly black in a bowl somewhere. I am pathologically unable to throw food away (extravagant I may be, but I'm never wasteful), so this chocolate-studded, orange-scented cakey bread is the perfect solution – for the cook as well as the cookee.

Besides, it's not even hard to make: you melt the butter, mash the bananas and just stir everything together. And that's it, truly. Your work here on earth is done.

* Roast Pumpkin, Radicchio and Feta Salad
* Shin of Beef Stew with Pasta
* Orange-scented, Chocolate-speckled Banana Bread

## Roast Pumpkin, Radicchio and Feta Salad

**Serves 8**

**900g (2lb) peeled and deseeded pumpkin, approximately 1kg (2¹/4lb pre-cut)**
**1 tablespoon vegetable oil**
**¹/2 red onion, cut into fine half moons**
**juice of 1–2 limes, to give 60ml (4 tablespoons) juice**
**50g (scant ¹/2 cup) pine nuts**
**250g (9oz) feta cheese, broken or cut into bite-sized pieces**
**1 radicchio head, cut into bite-sized pieces**
**2 tablespoons groundnut (peanut) oil, or other relatively tasteless vegetable oil**
**¹/4 teaspoon pumpkin oil**

Cut the pumpkin into 6cm (2¹/4-inch) pieces and put them into a roasting tin (pan) with the vegetable oil. Roast in an oven preheated to 200°C/400°F/Gas Mark 6 for about 45 minutes, until tender but not mushy. Take out of the tin and leave to cool. You can do this up to a day ahead if you put the cooked pumpkin pieces into the fridge, but remember to take them out in time so that they are at room temperature when you assemble the salad.

Steep the sliced onion in the lime juice for at least 15 minutes; longer won't matter. Toast the pine nuts by heating them in a dry pan, shaking the pan every now and again. When the nuts are scorched in parts, they are done. Transfer to a bowl and leave to cool.

Put the cold pumpkin pieces into a large bowl with the feta and add the now-puce onions, the dark red radicchio and half the pan-bronzed pine nuts, turning everything gently to mix with your hands. Mix the groundnut and pumpkin oil in the bowl the onion slices were steeping in, then dress the salad with them, mixing it gently with your hands again. Turn everything out on to a large, flattish plate and sprinkle with the remaining pine nuts.

# Shin of Beef Stew with Pasta

**Serves 8**

**3.5kg (8lb) shin of beef on the bone, or 2kg (4 1/2lb) diced stewing steak**
**1kg (2lb) onions**
**1kg (2lb) carrots if using shin with bone, or 750g (1 1/2lb) carrots if using diced stewing steak**
**125ml (1/2 cup) olive oil (not extra virgin) or vegetable oil**
**100g (2/3 cup) plain (all-purpose) flour**
**1 tablespoon dried leaf sage**
**2 teaspoons ground allspice**
**pared zest and juice of 1 large orange, to give 150ml (2/3 cup) juice**
**1 1/2 cans (750ml) Guinness**
**500ml (2 cups) water**
**4 bay leaves**
**salt and freshly ground black pepper**

**For the pasta:**
**500g (18oz) occhi di lupo or chifferi pasta, no. 33 in the de Cecco range, or other short, chunky shapes**
**5 tablespoons double (heavy) cream**
**40g (1/2 cup) Parmesan cheese, freshly grated**
**a good grating of fresh nutmeg, or 1/4 teaspoon ground nutmeg**

Peel and roughly chop the onions, peel the carrots, cutting them on the diagonal so that you have a pile of slanted oval slices. If I'm using the large slices of shin, with its bone in still, I cut the carrots into ovals 1cm (1/2 inch) thick; for stewing steak, where you start off with fewer carrots anyway, I cut them into 5mm (1/4-inch) ovals. Heat 4 tablespoons of the oil in a large saucepan or deep casserole, add the onions and carrots and fry for about 5 minutes, until they begin to soften.

Transfer the softened, oil-glossed vegetables to a bowl, then add the remaining oil to the pan. Put the flour into a large freezer bag along with some salt and pepper, the sage and allspice, and add the beef pieces to the bag. Toss to coat them in the flour (if you're using the larger bone-in pieces, it makes sense to mix the meat and flour in a large bowl rather than freezer bag, as you probably won't be able to toss them well in the flour otherwise). Sear the meat in the pan in batches, browning it a little and removing all of the beef to a large dish as you go.

When all the meat's browned and out of the pan, whisk or stir in the orange juice (reserving the pared strips of zest for the time being) and Guinness and let it come to the boil. Add the water and then return the meat and vegetables to the pan. Stir in the orange strips and bay leaves and turn the stew down to a soft simmer once it's come back to the boil. Cover and cook for 2 1/2 hours. This is best reheated a day or two after but, if you can't do that, you may feel better adding another half an hour to the cooking time just to make sure the meat is soft and mellow and tender.

When you are about to serve the fragrant stew, cook the pasta in plenty of boiling water according to packet instructions. Then drain and put back into the pan, pouring in the cream and sprinkling over the Parmesan and a good grating of fresh nutmeg. Spoon in a ladleful or so of the juice from the hot stew and stir it into the pasta, so that you end up with a flecked buff-coloured sauce. Serve with the stew.

# Orange-scented, Chocolate-speckled Banana Bread

**Serves 8**

**100g ($^3/_4$ cup) sultanas (golden raisins)**
**75ml ($^1/_3$ cup) tablespoons Grand Marnier**
**450g (1lb bananas), about 4 small ones, 300g (10oz) weighed without skin**
**125g (1 stick) butter, melted**
**150g ($^3/_4$ cup) caster (superfine) sugar**
**2 eggs**
**50g (scant $^1/_2$ cup) walnuts, chopped**
**grated zest of 1 small orange**
**175g ($1^1/_4$ cups) plain (all-purpose) flour**
**1 teaspoon baking powder**
**$^1/_2$ teaspoon bicarbonate of soda (baking soda)**
**75g ($^1/_2$ cup) milk chocolate chips**

Line a 450g (1lb) loaf tin (bread pan) with a paper liner. Put the sultanas and Grand Marnier into a small saucepan and bring to the boil. Remove from the heat and let the fruit plump up in the hot liquid.

Peel the bananas and mash them with a fork. Beat the melted butter and sugar together, then add the eggs one at a time, beating well after each addition. Add the mashed bananas and stir in the soaked sultanas with any remaining liquor, plus the chopped walnuts and the orange zest.

Sift the flour, baking powder and bicarbonate of soda into a bowl and then add to the cake batter a third at a time, stirring well after each addition. Finally tip in the chocolate chips and mix in gently.

Scrape the mixture carefully into the paper liner in the tin and bake in an oven preheated to 170°C/325°F/Gas Mark 3 for 1-$1^1/_4$ hours; when it's ready a cake tester should come out cleanish. Leave on a rack to cool in the tin.

# nineteen

# SUSUR LEE

## Susur's

Susur Lee was born in Hong Kong, where he did his apprenticeship at the Peninsula Hotel from the age of fourteen to twenty-one. He then moved to Toronto to pursue his culinary career, opening Lotus restaurant in 1987 as chef/owner. In 1997 he closed Lotus to become head chef of the renowned Club Chinoise in Singapore. In 2000 Susur's restaurant was opened, followed by Lee restaurant in 2004, both in Toronto. As well as his duties as executive chef at Susur's and consulting chef at Lee's, he makes numerous appearances as a guest chef and lecturer the world over.

**What are your favourite foods/tastes/flavours?**
Asian, Onami.

**What are your favourite utensils?**
Hands.

**What is your most useful piece of equipment?**
A Vita Mix blender.

**What is your favourite season?**
Summer.

**What is your favourite mealtime?**
Lunch.

**How do you decide what to cook?**
Personal culture, tradition.

**What is your favourite drink?**
Calamanci lime and fresh sugar cane.

**What are your likes and dislikes?**
I like things done my way; I dislike things not done my way.

**How can you inspire others to enjoy great food and cooking?**
Motivation by show and tell, less tell.

**How did you become a chef?**
My Mom was a bad cook.

**What are your top ten ingredients?**
Citrus, dry scallops, liquorice, garlic, chillies, seaweed, water, salt, fat, salted apricot.

**What are your top tips?**
Stay single for the first five years of training.

**Do you have any favourite junk food?**
Chinese preserved fruit.

**How do you feel about cooking for children?**
I love it.

**Can you give one piece of advice for the domestic cook?**
Don't try to cook like a chef.

* Orzo Sauté with Brown Butter
* Black Cod with Cantonese Preserved Vegetables
* Black Rice Pudding with Marsala Sabayon and Coconut

## Orzo Sauté with Brown Butter

**Serves 4**

**2 teaspoons vegetable oil**
**1 egg, lightly beaten**
**300g ($1^2/_3$ cups) orzo (rice-shaped pasta), partially cooked**
**50g ($3^1/_2$ tablespoons) butter, heated until golden brown, then strained**
**2 teaspoons mirin**
**1 tablespoon soy sauce**
**1 garlic clove, finely chopped**
**100g (2 cups) spinach, shredded**
**75g (3oz) fresh crabmeat**
**1 tablespoon pine nuts, toasted**
**1 spring onion (scallion), finely chopped**

Heat the oil in a small frying pan (skillet), pour in the beaten egg and make a thin, lightly cooked omelette. Turn it out of the pan, roll up and shred thinly, then set aside.

Sauté the orzo in the brown butter over a high heat until golden brown, then add the mirin, soy sauce and garlic. Fold in the spinach and crabmeat and cook for 2 minutes, until heated through.

Spoon the orzo into a bowl and garnish with the pine nuts, shredded omelette and spring onion.

# Black Cod with Cantonese Preserved Vegetables

**Serves 4**

**4 x 75g (3-oz) pieces of black cod**
**daikon sprouts or chive sticks, to garnish**

**For the marinade:**
**75g ($^1/_3$ cup) brown sugar**
**4 tablespoons soy sauce**
**2 tablespoons dark soy sauce**
**125ml ($^1/_2$ cup) Chinese cooking wine**

**For the Cantonese preserved vegetables:**
**2 garlic cloves, finely chopped**
**10g (1 tablespoon) fresh ginger, finely chopped**
**1 small red chilli, chopped**
**2 teaspoons fermented black beans, chopped**
**5 tablespoons canola oil**
**1 small onion, finely diced**
**1 leek, white part only, finely diced**
**30g (2 tablespoons) preserved radish, finely diced**
**50g ($^1/_4$ cup) granulated sugar**
**2 tablespoons Chinese cooking wine**
**2 teaspoons oyster sauce**
**30g (2 tablespoons) roasted red (bell) pepper, finely diced**

To make the marinade, put the sugar in a heavy-based pan, add about a tablespoon of water and heat gently until the sugar has melted. Raise the heat and cook, without stirring, until the sugar has turned into a rich brown caramel. Add the soy sauce, dark soy sauce and cooking wine and return to the boil. Remove from the heat and leave to cool completely. Put the cod in a dish, pour over the cooled marinade and leave for 25 minutes. Remove the cod and set aside.

To prepare the preserved vegetables, sauté the garlic, ginger, chilli and black beans in the oil until golden brown. Add the onion, leek and preserved radish, then reduce the heat and simmer for about 45 minutes, until all the vegetables are soft. Stir in the sugar, wine, oyster sauce and red pepper and cook for 20 minutes over a low heat to combine all the flavours. Remove from the pan and strain off excess oil.

Cook the cod for 6–7 minutes in an oven preheated to 200°C/400°F/Gas Mark 6. Finish under the grill (broiler) to achieve a caramelized crust. Place the fish in the centre of 4 serving plates and top with the warm vegetables. Garnish with daikon sprouts or chive sticks and serve.

# Black Rice Pudding with Marsala Sabayon and Coconut

**Serves 4**

**450g ($2^1/_3$ cups) black glutinous rice**
**3 cinnamon sticks and 5–7 cloves, tied up in a piece of muslin (cheesecloth)**
**1 thumb-sized piece of fresh ginger, smashed**
**125ml ($^1/_2$ cup) milk**
**125ml ($^1/_2$ cup) whipping cream**
**250ml (1 cup) coconut milk**
**100–175g ($^1/_2$ cup plus 2 tablespoons) caster (superfine) sugar**
**1 teaspoon vanilla extract**
**50g ($3^1/_2$ tablespoons) butter, chilled and diced**
**2 bananas**
**salt**
**toasted coconut, to serve**

**For the Marsala sabayon:**
**5 egg yolks**
**175g ($^3/_4$ cup plus 2 tablespoons) caster (granulated or superfine) sugar**
**a pinch of salt**
**125ml ($^1/_2$ cup) Marsala wine, or to taste**
**$^1/_2$ gelatine leaf**
**100ml (scant $^1/_2$ cup) double (heavy) cream, lightly whipped**

Put the rice in a pan with enough water to cover, add the spice bundle and the ginger and simmer until the rice is almost done, adding more water if necessary. Stir in the milk, cream and coconut milk. Add the sugar, vanilla extract and some salt and continue to cook until the rice is done. Remove from the heat and stir in the diced butter.

For the sabayon, put the egg yolks, sugar, salt and Marsala in a large bowl and place it over a pan of simmering water, making sure the water is not touching the base of the bowl. With an electric handheld beater, whisk until the mixture has increased in volume and is thick enough to leave a trail on the surface when dropped from the whisk.

Soak the gelatine in cold water for 5 minutes, then gently squeeze out excess water. Add to the sabayon and whisk to dissolve. Place the bowl in a larger bowl filled with ice so it cools down rapidly, then whisk the sabayon until completely cold. Fold in the whipped cream.

To serve, divide the rice between 4 bowls and slice the bananas over the top. Put the sabayon on top of that and sprinkle with toasted coconut.

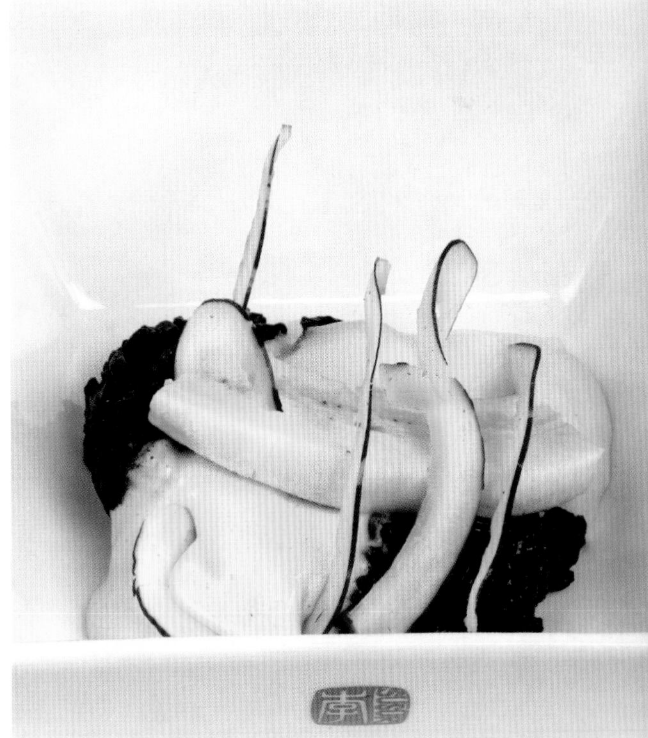

# twenty

# GIORGIO LOCATELLI

## Locanda Locatelli

**Brought up in the village of Corgeno, on the banks of Lake Maggiore in Italy, Giorgio Locatelli is considered one of the best Italian chefs in the UK. With a series of successful restaurants under his belt, including Zafferano and Spiga, he now owns the Michelin-starred Locanda Locatelli, where he prides himself on serving traditional Italian dishes personalised with his own creative touch. Giorgio has made two television series: 'Pure Italian' and 'Tony and Giorgio', which was filmed with entrepreneur, Tony Allan.**

**What are your favourite foods/tastes/flavours?**
My favourite food is pasta, my favourite flavour is saffron.

**What is your favourite utensil?**
At the moment it is the mezzaluna.

**What is your most useful piece of kitchen design and equipment?**
The compensation extraction canopy we have installed in the restaurant kitchen. It not only cleanses the air but also improves its quality by adding purified water to it.

**What is your favourite season?**
Autumn.

**What is your favourite meal?**
Breakfast: porridge (oatmeal).
Lunch: pasta.
Dinner: minestrone.

**How do you decide what to cook?**
My cooking is purely based on ingredients.

**What inspires you?**
The ingredients.

**What is your favourite drink?**
Wine – red and white.

**What are your likes and dislikes?**
I like almost everything; the only thing I dislike is chervil.

**How can you inspire others to enjoy great food and cooking?**
A good starting point is getting people to know more about what they eat.

**How did you become a chef?**
My family has a restaurant in Italy. I would always chip in, even when I was little, and because I was a terrible waiter I was sent to the kitchen.
I haven't looked back since.

**What are your top ten ingredients?**
Saffron, ginger, crab, pasta, white truffles, courgettes (zucchini), bottarga, all types of cured meats, all cheeses, pigeon.

**What are your kitchen secrets?**
I don't believe in secrets because my cooking evolves all the time.

**What are your top tips?**
When you cut a lemon, always cut it sideways, so the juice flows naturally when you squeeze it.

**Do you ever eat junk food?**
I don't eat junk food at all (toast with foie gras?).

**How do you feel about cooking for children?**
I don't see the difference between cooking for children and cooking for adults. It is a good investment, as what we feed (or not) our children will influence their tastes in the future.

**Can you give one piece of advice for the domestic cook?**
Never buy only chicken breasts or chicken legs, always buy the whole bird. It works out cheaper and you can make a fantastic stock out of the bones.

Parking P
BREVA

* Tortelli di Patate con Funghi Porcini (Potato Tortelli with Wild Mushrooms)
* Coda di Rospo in Salsa di Noci e Capperi (Monkfish with Walnuts and Capers)
* Zucotto (Chocolate, Cream and Nut Cake)



# Tortelli di Patate con Funghi Porcini (Potato Tortelli with Wild Mushrooms)

**Serves 4**

For the pasta:

**500g (3 1/2 cups) Italian '00' flour**
**a pinch of salt**
**1 egg**
**5 egg yolks**
**a little beaten egg for brushing**

For the filling:

**350g (12oz) Jersey Royal (or other new) potatoes, scrubbed**
**100g (7 tablespoons) butter**
**a sprig of rosemary**
**25g (2 tablespoons) Parmesan cheese, freshly grated**
**a pinch of salt**

For the sauce:

**300g (10oz) mixed wild mushrooms**
**2 tablespoons olive oil**
**3 garlic cloves, crushed**
**125ml (1/2 cup) white wine**
**1 tablespoon chopped chives**
**1 tablespoon chopped parsley**
**200ml (7oz) hot chicken stock**
**50g (3 1/2 tablespoons) butter**
**25–50g (2–3 1/2 tablespoons) Parmesan cheese, freshly grated**

First make the pasta dough. Sift the flour and salt into a food processor, then slowly pour in the egg and egg yolks through the feed tube, with the machine running. As soon as the mixture comes together into a dough, switch off the machine. Put the dough on a lightly floured work surface and knead for 10–15 minutes, until smooth and elastic. Wrap in cling film (plastic wrap) and chill for 1 hour.

To make the filling, cook the potatoes in boiling salted water until tender. Meanwhile, melt the butter in a small pan and add the rosemary sprig. Leave to infuse over a gentle heat for a few minutes, until the butter starts to colour, then set aside. Once the potatoes are cooked, drain and peel them, keeping them as warm as possible. Transfer the potatoes to a food processor and whiz until smooth, slowly pouring in the butter. Add the Parmesan and salt, then set aside to cool.

To make the tortelli, cut the pasta dough in half and flatten it slightly with a rolling pin. Pass each piece through a pasta machine on the widest setting, then fold in half and repeat, each time switching the machine to a finer setting, until the pasta is paper thin. Lay one of the pasta sheets on a work surface and place heaped teaspoons of the potato filling about 4cm (1 1/2 inches) apart all over it. Brush the other pasta sheet with beaten egg and lay it, egg-side down, on top of the filled sheet. Press the pasta sheets together around the filling and cut out the ravioli with a round pastry cutter or a knife, depending which shape you prefer. Cover with cling film and chill until ready to use.

To make the sauce, pick over the mushrooms, brushing off leaves or bits of earth with a pastry brush. Trim the stalks and tear the mushrooms lengthways into halves, quarters or eighths, depending on their size, so that the stalks remain attached to the cups. Heat the olive oil in a frying pan (skillet) and cook the garlic for a minute or so, then add the mushrooms and cook for a further 2 minutes. Pour in the wine and bubble for a few minutes to allow the alcohol to evaporate. Stir in the chives and parsley. Keep warm over a low heat.

Cook the tortelli in a large pan of boiling salted water for 2–3 minutes, until tender, then drain and return to the pan. Gently stir the tortelli together with the mushrooms, hot chicken stock, butter and Parmesan. Divide between warm serving bowls and serve immediately.

# Coda di Rospo in Salsa di Noci e Capperi (Monkfish with Walnuts and Capers)

**Serves 4**

**4 x 250g (9-oz) monkfish tails, skinned, or 4 thick monkfish steaks, weighing about 200g (7oz) each**
**4 tablespoons olive oil, plus extra for drizzling**
**5 tablespoons hot fish stock**
**50g (2oz) wild rocket (arugula)**
**2 tablespoons Giorgio's Vinaigrette (see Note below)**
**12 caper berries, rinsed and drained**
**sea salt and freshly ground black pepper**

**For the agrodolce:**
**100ml (7 tablespoons) white wine vinegar**
**100g (1/2 cup) white sugar**
**200g (7oz) capers, rinsed and drained**

**For the walnut sauce:**
**100g (generous 3/4 cup) walnuts**
**1 garlic clove, finely chopped**
**5 tablespoons olive oil**

First make the agrodolce: put the white wine vinegar and sugar in a small saucepan and bring gently to the boil. Simmer over a low heat for about 10 minutes, until it has reduced by half. Meanwhile, put the capers in a food processor and blitz until finely chopped (or chop them finely with a knife). Add to the reduced vinegar and sugar and cook over a very gentle heat for about 30 minutes, until all the liquid has evaporated. Leave to cool.

For the walnut sauce, place the walnuts and garlic in a food processor and blitz until finely processed. With the machine running, slowly drizzle in the olive oil until it forms a thick, glossy sauce. Season to taste.

Pat the monkfish dry with kitchen paper towels and season with salt and pepper. Heat the olive oil in a large frying pan (skillet) and brown the monkfish pieces one at a time, turning them until golden all over. Transfer to a roasting tin (pan) as they are done. Place the roasting tin in an oven preheated to 250°C/500°F/Gas Mark 10 for 4–6 minutes, until the monkfish is cooked through. Remove from the oven, cover with foil and leave to rest for 5 minutes.

Meanwhile, in a small bowl, mix together the agrodolce and walnut sauce, adding the hot fish stock as you mix. Toss the rocket leaves with the vinaigrette.

Spoon the agrodolce and walnut sauce into the centre of a serving platter and place the rocket on top, then the monkfish tails. Spoon over any juices from the roasting tin and give the whole lot an extra drizzle of olive oil. Scatter the caper berries around the plate and serve immediately.

**Note**

For Giorgio's Vinaigrette, put 1/2 teaspoon of salt in a bowl, add 3 1/2 tablespoons red wine vinegar and leave to dissolve for a minute. Whisk in 300ml (1 1/4 cups) extra virgin olive oil and 2 tablespoons water until the vinaigrette emulsifies and thickens. It will keep in the fridge for several months if stored in a sealed bottle.

# Zucotto (Chocolate, Cream and Nut Cake)

**Serves 4**

**200g (7oz) dark chocolate, 70 per cent cocoa solids**
**4 tablespoons cognac**
**4 tablespoons Vin Santo**
**1 litre (1 quart) double (heavy) cream**
**75g (1/2 cup) blanched almonds, roughly chopped**
**75g (2/3 cup) blanched hazelnuts, roughly chopped**
**150g (1 1/4 cups) icing (confectioners') sugar**
**25g (4 1/2 tablespoons) (unsweetened) cocoa powder**

For the sponge:
**6 eggs, separated**
**150g (1 1/4 cups) icing (confectioners') sugar**
**1 tablespoon honey**
**75g (2/3 cup) cornflour (cornstarch)**
**75g (1/2 cup) plain (all-purpose) flour, plus extra for dusting**
**melted butter for brushing**

First make the sponge. Put the egg yolks, icing sugar and honey in a large bowl and beat with a hand-held electric beater until pale and thick. In a separate bowl, whisk the egg whites until they form stiff peaks. With a large metal spoon, carefully fold them into the egg yolks. Sift the cornflour and plain flour and fold them in, too.

Brush a 20cm (8-inch) square cake tin (pan) with melted butter and dust with flour. Pour the cake mixture into the tin and bake in an oven preheated to 190°C/375°F/Gas Mark 5 for about 30 minutes, until golden and springy to the touch. Turn the sponge out on to a wire rack and leave to cool.

Finely chop the chocolate and leave 150g (5oz) of it in the fridge. Put the rest in a bowl set over a pan of gently simmering water. Turn off the heat and set aside to melt.

When the sponge is cool, cut off the crusty edges and cut the cake into slices about 1cm (1/2 inch) thick. Use to line a round bowl, 1.5 litres (6 cups) in capacity, making sure the cake comes all the way up to the top. Mix the cognac and Vin Santo together and, using a pastry brush, gently brush them over the pieces of cake.

Whip the double cream until stiff, stir in the nuts and finely chopped chocolate and divide this mixture in half. Stir the melted chocolate into one half. Place this mixture in the bottom of the cake-lined bowl and smooth the surface with a spoon. Fill the bowl to the top with the other cream mixture and then place a serving plate on top. Turn the bowl and plate upside down and chill in the fridge for at least 1 hour. Lift off the bowl, leaving the pudding on the plate, and dust with the icing sugar and cocoa powder. Cut into wedges to serve.

twenty one

# GRANT MACPHERSON

**Wynn**

**Before joining Wynn, Grant MacPherson was executive chef at Raffles Hotel, one of Asia's oldest and most lavish destinations. He held that same post at the venerable Datai Hotel in Malaysia. His CV (résumé) also includes stints at such prestigious resorts as the Regent, the Ritz-Carlton and the Four Seasons, as well as positions in some of England and France's finest restaurants.**

**What are your favourite foods/tastes/flavours?**
I love the sharp contrast of savoury and sweet in Cantonese cuisine; lemony-lime and more acidic flavours; garlic, ginger, tarragon and chervil.

**What are your favourite utensils?**
The Gray Kunz spoon and a fish slicer.

**What is your most useful piece of kitchen equipment?**
For indoors, Viking stoves; for outdoors, Viking barbecues.

**What is your favourite meal?**
Breakfast: brewed coffee and a pain au chocolat.
Lunch: Scottish meat pie, sausage rolls and warm Heinz beans.
Tea: Scottish smoked salmon finger sandwiches.
Dinner: a perfect rib eye, cooked rare, with béarnaise.

**How do you decide what to cook?**
It comes down to three things: the season, market availability and any whim.

**What inspires you?**
Tracking down the absolute freshest products and ingredients.

**What is your favourite drink?**
McEwan lager or Johnny Walker Blue with exactly one ice cube.

**What are your likes and dislikes?**
I am crazy for rock and roll, Corvettes and a good game of pool. I am less fond of ego and disorganization.

**How can you inspire others to enjoy great food and cooking?**
Jump behind the stove and go!

**How did you become a chef?**
Eating my way across five continents has inspired me to master my culinary skills.

**What are your top ten ingredients?**
Salt, pepper, Pont l'Eveque cheese, Scottish salmon, dry-aged beef, turbot, tomatoes, basil, sherry vinegar, virgin olive oil.

**What are your kitchen secrets?**
Be true to yourself.

**What are your top tips?**
Sharpen your knives, use only seasonal ingredients and always season.

**Do you have any favourite junk food?**
In and Out Burger's 'Double-double'.

**How do you feel about cooking for children?**
Keep it fresh and simple.

**Can you give one piece of advice for the domestic cook?**
Always taste before serving.

* Tempura of Baby Red Snapper with Root Vegetable Slaw and Sweet Basil Aioli
* Black-Jack Spiced Scottish Beef with Olive Smashed Potatoes and Ratatouille Vinaigrette
* New York Cheesecake with Blueberry Compote

## Tempura of Baby Red Snapper with Root Vegetable Slaw and Sweet Basil Aioli

**Serves 4**

**400g (14oz) red snapper fillet, skinned and cut into 8cm (3 1/4-inch) pieces**
**oil for deep-frying**

For the basil aioli:

**1 egg yolk**
**1 tablespoon Dijon mustard**
**1 teaspoon lemon juice**
**1 teaspoon basil purée**
**250ml (1 cup) grapeseed oil**
**salt and freshly ground black pepper**

For the root vegetable slaw:

**1 turnip, finely shredded**
**1 carrot, finely shredded**
**1 parsnip, finely shredded**
**100g (3 1/2oz) mangetout (snow peas), finely shredded**
**100g (1 1/3 cups) Chinese leaves, finely shredded**
**3 shallots, finely sliced**

For the tempura batter:

**75g (1/2 cup) plain (all-purpose) flour**
**2 tablespoons cornflour (cornstarch)**
**1 teaspoon baking powder**
**200ml (7oz) water**
**1 teaspoon vegetable oil**

To garnish:

**12 pink grapefruit segments**
**4 sprigs of basil**

First make the aioli. Put all the ingredients except the oil in a blender, then gradually add the oil, blending until the sauce has a consistency like mayonnaise.

For the root vegetable slaw, combine all the vegetables and toss with the basil aioli. Taste and adjust the seasoning.
To make the tempura batter, combine all the dry ingredients in a bowl, then gradually whisk in the water, followed by the vegetable oil, until you have a smooth batter.

Heat some oil in a large, deep pan or a deep-fat fryer to 190°C/375°F. Dip the pieces of snapper fillet in the batter and fry for 4–5 minutes, until the batter is crisp and the fish is cooked through. Drain on kitchen paper towels and serve immediately with the root vegetable slaw, garnished with the grapefruit segments and basil.

# Black-Jack Spiced Scottish Beef with Olive Smashed Potatoes and Ratatouille Vinaigrette

**Serves 4**

**1kg (2 1/4lb) beef fillet (tenderloin), free of fat and sinew**
**6 tablespoons oil**

For the 21 spices:
**15g (3 1/2 whole) nutmeg**
**15g (3 1/2 tablespoons) cloves**
**20g (1 1/2 tablespoons) white peppercorns**
**10g (2 1/2 teaspoons) black peppercorns**
**20g (ten 3-inch) cinnamon sticks**
**30g (1oz) mace**
**10g (2 1/2 tablespoons) coriander seeds**
**1/2 teaspoon fennel seeds**
**1 teaspoon curry powder**
**2 teaspoons ground ginger**
**a pinch of ground cardamom**
**1 teaspoon celery salt**
**1/2 teaspoon cayenne pepper**
**2 teaspoons dried thyme**
**2 teaspoons dried tarragon**
**2 teaspoons dried chervil**
**2 teaspoons dried rosemary**
**2 teaspoons dried sage**
**2 teaspoons dried marjoram**
**2 teaspoons dried basil**
**1 teaspoon dried dill**

For the ratatouille vinaigrette:
**1 small shallot, cut into 5mm (1/4-inch) dice**
**1 garlic clove, crushed**
**2–3 sprigs of thyme**
**50ml olive oil**
**60g (1/3 cup) red (bell) pepper, cut into 5mm (1/4-inch) dice**
**60g (1/3 cup) green (bell) pepper, cut into 5mm (1/4-inch) dice**
**60g (1/2 cup) courgette (zucchini), cut into 5mm (1/4-inch) dice**
**60g (1/2 cup) aubergine (eggplant), cut into 5mm (1/4-inch) dice**
**60g (1/2 cup) tomato, skinned, deseeded and cut into 5mm (1/4-inch) dice**
**3 tablespoons sherry vinegar**
**2 tablespoons chicken stock**
**salt and freshly ground black pepper**

For the olive smashed potatoes:
**450g (1lb) Fingerling potatoes or other waxy salad potatoes**
**100g (2/3 cup) Niçoise olives, pitted and chopped**
**3 tablespoons olive oil**
**100g (scant 1 cup) tomatoes, diced**
**1 1/2 tablespoons chopped coriander (cilantro)**
**1/2 teaspoon chopped garlic**
**salt and white pepper**

For the green beans:
**450g (1lb) green beans**
**3 tablespoons olive oil**

Grind all the whole spices to a powder, then mix with the remaining spices and the herbs. Roll the beef in the spice mix, tie it in several places with string and leave to rest overnight.

For the ratatouille vinaigrette, sauté the shallot, garlic and thyme in the olive oil until softened. Add the peppers, courgette and aubergine and cook gently until just tender. Stir in the diced tomato, followed by the sherry vinegar and chicken stock. Season to taste with salt and pepper and set aside.

To cook the beef, heat the oil in a roasting tin (pan), add the beef and brown on all sides. Transfer to an oven preheated to 220°C/425°F/Gas Mark 7 and roast for 25–30 minutes; this should give medium-rare meat. Remove from the oven and leave to rest in a warm place.

Meanwhile, cook the whole potatoes in boiling salted water until tender, then drain well. Fork mash with the olives, olive oil, tomatoes, coriander and garlic and season to taste. Keep warm.

Cook the green beans in boiling salted water until just tender, then drain and toss with the olive oil.

To serve, put the potatoes in the centre of 4 plates and pour a little of the vinaigrette over. Top with the green beans. Cut the beef into 4 portions and place on the potatoes and beans. Top with the remaining ratatouille vinaigrette.

# New York Cheesecake with Blueberry Compote

**Serves 4**

**350g ($1\frac{1}{2}$ cups) cream cheese**
**110ml (scant $\frac{1}{2}$ cup) soured cream**
**a pinch of salt**
**125g (heaped $\frac{1}{2}$ cup) caster (superfine) sugar**
**$1\frac{1}{2}$ tablespoons lemon juice**
**seeds from $\frac{1}{2}$ vanilla pod (vanilla bean)**
**2 eggs**
**30g (2 tablespoons) butter, melted**

For the base:

**125g (1 stick) butter**
**150g ($\frac{3}{4}$ cup) caster (superfine) sugar**
**$\frac{1}{2}$ teaspoon salt**
**1 teaspoon grated orange zest**
**1 teaspoon grated lemon zest**
**1 egg, lightly beaten**
**2 tablespoons milk**
**310g ($2\frac{1}{4}$ cups) plain (all-purpose) flour**
**10g (1 tablespoon) baking powder**

For the blueberry compote:

**75g ($\frac{1}{3}$ cup) caster (superfine) sugar**
**2 tablespoons water**
**$1\frac{1}{2}$ teaspoons lemon juice**
**a small pinch of ground cinnamon**
**$\frac{1}{8}$ teaspoon freshly ground black pepper**
**225g (8oz) blueberries**

First make the base. Cream together the butter, sugar, salt and zest until the mixture is pale and fluffy. Add the egg and milk and mix in thoroughly. Sift together the flour and baking powder and fold in gently; do not over mix. On a lightly floured surface, roll out the mixture to about 5mm ($\frac{1}{4}$ inch) thick and cut out 4 rounds to fit the base of 4 ring moulds, 6–7cm ($2\frac{1}{2}$–$2\frac{3}{4}$ inches) in diameter and 6cm ($2\frac{1}{4}$ inches) high. Alternatively you could use 4 individual rectangular moulds or a 24–28cm ($9\frac{1}{2}$–11 inch) round cake tin (pan). Place on a baking sheet and bake in an oven preheated to 160°C/325°F/Gas Mark 3 for about 15 minutes, until pale golden brown.

For the topping, combine the cream cheese, soured cream, salt, sugar, lemon juice and vanilla seeds in an electric mixer and beat on a low speed until all is incorporated. Beat in the eggs one at a time and then mix in the melted butter. Pour into the moulds and bake in an oven preheated to 180°C/350°F/Gas Mark 4 for 20 minutes or until set. Remove from the oven and leave to cool on a wire rack.

To make the blueberry compote, combine the sugar, water, lemon juice, cinnamon and pepper in a saucepan and bring to a simmer. Add the blueberries, remove from the heat and leave to steep for 1 hour. Strain the liquid off the blueberries into a clean pan and simmer until reduced by two-thirds. Pour the reduced cooking juices back over the blueberries and set aside. Turn the cheesecakes out of their moulds and serve accompanied by the blueberry compote.

# twenty two

# NOBU MATSUHISA

**Nobu**

Better known as Nobu, Nobuyuki Matsuhisa is probably the most famous Japanese chef in the world. He draws heavily on his classic Japanese training as a sushi chef in Tokyo, as well as on South American influences gained during his extensive travels. This innovative 'new-style' Japanese cuisine has become both his trademark and the foundation of his success. Nobu now has thirteen restaurants worldwide.

**What are your favourite foods/tastes/flavours?**
Sushi.

**What are your favourite utensils?**
Sushi knives.

**What is your most useful piece of kitchen equipment?**
A sushi bar.

**What is your favourite season?**
Autumn.

**What is your favourite mealtime?**
Dinner.

**How do you decide what to cook?**
With the best-quality ingredients available.

**What inspires you?**
Travel.

**What is your favourite drink?**
Hokusetsu saki.

**What are your likes and dislikes?**
I dislike strange foods, I like snake and fish.

**How can you inspire others to enjoy great food and cooking?**
I am always thinking about what my customers would like to eat.

**How did you become a chef?**
It was always my dream from a young age.

**What are your top ten ingredients?**
Soy, yuzu, miso, rice, wasabi, ginger, jalepeno, olive oil, rice vinegar, konbu.

**What are your kitchen secrets?**
Team work.

**What are your top tips?**
Good food and good service.

**Do you ever eat junk food?**
No.

**How do you feel about cooking for children?**
I love to show children my style of cooking.

**Can you give one piece of advice for the domestic cook?**
Try not to overcomplicate things; simple is best.

* Spicy Mushroom Soup
* Saikyo Grilled Salmon
* Mochi Ice-cream Balls



# Spicy Mushroom Soup

**Serves 4**

**2 tablespoons Japanese light soy sauce, also labelled as usukuchi soy**
**1 tablespoon sake**
**1 teaspoon Maldon sea salt**
**150g (2 cups) assorted mushrooms, such as shiitake, oyster, enoki or whatever is available, sliced**
**1 teaspoon chilli and garlic paste**
**a few drops of Japanese sesame oil**
**finely shredded spring onions (scallions), to serve**

**For the clear stock (dashi):**
**1 litre (1 quart) water**
**5cm (2-cm) piece of konbu (Japanese dried seaweed)**
**25g (1oz) dried bonito flakes**

First make the dashi. Bring the water and konbu to a gentle boil, then remove from the heat, add the bonito flakes and leave to infuse. Strain when cool.

Heat up the dashi with the soy sauce, sake and salt. Then add the sliced mushrooms and leave to infuse for 15 minutes, making sure the soup is just under boiling point.

Finally add the chilli and garlic paste and sesame oil. Check the seasoning for salt, then sprinkle with finely shredded spring onions and serve.

# Saikyo Grilled Salmon

**The salmon portions for this dish may seem quite large but they will shrink after marinating and cooking. Serve with salad, steamed rice or stir-fried vegetables.**

**Serves 4**

**100ml (7 tablespoons) sake**
**100ml (7 tablespoons) mirin**
**150g (3/4 cup) caster (superfine or granulated) sugar**
**300g (10oz) white miso paste**
**4 x 200g (7-oz) salmon fillets, skin on**
**lemon wedges, to serve**

Heat the sake in a large, heavy-based pan and ignite it to burn off the alcohol. Add the mirin and sugar and stir over a low heat until the sugar has dissolved. Carefully whisk in the miso paste a little at a time, making sure the mixture is smooth. Raise the heat a little and cook for about 20 minutes, stirring constantly to make sure the mixture does not burn on the base of the pan. Strain and leave to cool completely. It can be stored in the refrigerator for up to 1 month.

Place the salmon fillets in a non-metallic container, large enough to hold them in a single layer, and pour some of the cooled marinade over them, making sure that the fish is completely surrounded; save a little of the marinade for later. Leave in the fridge to marinate for 24 hours, turning the fillets over once during this time.

When ready to cook, preheat an overhead grill (broiler) and remove the salmon fillets from the marinade, wiping off any excess. Place the fillets on a non-stick baking tray and grill, skin-side down for 5–6 minutes, taking care that they do not get too dark or caramelized. Turn the salmon over to cook the skin side until nice and crisp. Serve with lemon wedges and a little of the reserved marinade on the side.

# Mochi Ice-cream Balls

**Do not make this dish on a humid day, as the paste will sweat and become unusable.**

**Serves 4**

**100g (1 cup) mochi flour, often labelled as Japanese rice flour**
**210ml (7½oz) water**
**95g (scant ½ cup) caster (superfine) sugar**
**any of your favourite ice cream flavours, to serve**

Mix the mochi flour and water together, ensuring there are no lumps, then mix in the sugar. Put the mixture in a non-stick pan and cook over a low to medium heat, stirring vigorously, for 8 minutes, until it is stiff and elastic; take care not to let it catch on the side of the pan. Turn the paste out on to a lightly floured board and leave to cool. Meanwhile, scoop the ice cream into small balls, no more than 2cm (¾ inch) in diameter, and return to the freezer.

When the mochi paste is cold, roll it out to about 3mm (⅛ inch) thick and dust with flour. Place on a baking tray and put it into the freezer for 1 hour.

Remove the paste from the freezer and cut out rounds using a 4-5cm (about 2-inch) cutter. Place a ball of ice cream in the centre of each one and wrap it up in the mochi paste. Return to the freezer.

twenty three

# ANDY McLEISH

## Chapter One

Head chef at Chapter One restaurant in Farnborough, Kent, Andrew McLeish has been instrumental in developing an award-winning modern European menu, which in 2001 won a Michelin star – an accolade it continues to retain. In 2004 Chapter One was awarded its fourth AA Rosette and was also named the AA's Restaurant of the Year. McLeish's career includes stints at Chez Nico, the Ritz, the Mandarin Oriental Baan Taling Ngam in Thailand, and the Dining Room at the Landmark, London, where he was head chef.

**What is your favourite season?**
I like autumn and winter, as there is plenty of game around. During the game season I always have at least one game dish on the menu, and they are extremely popular at Chapter One. It is strange - chefs working in the centre of London tell me that dishes such as game and rabbit are never that popular but here in Kent at Chapter One, they are always the best sellers.

**How do you decide what to cook?**
It is all based on the seasons and what is best at the time. After that, every thing else just falls into place.

**What is your favourite drink?**
Gin and tonic.

**What are your likes and dislikes?**
I like simple food where the produce speaks for itself. I dislike overworked and contrived food.

**How can you inspire others to enjoy great food and cooking?**
By letting them take part and taste the food. They should enjoy eating out.

**How did you become a chef?**
It was a dream from an early age. Ever since my Mum was ill one Christmas and I cooked Christmas lunch for the whole family - turkey with all the trimmings!

**What are your kitchen secrets?**
There are no secrets in my kitchen - just passion and hard work.

**Do you have any favourite junk food?**
A doner kebab and a pint of Boddingtons.

**How do you feel about cooking for children?**
I don't believe in doing separate menus for kids and I certainly don't believe in plying them with sausage and chips. Children can eat healthily - smaller portions of good food. In the restaurant we offer half portions from the à la carte menu at half price and then the children can eat the same as mum and dad, which can help teach them that there is more to food than chicken nuggets! However, if a child wants something simple, like a pasta dish or some chicken, we will of course cook it for them.

**Can you give one piece of advice for the domestic cook?**
Prepare as much in advance as possible so you can enjoy the evening.

* Cornish Mackerel with Puy Lentils and Artichoke Purée
* Roast Pheasant with Potato Purée, Savoy Cabbage and Raisin and Wild Mushroom Sauce
* Lemon Posset with Raspberry Salad

## Cornish Mackerel with Puy Lentils and Artichoke Purée

**I chose this dish because mackerel is often overlooked by professional kitchens as it is so cheap. In fact it has a beautiful flavour and a crisp skin, which goes beautifully with the earthiness of the artichokes and lentils. It is a very simple but effective dish.**

**Serves 4**

**1 globe artichoke**
**600ml (2 1/2 cups) good chicken stock, preferably home-made**
**20ml (4 teaspoons) double (heavy) cream**
**4 tablespoons vegetable oil**
**1 carrot, cut into 4**
**1 onion, cut in half, leaving the root on**
**3 garlic cloves, cut in half**
**50g (2oz) pancetta trimmings**
**100g (1/2 cup) Puy lentils**
**2 large mackerel, filleted**
**15g (1 tablespoon) butter**
**lemon juice**
**salt and freshly ground white pepper**

Snap the stalk off the artichoke and pull off all the leaves. Trim off any remaining bits of stalk or leaf with a small knife, then scoop out the choke with a spoon and discard. Dice the artichoke heart into about 10 pieces. Place in a saucepan with 200ml (7oz) of the chicken stock and simmer until the artichoke is tender and the stock has reduced by about half. Place the artichoke and its cooking liquid in a mini food processor with the cream and blend until smooth. Pass through a fine sieve to remove any artichoke hairs, then season to taste. Set aside.

Heat 2 tablespoons of the vegetable oil in a heavy-based pan, add the carrot, onion, garlic and pancetta and cook until golden brown. Add the Puy lentils, followed by the remaining chicken stock. Cover and simmer for 20–30 minutes, until the lentils are soft. Do not boil, or the lentils will split. Drain off excess liquid, if necessary, and remove the carrot and onion. Cover the lentils and keep warm.

Score the skin of the mackerel from belly to fin at 5mm (1/4-inch) intervals. Heat the remaining oil in a large, non-stick frying pan (skillet). Season the mackerel fillets, then add them to the pan, skin-side down, and cook for 3–4 minutes, until crisp. Turn them over, add the butter and a drop of lemon juice to the pan and spoon them over the fish. Transfer the fish to kitchen paper towels.

Arrange the Puy lentils in the centre of 4 serving plates. Reheat the artichoke purée if necessary and spoon it to either side of the lentils. Place the mackerel on top of the lentils, add a spoonful of the pan juices and serve.

**Opposite: Roast Pheasant with Potato Purée, Savoy Cabbage and Raisin and Wild Mushroom Sauce**

# Roast Pheasant with Potato Purée, Savoy Cabbage and Raisin and Wild Mushroom Sauce

**This is a hugely popular dish when we have it on the menu at Chapter One. The pheasant has a distinctive buttery flavour that goes well with the sweet raisins and a nice bottle of red wine on a cold winter's day.**

**Serves 4**

**4 large Maris Piper (main-crop Idaho) potatoes**
**2 hen pheasants**
**7 garlic cloves, chopped**
**1/2 bunch of thyme**
**1 tablespoon olive oil**
**150g (1 1/4 sticks) butter**
**2 shallots, sliced**
**200g (7oz) mixed wild mushrooms, preferably ceps (porcini), chanterelles and morels**
**200ml (7oz) double (heavy) cream**
**lemon juice**
**50g (1/3 cup) raisins, soaked in hot water until plump**
**1 pointed cabbage, cut into chunks**
**salt and freshly ground black pepper**

Bake the potatoes in an oven preheated to 220°C/425°F/Gas Mark 7 until tender. Meanwhile, remove the legs from the pheasants, which can be kept to use in another recipe. Season the pheasants with salt and pepper and push 3 chopped garlic cloves and 5 thyme sprigs into the cavity of each bird.

Heat the olive oil in a large, heavy roasting tin (pan), add the pheasants and cook until golden all over. Transfer to the hot oven and cook for a total of 12 minutes – 4 minutes on each side. Remove from the roasting tin and leave to rest for a few minutes in a warm place.

Put the roasting tin on the hob (stovetop), add 50g (3 1/2 tablespoons) of the butter, then add the remaining garlic and the shallots. Chop the remaining thyme and add that too. Sauté gently until softened, then add the mushrooms and sauté until golden and tender. Add half the double cream and bring to the boil. Season with salt, pepper and a drop of lemon juice, then add the drained raisins and set aside.

When the baked potatoes are done, scoop out the flesh while still hot and pass through a fine sieve. Bring the remaining cream to the boil with 50g (3 1/2 tablespoons) of the butter and beat in the potato to give a smooth purée. Season with salt and pepper.

Cook the cabbage in boiling salted water until tender, then drain well and return to the pan. Mix with the remaining butter and adjust the seasoning.

Take the pheasant breasts off the bone – the meat should be slightly pink. Place a spoonful of potato purée on each serving plate with some pointed cabbage. Place the pheasant breasts on top of the cabbage, then the creamed mushrooms on top of the pheasant, and serve.

# Lemon Posset with Raspberry Salad

**This dessert is famous for its simplicity and foolproof method and is also very refreshing and tasty. It can be made well in advance.**

**Serves 4**

**450ml (2 cups) double (heavy) cream**
**125g (generous 1/2 cup) caster (superfine) sugar**
**grated zest and juice of 1 1/2 lemons**
**1 punnet of raspberries**
**1 tablespoon icing (confectioners') sugar**

Put the cream, sugar and lemon zest in a heavy-based saucepan and bring to the boil. Pour on to the lemon juice and then strain through a sieve into 4 glasses. Leave to cool, then place in the fridge until set.

Wash the raspberries, pat dry and dust with the icing sugar. Leave for 10 minutes, until the raspberries begin to break up. Then place a generous spoonful of the raspberry salad on top of each lemon posset and serve.

twenty four

# MATT MORAN

## Aria

Matthew Moran spent his childhood in rural New South Wales, Australia, where he developed his understanding of the importance of fresh produce. This principle has stayed with him and paved the way for his successful career on the Sydney food scene. After completing his apprenticeship at La Belle Helene restaurant, he further developed his cooking passion under Stefano Manfredi. Matthew has successfully opened three restaurants, Paddington Inn Bistro, Moran's and current award winner, Aria. His reputation as a leader in innovative and cutting-edge cuisine results from his dedication and passion for produce, preparation, presentation and service.

**What are your favourite foods/tastes/flavours?**
My tastes change all the time, depending on what is in season. My favourite food is fresh seasonal produce.

**What are your favourite utensils?**
The best utensils to invest in are some good chef's knives.

**What is the most useful piece of kitchen design and equipment?**
I believe a design that allows a streamlined work area creates the best flow of service. If you design the different sections correctly, this will maximize the kitchen's efficiency.

**What is your favourite season?**
Spring, because of all the new produce.

**What is your favourite meal?**
There is nothing like breakfast on the beach.

**How do you decide what to cook?**
My menu is highly influenced by seasonal produce.

**What is your favourite drink?**
A beer after a busy service.

**How can you inspire others to enjoy great food and cooking?**
During the year we host a range of educational promotions, from behind-the-scenes chefs' tours and market tours to cooking classes and demonstrations. Once people are invited into your kitchen and see all the hard work that goes on behind the scenes and the wonderful produce we use, I think they can appreciate the Aria culture better and have more confidence in trying new things at home.

**How did you become a chef?**
I left school in year ten to pursue an apprenticeship and I fell in love with the art of cooking.

**How do you feel about cooking for children?**
I have a three-year-old son and I really enjoy cooking for him. I think it is important to educate children about good food and encourage healthy eating habits from an early age.

**Can you give one piece of advice for the domestic cook?**
If you use the best-quality produce you will achieve better results.

* Seared Scallops with Peking Duck and Ginger and Shallot Dressing
* Roast Rack of Lamb with Spiced Aubergine and Spring Vegetables
* Apple Jelly with Rhubarb

## Seared Scallops with Peking Duck and Ginger and Shallot Dressing

**Serves 6**

**2.5cm (1-inch) piece of fresh ginger, finely shredded**
**1 tablespoon vegetable oil**
**150g (5oz) shiitake mushrooms**
**1 large, Chinese-style barbecued Peking duck – available from Chinese food stores and some large supermarkets**
**2 tablespoons coriander (cilantro) leaves**
**2 spring onions (scallions), chopped**
**180g (6oz) fine pasta, such as tagliolini or noodles**
**18 large scallops**
**1 teaspoon toasted sesame seeds**

For the dressing:

**1 teaspoon hoisin sauce**
**2 1/2 tablespoons rice wine vinegar**
**5 tablespoons grapeseed oil**

To make the dressing, whisk all the ingredients together in a bowl until they have emulsified into a vinaigrette. Set aside. Fry the shredded ginger in the oil until crisp, then set aside. Poach the shiitake mushrooms in boiling water for 20 seconds, then drain well. Take the duck meat off the bone and tear or chop it into chunks. Place in a large bowl with the shiitake mushrooms, coriander and spring onions.

Cook the pasta in a large pan of boiling salted water until tender, then drain. Add the pasta to the duck mixture, pour in enough of the dressing to coat everything and toss well.

Sear the scallops in a lightly oiled hot pan for about 2 minutes, until golden.

To serve, place the duck and pasta salad in the middle of each plate and arrange the scallops around the edge. Drizzle a little of the dressing around the plate and garnish with the fried ginger and toasted sesame seeds.

# Roast Rack of Lamb with Spiced Aubergine and Spring Vegetables

**Serves 6**

**2 bunches of baby turnips**
**60g (2oz) baby carrots**
**60g (2oz) asparagus**
**60g (2oz) white asparagus**
**40g ($1^1/_2$ oz) green beans**
**40g ($^1/_3$ cup) shelled peas**
**6 x 3-rib racks of lamb**
**160g (about 5oz) fresh spinach**
**40g ($1^1/_2$oz) vine-ripened cherry tomatoes**
**4 tablespoons Herb Oil Vinaigrette (see Note below), plus extra to serve**
**salt and freshly ground black pepper**

For the spiced aubergine:

**400g (14oz) aubergines (eggplants)**
**50g (2oz) mango chutney**
**1 red chilli, finely chopped**
**a pinch each of cumin and coriander seeds, toasted in a dry frying pan (skillet) and then ground**
**1 tablespoon chopped coriander (cilantro)**

For the sauce:

**1 onion, chopped**
**$^1/_2$ garlic clove**
**50g ($^1/_3$ cup) carrot, chopped**
**25g ($^1/_3$ cup) mushrooms, chopped**
**1 celery stick, chopped**
**1 tablespoon skinned, deseeded and finely diced tomato**
**$^1/_2$ glass of dry white wine**
**500ml ($2^1/_4$ cups) chicken stock**

To make the spiced aubergine, prick the aubergines with a fork, then place on a baking sheet and roast in an oven preheated to 190°C/375°F/Gas Mark 5 until very soft. Place in a bowl, cover with cling film (plastic wrap) and leave to steam for a few minutes. Remove from the bowl and cut in half, then drain off any liquid. Scoop out the flesh from top to bottom, keeping it as intact as possible. Fold all the remaining ingredients into the aubergine flesh and season to taste with salt and pepper. Cook the turnips, carrots, asparagus, green beans and peas separately in a large pan of boiling water, removing them with a slotted spoon when tender. Set aside.

Season the racks of lamb and sear in a very hot ovenproof frying pan (skillet) until browned. Transfer to an oven preheated to 200°C/400°F/Gas Mark 6 and roast for 5–8 minutes, until cooked medium rare. Remove from the oven, transfer to a warm plate and leave to rest for 15 minutes.

Meanwhile, for the sauce, put the onion, garlic, carrot, mushrooms and celery in the pan in which the meat was cooked and cook over a gentle heat until lightly browned. Drain off excess fat, raise the heat to medium-high and add the tomato. Stir well, then add the wine and cook until it has reduced, stirring to scrape up the sediment from the base of the pan. Add the chicken stock, bring to the boil and simmer until reduced by about two-thirds. Strain through a fine sieve into a clean pan and simmer until reduced to a sauce consistency. Season to taste and keep warm.

Blanch the spinach in a large pan of boiling salted water until just wilted, then drain well and season to taste. Put the spiced aubergine in a saucepan and reheat gently. Reheat the spring vegetables in a pan of boiling water, drain well and place in a large bowl. Add the cherry tomatoes and toss with enough herb oil vinaigrette to coat.

To serve, place the spinach in the centre of each serving plate and top with the spiced aubergine. Arrange the vegetables on top. Carve each rack of lamb into 3 cutlets (chops) and place them around and on top of the vegetables. Drizzle with the sauce and a little herb oil vinaigrette.

**Note**

For the Herb Oil Vinaigrette, mix together 5 tablespoons of vegetable oil, 5 tablespoons of olive oil, 15g (heaped 4 tablespoons) chopped basil and 15g (heaped 4 tablespoons) chopped parsley and set aside for 1 hour to allow the flavours to infuse. Strain through a fine piece of muslin (cheesecloth) and discard the herbs. Whisk together 2 tablespoons Chardonnay vinegar, 2 tablespoons champagne vinegar and 1 tablespoon of lemon juice, then whisk in the herb oil until emulsified.

# Apple Jelly with Rhubarb

**Serves 6**

**320ml ($1^1/_4$ cups plus 1 tablespoon) water**
**60g ($^1/_4$ cup plus 1 tablespoon) caster (superfine) sugar**
**15g ($^1/_2$oz) gelatine leaves**
**300ml ($1^1/_4$ cups) fresh apple juice**

For the baked rhubarb:

**200g (1 cup) caster (superfine) sugar**
**160ml ($^1/_2$ cup) water**
**5 tablespoons champagne**
**1 vanilla pod (vanilla bean), slit open**
**about 250g (9oz) rhubarb, peeled and cut into 4cm ($^1/_2$-inch) lengths**

For the rhubarb syrup:

**100g rhubarb (scant 1 cup), cut into small cubes**
**20g (heaped $^1/_2$ tablespoon) caster (superfine) sugar**
**7 tablespoons water**

For the garnish:

**1 Granny Smith apple**
**100g (7 tablespoons) crème fraîche**
**10g ($^1/_3$oz) celery cress, optional**

To make the jelly, put the water and caster sugar in a pan and bring to the boil. Meanwhile, cover the gelatine in cold water and leave for 5 minutes, until soft. Remove the sugar syrup from the heat, then gently squeeze out excess water from the gelatine and add the softened gelatine to the syrup. Stir until it has dissolved, then set aside to cool. Stir in the apple juice and pour into 6 ramekins or dariole moulds. Chill until set.

For the baked rhubarb, put the sugar, water, champagne and vanilla pod into a saucepan and bring to the boil, stirring to dissolve the sugar. Place the rhubarb in a baking dish and pour the hot syrup over it. Cover with foil and bake in an oven preheated to 180°C/350°F/Gas Mark 4 for 10 minutes or until tender; be careful not to overcook it; it should still hold its shape. Remove from the oven and leave to cool.

To make the syrup, put the rhubarb and sugar in a heavy-based pan and heat gently until the rhubarb starts to caramelize. Add the water and bring to the boil, then set aside for 1 hour to allow the flavours to infuse. Strain off the syrup, discarding the rhubarb, and leave to cool.

To serve, turn the jellies out of their moulds and place one in the centre of each plate. Pour the rhubarb syrup around the jelly and scatter the rhubarb sticks over it. Using a small scoop, such as a parisienne cutter or melon baller, make some apple balls from the Granny Smith apple and scatter these around the plate too. Place 3 small quenelles [oval shapes] of crème fraîche on each plate, using 2 teaspoons to shape them, then finish with some celery cress, if using.

# twenty five

# ANTON MOSIMANN

## Mosimann's

Anton Mosimann's philosophy is to use the freshest ingredients, cooked in the simplest way, to produce good, honest food. This is the concept behind his *cuisine naturelle*, which he pioneered 20 years ago. Anton Mosimann has run Mosimann's Private Dining Club in London since 1988, together with Mosimann's Party Service and Mosimann's Academy, the cookery school. He holds the Royal Warrant for catering services to His Royal Highness The Prince of Wales and in 2004 was awarded the OBE.

**What are your favourite foods/flavours?**

I feel simplicity is the key. I enjoy all foods and flavours and love to try different recipes and products. For example, I love a freshly steamed piece of fish, such as halibut, with black bean sauce, coriander and ginger – I just love that oriental mix, and of course with that I would have a glass of my favourite drink, Mosimann Champagne, to complement the flavours. Although I am a believer in keeping it simple, food never has to be boring – in fact the more exotic the food, the better I like it. There is nothing I dislike, although I have never tried what they call 'junk food'.

**What is your most useful piece of kitchen equipment?**

I like steamed food, so my favourite piece of equipment has to be a steamer. It's an essential tool for any kitchen and is very straightforward to use. What you put in, you get out. For me, it is one of the best ways to cook. It doesn't have to be expensive, it can be a very simple steamer, such as a Chinese dim sum basket. Of course, a good cleaver is important, too. I love to work with a Chinese knife. But I think the best invention of recent years is the induction hob, and using a wok with this technology is just great.

**What is your favourite season?**

I wouldn't say that I have a favourite season, as the produce of each is so different. It's wonderful to see the fresh produce coming on to the market. For instance, grouse is one of my favourite foods, and every year I look forward to the Glorious Twelfth (when grouse season starts in Britain). In fact, several weeks beforehand I get quite excited about this wonderful bird!

**What is your favourite mealtime?**

I cannot say that I have a favourite mealtime. I love them all – breakfast, lunch and dinner, they are all different, and of course it all depends on which country I am in at the time.

**How do you decide what to cook?**

I go for what is available at the time. I visit the markets and get the freshest possible produce, so it can change daily, but I just love fresh food and the market will decide for me. That is why it is impossible to tell anyone what my 'top ten ingredients' would be.

**What inspires you?**

The produce, the market, the freshness, but it's also the people at the market. The local market is the ideal starting point for getting to know the culture of any country. I have just returned from a trip to Southeast Asia, where I learned so much about basic ingredients. The countries I visited included Cambodia, Myanmar and Laos, where I found incredibly tasty, fresh food. It was fantastic! That inspires me to understand different cultures and look at their basic recipes and how I can develop and incorporate them into my own dishes.

**How can you inspire others to enjoy great food and cooking?**

Hopefully I inspire others by advising them to keep it simple, to use not necessarily the most expensive but the

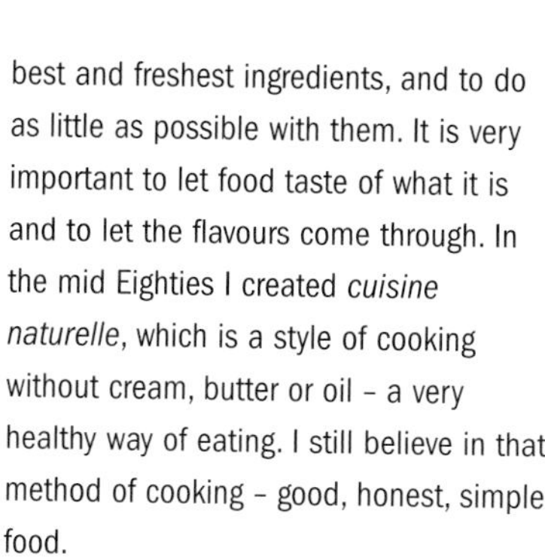

best and freshest ingredients, and to do as little as possible with them. It is very important to let food taste of what it is and to let the flavours come through. In the mid Eighties I created *cuisine naturelle*, which is a style of cooking without cream, butter or oil – a very healthy way of eating. I still believe in that method of cooking – good, honest, simple food.

**How did you become a chef?**
For me, there was never any question in my mind that cooking would be my life. My parents owned a restaurant in Switzerland so I grew up in this environment. From a very early age I just loved cooking. Both my parents were in the kitchen, so automatically I helped, peeling onions, baking bread. At first I had to stand on a stool in order to be able to watch what was going on. I would do my homework in the restaurant; we had no sitting room, no family room, everything happened in the restaurant. It was closed one day a week, and when I was about eight years old I would have my friends, who were older than me, round to cook a meal for them. It has always been my passion.

**What are your kitchen secrets?**
When people ask me my kitchen secrets I do not wish to bore them with details of which way to stir. More important is to enjoy your cooking. It means a lot to me to have happy, motivated staff – I go around every day and shake hands with my staff and have a chat. There is no shouting in my kitchen. I don't believe in it. I never did. It creates an unpleasant atmosphere. So if you have the best produce and happy staff you have happy customers. That's the same in the domestic kitchen. If you feel good about the food you are preparing, it will taste good, and you will enjoy the meal you have created. I advise everyone who has not yet discovered these pleasures to try it. And at the same time, once again, 'Keep it simple.' One of my favourite quotes is, 'Everything simple is beautiful and everything beautiful is simple.' Especially in cooking. Look at Nature – we have such wonderful ingredients! Don't overdo it, keep the colours, keep the textures. It's wonderful to combine food colours and textures together, like an artist. When creating a new recipe, look at the freshness and quality of the produce, cook in different ways: steam it, grill it, poach it, and keep the natural flavours of the food. For me, that's very important. Let fish taste of fish, meat of meat, and chicken of chicken.

**How do you feel about cooking for children?**
Children are the future generation and it's never too early for them to learn about cooking. We run courses for kids at the Mosimann Academy, which are fun as well as educational. The children can have a good time and hopefully also learn something about the quality of products and different cooking methods. It is very important that we train our youngsters as early as possible to understand not only the ifs and buts of cooking but also the importance of eating more healthily and having fewer so-called junk and processed foods, which most of the time are full of fat and sugar.

* Carpaccio of Scottish Salmon and Scallops with Lime, Herbs and Olive Oil
* Poached Chicken Breasts with Baby Leeks and Trompette Mushrooms, Tomato Dressing and Market Vegetables
* Raspberries in Puff Pastry

## Carpaccio of Scottish Salmon and Scallops with Lime, Herbs and Olive Oil

**Serves 4**

**400g (14oz) very fresh Scottish salmon fillet, preferably a thick centre cut, so it is the same width all along, bones and skin removed**
**8 very fresh scallops**
**juice of 2 limes**
**50ml ($3\frac{1}{2}$ tablespoons) olive oil**
**$1\frac{1}{2}$ tablespoons chopped dill**
**$1\frac{1}{2}$ tablespoons chopped chives**
**salt and freshly ground pepper**
**fresh chervil, to garnish**

Cut the salmon into paper-thin slices across the grain. Remove the coral from the scallops and slice the scallops thinly. Arrange the salmon and scallop slices on 4 plates.

Mix the lime juice, olive oil, dill and chives together in a bowl and season with salt and pepper to taste.

About 10 minutes before serving, lightly brush the salmon and scallops with the lime juice and oil mixture. Place a small sprig of chervil on each plate and serve.

# Poached Chicken Breasts with Baby Leeks and Trompette Mushrooms, Tomato Dressing and Market Vegetables

**Serves 4**

**4 x 150g (5-oz) skinless chicken breasts (breast halves)**
**8 baby leeks**
**100g ($3^1/_2$oz) fresh trompette mushrooms, or 10g ($^1/_3$ oz) dried ones**
**chicken stock to cover**
**salt and freshly ground black pepper**
**fresh herbs, to garnish (optional)**

For the tomato dressing:

**3 plum tomatoes**
**100ml (7 tablespoons) olive oil**
**2 tablespoons champagne vinegar**
**$4^1/_2$ tablespoons reduced chicken stock**
**2 teaspoons French mustard**
**2 tablespoons finely chopped chives**
**2 tablespoons finely chopped chervil**
**$1^1/_2$ teaspoons finely chopped dill**

To serve:

**market vegetables, such as carrots, courgettes (zucchini), baby leeks, broccoli**

Place the chicken breasts on a chopping board and, using a very sharp knife, slice them horizontally in half, leaving them joined at one edge. Open them out so they form a butterfly shape, then cover with cling film (plastic wrap) and gently flatten with a rolling pin. Blanch the leeks in boiling salted water until just tender, then drain. Cool in iced water and set aside.

If using dried mushrooms, soak them in warm water for 10 minutes, then tear them in half and wash thoroughly to remove any sand and dirt. Drain well. If using fresh mushrooms, simply clean them and tear them in half.

Spread a piece of cling film out on a chopping board. Sprinkle with salt and pepper. Spread one of the chicken breasts out on the cling film and season with salt and pepper. Place 2 leeks and some trompette mushrooms along the centre of the chicken and roll up. Then roll the cling film over the breast into a sausage shape, twist both ends and knot. Repeat with the remaining chicken breasts. Poach for 10–12 minutes in enough hot chicken stock to cover, then remove from the stock and keep warm.

While the chicken is poaching, blanch the tomatoes in boiling water for about 10 seconds, then remove from the pan and drop into ice-cold water. Peel off the skin, cut each tomato into quarters, then scrape out the seeds and dice the flesh.

Whisk together the olive oil, vinegar, reduced chicken stock and mustard. Season to taste and set aside. Just before serving, gently warm the dressing in a small pan and add the herbs and tomatoes.

Blanch the vegetables individually in boiling salted water, then drain and keep warm. Season with salt and pepper.
To serve, remove the cling film from the chicken breasts and cut each one in half at an angle. Place in the centre of 4 plates, along with the market vegetables, and drizzle over the tomato dressing. Garnish with fresh herbs, if you wish.

# Raspberries in Puff Pastry

225g (8oz) puff pastry
1 egg yolk, beaten
icing (confectioners') sugar for dusting
200g (7oz) fresh raspberries
4 sprigs of mint

For the raspberry sauce:
250g (9oz) raspberries
80g (6½ tablespoons) caster (superfine) sugar
juice of 1 lemon
3 tablespoons framboise (raspberry liqueur)

For the pastry cream:
175ml (¾ cup) milk
2 vanilla pods (vanilla beans)
3 egg yolks
2½ tablespoons caster (superfine) sugar
15g (2 tablespoons) cornflour (cornstarch)
2 tablespoons whipped cream
2 teaspoons framboise (raspberry liqueur)

Lay the puff pastry on a flat surface and roll it up tightly. Cut the roll of pastry into 12 even pieces. Place each piece flat, roll it out and cut it into a circle about 5cm (2 inches) in diameter. Prick the pastry circles with a fork and then brush with the beaten egg yolk. Place on a baking sheet and bake in an oven preheated to 180°C/350°F/Gas Mark 4 for 12–15 minutes. Remove from the oven, sprinkle evenly with icing sugar and return briefly to the oven to glaze. Remove and allow to cool.

To make the sauce, purée the raspberries in a blender, then mix in the caster sugar. Flavour with the lemon juice and framboise. Strain through a fine sieve to remove the pips (seeds) and set aside.

For the pastry cream, gently warm the milk and vanilla pods in a pan. Whisk the egg yolks and sugar together until the sugar has dissolved. Add a dash of the milk to the eggs, whisk the mixture together and pour back into the pan. Heat gently, stirring constantly, until the mixture begins to thicken; do not allow it to boil. Mix a dash of water with the cornflour and add this to the pan. Cook, stirring, until the mixture thickens even more, then remove the pan from the heat. Allow the pastry cream to cool, then fold in the whipped cream and framboise. Leave the pastry cream in the fridge until you are ready to serve.

To serve, place one layer of pastry on each plate, put some of the pastry cream in the centre, then a layer of raspberries to the edge of the pastry. Repeat until you have 3 layers of pastry. Place a little pastry cream on top and 3 fresh raspberries. Pour a little of the raspberry sauce around each plate, finish with a sprig of mint and lightly dust with icing sugar.

twenty six

# DAVID NICHOLLS

## Mandarin Oriental Hyde Park Hotel

**David Nicholls is one of the UK's most respected chefs, and is firmly established amongst the world's finest hotel chefs. At the tender age of twenty-two, he became one of the country's youngest chefs to receive a Michelin star, at the Old Lodge in Limpsfield. He was chef at the Ritz in London before taking over his current role at the Mandarin Oriental Hyde Park, London. Under David's guidance, its restaurant, Foliage was awarded a Michelin star in 2002, which has been retained ever since.**

**What are your favourite foods/tastes/flavours?**
I love Indian and Asian foods. I think Indian food in the UK is completely misrepresented – we box it with chicken korma, rice and naan bread. In reality, Indian food is very exciting and diverse, with its use of flavours and spices – almost as diverse as Chinese or Japanese food.

**What are your favourite utensils?**
Probably a very old knife I use for most things. However, I couldn't be without my liquidizer (blender) and mandoline. Also, I have an old dim sum bamboo basket – fantastic for steaming.

**What is the most useful piece of kitchen design and equipment?**
Space and clever storage areas. My wood-fired oven is an absolute must for cooking and adding flavour to food.

**What is your favourite season?**
Spring – I love everything that starts to grow, the colours and the textures.

**What is your favourite mealtime?**
I hardly ever eat breakfast or lunch so it must be dinner, although afternoon tea is fun if done well. But since you really have more time for dinner, that's my favourite, as I get to sit with Claire and my two boys, Daniel and Dean, and talk.

**How do you decide what to cook?**
It depends mainly on how I feel. However, ingredients and mood are key – in spring and summer, lots of very light dishes, salads etc., getting more robust in autumn and winter.

**What inspires you?**
Ingredients normally but often smell, too. If I am in a supermarket and smell something like fresh bread, I'll buy some and do something to eat with it. Also good restaurants, a great recipe, or watching TV.

**What is your favourite drink?**
Mint tea, I drink gallons of it – preferably fresh mint. I am also partial to good red wines.

**What are your likes and dislikes?**
I like most things but I am not a great lover of fish roe. I hate restaurants putting things on the menu that are not good quality. For example, truffle risotto if the truffles are cheap and flavourless – I'd prefer a spring onion risotto.

**How can you inspire others to enjoy great food and cooking?**
By cooking for family and friends at home. Also, I am always advocating friends' restaurants, telling people they ought to go and how good they are; this inspires people, I think.

**How did you become a chef?**
We came from a very poor mining community but we always had great food. My mum was a fantastic cook and my brother, Robert, sister, Susan, and I were always made to cook and be involved. I started working in a local hotel and I remember being really excited about food. I loved the way foods worked together or could be a disaster.

**What are your top ten ingredients?**
Sea salt, aged balsamic vinegar, olive oil, fresh herbs, foie gras, shellfish, vanilla, ripe soft fruits such as mangoes, cheeses, morel mushrooms.

**What are your kitchen secrets?**
My kitchen secret is that I am really only 32. I am wearing this body for someone else. Seriously – I don't have any.

**What are your top tips?**
After cooking vegetables, always refresh them in ice-cold water. This helps them keep their colour and prevents overcooking. A few minutes before you serve them, plunge them into boiling water to reheat, then drain and finish with a little butter. With spinach, wash and drain it well, then cook it quickly in a very hot pan with a knob of butter.

**Do you ever eat junk food?**
I have been known to sample a famous burger on the odd occasion. However, we do have a good Indian near us and the food is excellent – not junk food, but quick and easy.

**How do you feel about cooking for children?**
Great, if it's about education – the more they try, the better at eating they become. But I think you should let kids be kids and enjoy what they want to eat – the serious stuff comes much later.

**Can you give one piece of advice for the domestic cook?**
Read the recipe, get everything ready – have a cup of tea or a glass of wine – then read the recipe again and go for it. But think about what the writer is trying to get you to do, and what the end result is going to be.

* My Anything Salad
* Fillet of Beef Cooked in Herb Bread with Madeira Sauce
* Orange and Raspberry Gratin with Mango Ice Cream

# My Anything Salad

**I always plan to eat a main course and dessert, and seldom prepare a starter (appetizer). Then at the last minute I raid the fridge and make a salad using anything that's available. Either follow the recipe below or substitute ingredients as necessary. Instead of the dressing given below, you could use a dressing of your choice – Caesar would be ideal.**

**Serves 4**

**50g (2oz) sugarsnap peas**
**50g (2oz) green beans**
**6 asparagus spears, cut into 5cm (2-inch) lengths**
**4 tablespoons olive oil**
**50g (2/3 cup) button mushrooms, cut into quarters**
**1 red onion, sliced**
**100g (2/3 cup) new potatoes, boiled in their skins, then sliced**
**a bunch of spring onions (scallions), chopped**
**2 slices of toast, crusts removed and cut into 1cm (1/2-inch) dice**
**10 cherry tomatoes, cut in half**
**2 cooked chicken breasts (breast halves), either roasted or fried, diced**
**3 eggs**
**25g (1oz) Parmesan cheese shavings**
**mixed salad leaves, such as curly endive, lollo rosso, rocket (arugula), spinach, Cos (romaine), cress, etc.**
**salt and freshly ground black pepper**

For the dressing:
**1/2 teaspoon garlic purée**
**1 egg yolk**
**1/2 teaspoon Dijon mustard**
**1 tablespoon freshly grated Parmesan cheese**
**1 tablespoon white wine vinegar**
**4 1/2 tablespoons olive or vegetable oil**
**Worcestershire sauce to taste**
**3 tablespoons hot water, if necessary**

To make the dressing, whisk the garlic purée, egg yolk, mustard, cheese and vinegar together, then gradually whisk in the oil. Season to taste with salt, pepper and Worcestershire sauce. Add the water, if necessary, to give the consistency of double (heavy) cream.

Cook the sugarsnaps, green beans and asparagus in boiling salted water, then drain and refresh in cold water. Drain again and set aside.

Heat the olive oil in a pan, add the mushrooms and onion and cook until tender and lightly coloured. Add the green vegetables, toss together and season to taste. Remove from the heat and add the potatoes, spring onions, toast croûtons, cherry tomatoes and diced roast chicken. Season with salt and pepper and transfer to a large mixing bowl.

Boil the eggs for 3 minutes, then break them into the bowl and spoon into the mixture. Add the dressing, then add the mixed leaves and toss everything together. Finally add the Parmesan cheese shavings, adjust the seasoning and serve.

# Fillet of Beef Cooked in Herb Bread with Madeira Sauce

**Have a very sharp carving knife ready for the beef. The crust is extremely rich and delicate, simply a triumph when done well. Serve with mixed green vegetables.**

**Serves 4**

**500g (18oz) beef fillet (tenderloin)**
**oil for frying**
**Dijon mustard**
**300ml ($1^1/_4$ cups) double (heavy) cream**
**4 eggs**
**4 tablespoons chopped green herbs**
**1 teaspoon crushed garlic or garlic purée**
**6 slices of medium-sliced white bread, crusts removed**
**salt and freshly ground black pepper**

For the Madeira sauce:
**50g (2oz) shallots, sliced**
**75g (1 cup) shiitake mushrooms, sliced**
**$3^1/_2$ tablespoons Madeira (or port)**
**300ml ($1^1/_4$ cups) chicken stock**
**4 tablespoons double (heavy) cream**
**175g ($1^1/_2$ sticks) butter, diced**

Season the beef fillet with salt and pepper. Pour just enough oil in a frying pan (skillet) to cover the base and place over a fairly high heat. When it is hot, add the beef fillet and cook until well browned on all sides. Remove from the heat and leave to cool. Brush liberally all over with Dijon mustard and season with salt and pepper again.

Generously oil a sheet of baking parchment paper, large enough to wrap round the beef. Lightly whisk the cream and eggs together, then add the chopped herbs and crushed garlic. Soak the bread in the cream and egg mixture until it absorbs some of the liquid (not too much, though). Drain off any excess liquid and lay 4 slices of the bread on the piece of baking parchment to form a square. Place the beef fillet on top and encase it in the bread, using the remaining 2 slices to form a crust around it. Roll up the meat in the parchment and tie the parcel with string, retaining the shape of the fillet. Bake for 30 minutes in an oven preheated to 200°C/400°F/Gas Mark 6. Meanwhile, make the sauce. Put the shallots and mushrooms in a pan, add the Madeira and bring to the boil. Add the chicken stock and simmer until reduced to a tenth of its original volume. Add the cream, bring back to the boil and simmer gently until reduced by half. Over a low heat, gradually whisk in the butter, then season to taste.

When the beef is done, remove from the oven and leave to rest for 5 minutes. Remove the baking parchment and slice the beef into 4. Place on 4 serving plates, pour over the sauce and serve.

# Orange and Raspberry Gratin with Mango Ice Cream

**This dessert can be made 2 or 3 hours before required. Keep refrigerated and add the ice cream when serving. If you haven't got a blowtorch, just serve this without glazing. Putting it under a grill (broiler) would start to cook the fruit.**

**Serves 4**

**4 very large oranges**
**150g (5oz) raspberries**
**80g ($6^{2}/_{3}$ tablespoons) caster (superfine) sugar**
**2 tablespoons water**
**4 egg yolks**
**175ml ($^{3}/_{4}$ cup) double (heavy) cream, semi-whipped**
**2 tablespoons Grand Marnier**

**For the mango ice cream:**

**250g (9oz) mango flesh (you can use drained canned mangoes or very ripe fresh ones)**
**250g ($1^{1}/_{4}$ cups) caster (superfine) sugar**
**250ml (1 cup plus 2 tablespoons) double (heavy) cream**

First make the ice cream. Place all the ingredients in a liquidizer (blender) or food processor and blend for 1–2 minutes, until very smooth. Place in an ice-cream maker and churn until set. If you don't have an ice-cream maker, simply place the mixture in a bowl and put it in the freezer for 4 hours, whisking lightly every 30 minutes, until frozen.

Cut all the peel and pith off the oranges, then cut out the segments from between the membrane. Arrange the segments around 4 plates like spokes on a wheel. Place the raspberries between the orange segments.

Put the sugar and water in a pan, heat gently until the sugar has dissolved, then boil for 30 seconds. Meanwhile, whisk the egg yolks well in a bowl. Gradually pour the hot sugar syrup over the egg yolks, whisking constantly with a hand-held electric beater. Continue to whisk until cold. Fold in the semi-whipped cream and the Grand Marnier. Spoon this mixture over the oranges and raspberries and glaze using a blowtorch. Scoop a generous ball of mango ice cream into the centre of each portion and serve.

# twenty seven

# JAMIE OLIVER

## Fifteen

Jamie Oliver started cooking at his parents' pub at the age of eight and has since worked with some of the world's top chefs, including Antonio Carluccio and Gennaro Contaldo at the Neal Street Restaurant and Rose Gray and Ruth Rogers at the River Café. Jamie's five cookbooks have all been international bestsellers, selling over 11 million copies worldwide. His television shows are broadcast in forty-six countries. He is co-founder of Fifteen restaurant and involved with the charity, Fifteen Foundation, which helps disadvantaged youngsters to become chefs. He recently led a nationwide campaign to improve school dinners in the UK.

**What are your favourite foods/flavours?**
Chilli, tomatoes, olive oil, fish, sour things.

**What are your favourite utensils?**
Pestle and mortar, a good heavy frying pan (skillet) and a thick chopping board.

**What is your most useful piece of kitchen design or equipment?**
Magimix food processor, big open spaces, wooden surfaces. Clear out all the junk hanging around on your worktops.

**What is your favourite season?**
All of them. Each has its own amazing produce and this keeps me thinking.

**What is your favourite meal?**
Breakfast: good scrambled egg bruschetta with chopped chilli over the top.
Lunch: pasta with salad.
Dinner: anything roasted.

**How do you decide what to cook?**
By seeing what's good down at the shops or the market. If a chicken or a duck looks beautiful, I'll have it.

**What inspires you?**
Produce, producers, the countryside, my veg garden, my students, my wife, conversations and reading.

**What is your favourite drink?**
An Italian cocktail called Milano e Torino, with loads of ice.

**What are your likes and dislikes?**
Likes – anything fast that scares me; anything funny.
Dislikes – Clarissa Dickson Wright, parking attendants and traffic wardens, people who aren't open-minded and people who aren't kind.

**How can you inspire others to enjoy great food and cooking?**
Try to encourage parents to cook with their kids, to improve school dinners; with my TV programmes, books and magazine columns.

**What are your top ten ingredients?**
Too many to choose – I love everything.

**What are your kitchen secrets?**
After seven years of being on TV, and having written five books, I've exhausted them all!

**What are your top tips?**
Pour a little boiling water over woody herbs such as rosemary and thyme before you use them. It helps release the fragrant oils in their leaves.
Next time you're doing a roast chicken, parboil a lemon with your potatoes and then pop the hot lemon inside the bird. It helps cook the chicken on the inside and the outside.

**What is your favourite junk food?**
Quesadillas filled with cheese and chilli, with guacamole and soured cream.

**How do you feel about cooking for children?**

Oh, there's so much to talk about here. Basically it's essential to cook for kids – it's rewarding and loads of fun.

**Can you give one piece of advice for the domestic cook?**

Before you start trying new things, practise the things that you can do already so that you do them properly – get your confidence up and then start experimenting. Don't buy big sets of knives. All you need is a chopper, a paring knife and a serrated knife. The two other things I would suggest you have in the kitchen are a speed peeler and a pair of tongs, as these will cover most jobs.

## Salad of Haloumi, Pomegranate, Little Gem and Watercress with a Lemony Crème Fraîche Dressing

**1/2 garlic clove**
**3 anchovies**
**200ml (7oz) crème fraîche**
**finely grated zest and juice of 1 lemon**
**1/2 small loaf of rustic bread**
**2 glugs of olive oil**
**4 Little Gem lettuces**
**2 handfuls of watercress**
**1 fennel bulb**
**250g (9oz) haloumi cheese, cut into 12 slices**
**1 pomegranate**
**sea salt and freshly ground black pepper**

For the dressing, pound together or finely chop the garlic and anchovies. Mix in the crème fraîche, then the lemon zest and juice, and season to taste with freshly ground black pepper.

Tear the bread into rough pieces about 2-3cm (3/4-1 1/4 inches) and scatter them in a roasting tin (pan). Drizzle with a little olive oil, toss with a good pinch of sea salt and bake in an oven preheated to 200°C/400°F/Gas Mark 6 for 10 minutes or until crunchy.

Trim the bottoms of the Little Gems and break up each one, keeping the leaves whole. Give the watercress and lettuce leaves a quick wash, then dry in a salad spinner and lay on a large serving plate. Cut the top off the fennel and hang on to the feathery parts. Trim the bottom of the bulb and discard the scruffy outer layers. Cut the bulb in half and slice as thinly as possible from the root to the tip, then add to the rest of the leaves. Next, fry the slices of haloumi on both sides in a little olive oil until golden. Drain on kitchen paper towels and add to the salad leaves with the croûtons. Season, give the whole lot a gentle toss, then drizzle over the crème fraîche dressing.

Chop the feathery fennel tops and bash the pomegranate to get the seeds out, then scatter the fennel and pomegranate seeds over the salad.

# Crab Risotto with Peas and Fennel

**1.5 litres (6 cups) fish stock**
**a knob of butter**
**1 small white onion, finely chopped**
**1/2 fennel bulb, finely chopped, fronds reserved**
**400g (2 cups) risotto rice, such as vialone nano or carnaroli**
**250ml (1 cup) white wine or vermouth**
**250g (9oz) fresh crabmeat, white and brown kept separate**
**120g (generous 2/3 cup) raw shelled baby peas**
**zest and juice of 1 lemon**
**extra virgin olive oil**
**1 red chilli, deseeded and finely chopped**
**salt and freshly ground black pepper**

Heat the fish stock gently and keep warm.

Melt the butter in a deep saucepan, add the onion and fennel and sweat gently, with the lid on and the heat turned down low, for 10 minutes, until the vegetables are very soft. Add the rice, bring the heat up to medium and stir until the grains of rice are mixed in well with the soft vegetables and butter. Add the wine or vermouth, stir well and simmer until the rice has absorbed all the liquid. Start adding the hot stock a bit at a time, stirring until the liquid has been absorbed before you add the next ladleful. Keep going like this until the stock is almost all used up and the rice is almost cooked.

Add the brown crabmeat, half the peas and the rest of the stock to the risotto. Stir and simmer gently until the rice is just cooked, with a little bite left. Fold in the white crabmeat, cover with a lid, then remove from the heat and leave for 3 minutes.

Stir the risotto gently; it shouldn't be too thick or too thin, it should just ooze. Add a little more hot stock or water if necessary, season well with salt and pepper and add a squeeze of lemon juice to give it a bit of zing. Drizzle with olive oil and scatter with the rest of the peas, the chopped fennel fronds, chilli and lemon zest before serving.

# Raspberry and Blackberry Meringue with Hazelnuts, Caramel and Chantilly Cream

**4 large (extra-large) organic egg whites**
**400g (2 cups) caster (superfine) sugar**
**100g (generous 3/4 cup) skinned hazelnuts**
**1 punnet of raspberries**
**1 punnet of blackberries**
**200ml (7oz) water**
**a small bunch of mint, smallest leaves picked**

For the Chantilly cream:

**400ml (1 3/4 cups) double (heavy) cream**
**100g (scant 1 cup) icing (confectioners') sugar, sifted**
**seeds from 1 vanilla pod (vanilla bean)**

Line a baking tray with a sheet of baking parchment paper and set aside. Beat the egg whites in a food mixer on medium speed until they form stiff peaks. Keep beating and gradually add half the caster sugar. When you've finished adding it, turn the speed up high and beat for 3–4 minutes, until you have a smooth, glossy, thick, white meringue.

Spread the meringue on to the baking parchment and shape it into a rectangle about 30 x 10cm (12 x 4 inches). Gently place in an oven preheated to 140°C/275°F/Gas Mark 1 and bake for an hour, or until the meringue is creamy coloured and crisp on the outside but soft inside. Remove from the oven and leave to cool.

Place the hazelnuts on a baking tray and pop them into the oven for about 10 minutes, until they are light brown. Crush them lightly in a pestle and mortar and put to one side.

For the Chantilly cream, whip the cream with the sifted icing sugar and the vanilla seeds just until it's stiff.

Press the centre of the meringue with your fingers so you create a hollow. Sprinkle in some of the crushed hazelnuts, then some berries and some Chantilly cream. Keep filling up the meringue in layers of crushed hazelnuts, berries and Chantilly cream until you have used all the ingredients.

To make the caramel, put the remaining caster sugar and the water in a small, heavy-based pan and stir until the sugar has dissolved. Place on the heat, bring to the boil and simmer until it turns into a golden brown caramel. Carefully drizzle the caramel over the meringue, then scatter with the smallest mint leaves from the bunch.

# twenty eight

# NEIL PERRY

## Rockpool

**Neil Perry is one of Australia's most influential chefs. He has managed several quality restaurants in Sydney and today concentrates on his flagship brands, Rockpool restaurant, for which he became famous, and Rockpool Consulting. Neil is also the author of three cookbooks (*Rockpool*, *Simply Asian* and *The Food I Love*) and four classical CDs, creator of a large range of Neil Perry Fresh Food Products and a television presenter on the Lifestyle Channel's 'Rockpool Sessions', 'Food Source' and 'Fresh and Fast'.**

**What are your favourite foods/tastes/flavours?**
Being Australian, I have a very eclectic palate. We are so multicultural and have such a diverse array of fresh produce available that it is possible to eat something different every day. But I love seafood, duck fat, pork fat and chilli. I guess I just can't get the love of Asian food out of me.

**What is your favourite utensil?**
I love my mortar and pestle. The smell of things being crushed between stone is wonderful.

**What is your most useful piece of kitchen equipment?**
I think it is important to have enough worktop space, a large sink and a stove that is well extracted, as I love cooking on a high heat as well as low-temperature slow cooking.

**What is your favourite season?**
I love winter in Australia, as the fish are in prime condition and fennel, celeriac and artichokes are around.

**What is your favourite meal?**
Freshly extracted juice and Bircher muesli for breakfast. For lunch or dinner I would have to say I'm in heaven when eating abalone steamboat, a fabulous Chinese dish.

**How do you decide what to cook?**
Whatever looks freshest at the market.

**What inspires you?**
Beautiful produce, walking through a great fresh food market, cooking with fabulous young cooks, eating in great restaurants, eating street food in exotic locations, reading a cookbook with a marvellous philosophy.

**What is your favourite drink?**
Burgundy, but only a good one.

**What are your likes and dislikes?**
I love attention to detail, I hate lack of it.

**How can you inspire others to enjoy great food and cooking?**
By selecting great fresh produce and cooking it perfectly, to allow the quality to speak to the diner.

**How did you become a chef?**
I have loved food all my life, and it was my father's love of all things fresh that inspired me. He was a butcher, a fisherman and a gardener, but above all he was a brilliant, adventurous cook.

**What are your top ten ingredients?**
Extra virgin olive oil, the best-quality red wine vinegar, sea salt, freshly ground pepper, lemon, lime, fresh chilli, fish sauce, soy sauce, palm sugar.

**What are your kitchen secrets?**
There are no secrets, just choose quality ingredients and cook them with sympathy.

**What are your top tips?**
Do the little things well; it will make a big difference to your cooking.

**What is your favourite junk food?**
A hamburger if I make it or if I'm at Café Zuni.

**How do you feel about cooking for children?**
I love it. They are tomorrow's grown-ups and we want them to eat well and appreciate good food.

**Can you give one piece of advice for the domestic cook?**
Be organized and don't panic. Cooking is a learned craft, not an inherent art. Like swimming, we all have to be taught or we sink to the bottom and drown.

* Italian-style Courgette and Parmesan Soup
* Spaghetti Vongole
* Panna Cotta with Fresh Raspberries

## Italian-style Courgette and Parmesan Soup

**Serves 4**

**4 tablespoons extra virgin olive oil**
**3 garlic cloves, chopped**
**25g (3 tablespoons) basil leaves, chopped**
**1kg ($2^1/_4$lb) courgettes (zucchini), cut lengthways into quarters, then into 1cm ($^1/_2$-inch) slices**
**750ml ($3^1/_3$ cups) chicken stock**
**4 tablespoons single (light) cream**
**20g (5 tablespoons) flat-leaf parsley, chopped**
**50g ($^1/_2$ cup) Parmesan cheese, freshly grated**
**sea salt and freshly ground black pepper**

Heat the oil in a heavy-based pan, add the garlic, basil, courgettes and some salt and cook slowly for about 10 minutes. Add a little pepper and the stock and simmer, uncovered, for 8 minutes.

Put three-quarters of the soup into a food processor and process until smooth. Return to the pan, reheat gently and stir in the cream, parsley and Parmesan. Adjust the seasoning, if necessary, and serve.

## Spaghetti Vongole

**Only use clams that are tightly closed. Wash them in several changes of running water and discard any that don't open when cooked.**

**Serves 4**

**400g (14oz) spaghetti**
**olive oil**
**4 garlic cloves, finely chopped**
**4 shallots, finely chopped**
**150ml ($^2/_3$ cup) white wine**
**1kg ($2^1/_4$lb) live clams, thoroughly cleaned**
**$^1/_2$ bunch of flat-leaf parsley, chopped**
**sea salt and freshly ground black pepper**

Cook the spaghetti in a large pan of boiling salted water for 6–7 minutes, until *al dente*.

Meanwhile, heat some olive oil in a large pan, add the garlic, shallots and white wine and bring to the boil. Add the clams and cover with a tight-fitting lid. Steam over a high heat for a few minutes, shaking the pan occasionally, until the shells open.

When the spaghetti is done, drain it and add to the clams. Toss through with plenty of chopped parsley. Season to taste and serve immediately.

# Blueberry

## Blueberries can be an expensive addition to your supermarket trolley, so why not grow your own?

These delicious, plump berries are packed with health-boosting compounds and are loved by adults and children alike!

T&M has carefully chosen varieties which are easy to grow and which will reliably produce a good crop of juicy berries year after year. The plants make attractive patio plants, covered in sweetly-scented, creamy-white flowers in the spring, whilst in autumn the leaves change colour to a delightful crimson.

**Harvest:** July to September
**Delivery:** All year round

## Blueberry collection sweet-flavoured berries from July to September

2

Autumn foliage

White flowers

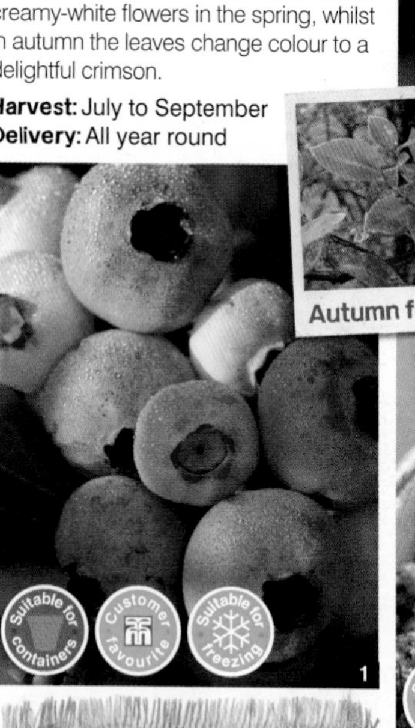

### Blueberry Collection

Fruits from July to mid September
**Brigitta, Chandler and Earliblue**

(3 x 1.5 litre pots, 1 of each)
**T99537P ~~£56.97~~ £29.99**

### Premium Collection

(3 x 3 litre premium plants, 1 of each)
**T99571P ~~£68.97~~ ONLY £34.99**

**Save £33.98**

### 1. Blueberry Chandler

Self fertile **Harvest:** Aug-Sept

**Firm, tasty berries** each weighing up to 2g are produced from the beginning of August until mid-September, helping to extend your picking season.

**T13868** (1 x 1.5 litre potted plant) £18.99
**Premium plant**
**T14219** (1 x 3 litre potted plant) £22.99

### 2. Blueberry Earliblue

Self fertile **Harvest:** July

An **early-maturing** variety, producing large, **sweetly-flavoured berries** that hang in medium-sized clusters from the beginning of July. A stout bush that will grow up to 1.8m (6ft) high.

**T44608** (1 x 1.5 litre pot) £18.99
**Premium plant**
**T14245** (1 x 3 litre potted plant) £22.99

### 3. Blueberry Brigitta

Self unfertile - requires a pollinator
**Harvest:** Aug-Sept

A **late-season variety,** producing large, firm fruits on upright bushes that will eventually reach 1.8m (6ft) tall. The **richly-flavoured fruits** have a 'crisp' texture making them ideal for freezing, as well as eating fresh from the bush.

**T13867** (1 x 1.5 litre potted plant) £18.99
**Premium plant**
**T14218** (1 x 3 litre potted plant) £22.99

**More information available at www.thompson-morgan.com**

# Autumn planting onions, shallots

**Plant:** from early September, although commercial trials have shown early October is the prime planting time.
**Harvest:** late June/early July
**Delivery:** from Sept until early Nov 2014

## For an early crop of onions, plant these varieties in the autumn

Autumn planting, when soils are still warm acts as a great space filler for otherwise empty winter soils, helping to prevent soil erosion, nutrient leeching and the spread of unwanted weeds.

New
Choose Red Cross - more reliable than trusted Electric!
2

Drought tolerant and excellent overwintering onion

**1. Electric**

Shiny red-skinned, semi globe-shaped bulbs with **pink-tinged crisp flesh** ideal for salads or in stir fries.

**T46560** (75 sets) £3.99
**T46567C** (150 sets) £6.99 SAVE 99p

**2. NEW Red Cross**

Selected for it's overwintering abilities, Red Cross is **perfect for adding to the earliest of summer salads** when planted in autumn, distinct red skin and white flesh produce defined red rings when sliced. Unusually for an autumn planter, Red Cross can store for up to 3 months.

**T56507** (75 sets) £3.99
**T56508** (150 sets) £6.99 SAVE 99p

**3. Red, White & Brown Mix**

This mix of Electric, Snowball and Tornado is **perfect for gardeners with limited space** who want to grow a range of onion colours.

**T46561** (75 sets) £3.99
**T46568C** (150 sets) £6.99 SAVE 99p

**Don't forget to add...**

**Chempak® Onion Fertiliser**
T14176C
(1kg) £9.99

CHEMPAK ESSENTIALS RANGE ORGANIC ONION FERTILISER

Growing hints & tips

BEST IN CLASS
for blight resistance
or your money back*
Special offer
5 Potato Sacks
HALF PRICE
ONLY £6.49
when you buy 20 tubers or more of potatoes


## Don't forget to add...

**Potato Sacks**

**T13888P** (5 sacks) £12.99

**T99554P** (10 sacks) £19.99

Also makes a tasty salad potato

Pre 1950's VARIETY

# Maincrops

**Plant:** from March to May
**Harvest:** For early maincrops from early to mid August, for maincrops from late August to September
**Delivery:** from January until May 2015

### 6. Desirée early maincrop

**Uses:** Bake/roast/general purpose
**Blight score:** Foliage 4/9 Tubers 5/9

The **world's most popular red potato!** With its pale yellow, firm, quite waxy flesh, Desirée is extremely versatile for all cooking methods. Drought resistant.

**T14026** (20 tubers) £5.99
**T99615P** (60 tubers) £13.99 SAVE £3.98

### 7. Pink Fir Apple maincrop

**Uses:** Salad

These attractive knobbly, pink-skinned tubers with yellow, waxy flesh should be **cooked whole** and are completely **delicious hot or cold.** Be decadent and deep fry them - **each tuber will make a single tasty chip!** To reach perfection allow up to 22 weeks before harvesting.

**T14080** (5 tubers) £4.49
**T14031** (20 tubers) £5.99 SAVE £11.97

### 8. Sárpo Mira maincrop

**Uses:** Bake/roast/chips/general purpose
**Blight score:** Foliage 9/9 Tubers 9/9

For optimum tuber quality, cut down haulms by early September and allow 3 weeks for the tubers to 'set skin' prior to lifting. Tubers will then be **perfect for all cooking purposes** for many months.

**T14052** (20 tubers) £4.99
**T99633P** (60 tubers) £12.99 SAVE £1.98

### 9. Setanta maincrop

**Uses:** Roast/bake/chip
**Blight score:** Foliage 4/9 Tubers 9/9

**Voted the best roast potato in T&M trials!** Setanta won over its 6 competitors with its attractive, **golden crisp skins** and **melt-in-the-mouth buttery flesh**. Setanta is the **perfect choice for the home and organic gardener.**

**T14625** (20 tubers) £5.99
**T99679P** (40 tubers) £9.99 SAVE £1.99

BEST IN CLASS
for roasting
or your money back*

# Popular potatoes

**Delivery:** from January until May 2015

## As always we have a fantastic range of potatoes for you to grow.

Whether you want tried and trusted favourites or are looking for new varieties, you won't be disappointed when you cook your fresh home-grown crops. We've selected a few of the most popular potato varieties here but please check our website for the full range www.thompson-morgan.com

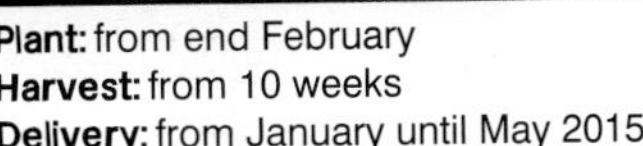


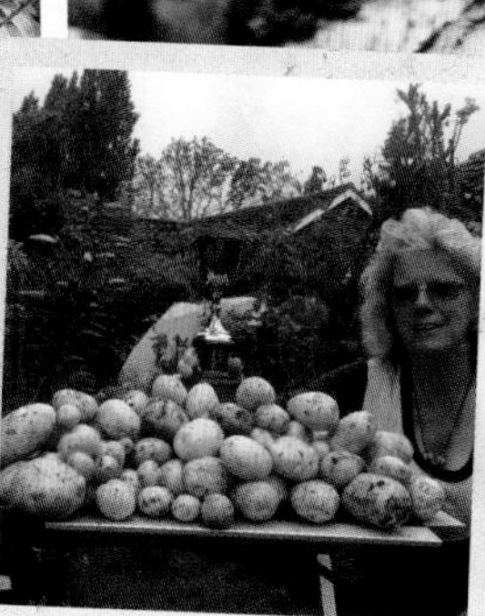
Bumper harvest of Maris Peer from just 3 x 8 litre bags!

**Plant:** from end February
**Harvest:** from 10 weeks
**Delivery:** from January until May 2015

### 1. Potato Growing Bags

Following on from this year's technical trials, we now recommend planting a **single tuber in a 8 litre bag** - we noted a **186% increase in yield**!

**T47568P** (5 x 8 litre bags) £5.99

**T51558P** (20 x 8 litre bags) £9.99

### Potato Growing Bag Collections

Increase your potato harvest with these collections.

**T56499P (5 bags and 5 tubers of Jazzy) £8.99**

**T56498P (5 bags and 5 tubers of Abbot) £7.99**

**T47655P (5 bags and 5 tubers of Maris Peer) £6.99**

## First earlies

**Plant:** from March
**Harvest:** from 13 weeks
**Delivery:** from January until May 2015

### 2. Lady Christl first early

**Uses:** New potato/general purpose

Holding an RHS AGM as a garden variety for growing in patio bags, this is probably the **most popular** modern, waxy first early. It produces **high numbers** of pale tubers, and also has good disease resistance.

**T14050** (5 tubers) £3.99

**T14010** (20 tubers) £5.99

**T99623P** (40 tubers) £9.99 SAVE £21.93

### 3. Pentland Javelin first early

**Uses:** New potato/salad/general purpose

Easy to grow, a very tasty white, waxy-fleshed new potato which is ideal for boiling and salad use. Shows **good all-round disease resistance**.

**T14018** (20 tubers) £5.99

**T99626P** (40 tubers) £9.99 SAVE £1.99

## Second earlies

**Plant:** from March
**Harvest:** from July
**Delivery:** from January until May 2015

### 4. Maris Peer second early

**Uses:** Salad/new/boil

More than 50 years old and classed as a 'heritage variety', **Peer still wins on flavour in modern taste tests.** The short oval, white-skinned with cream flesh tubers remain firm on cooking.

**T14164** (5 tubers) £3.99

**T14064** (20 tubers) £5.99 SAVE £9.97

### 5. Kestrel second early

**Uses:** General purpose

Visually stunning with its blue eyes, Kestrel produces a **reliable yield** of longer oval, quite waxy tubers with **superb flavour.** A favourite of gardeners due to its slug and disease resistance; it is also very **popular with exhibitors** (see opposite for our prize winning potatoes)

**T14032** (20 tubers) £5.99

# Choose Abbot for faster and better flavour than customer favourite Rocket

In the race to bring you the earliest first early potato variety, it seems the plant breeders forgot all about flavour when launching Rocket on the market. Finally, Thompson & Morgan is able to bring you a full-flavoured first early with the introduction of Abbot – the perfect option for bringing full flavour to your first crop of the season.

We're so confident that Abbot is better than Rocket that we are offering you the chance to find out for yourselves! Buy a 20 or 60 tuber pack of Rocket and try Abbot for just 99p!

**Plant:** from March
**Harvest:** from 10 weeks
**Delivery:** from January until May 2015

Early and tasty!

3

## 3. NEW Abbot first early

**Uses:** New potato/boil/chip/early summer baker

Produces **heavy yields of uniform short-oval tubers.** Thin, pale skin covers firm, waxy, white flesh. Abbot will be **ready for lifting alongside Rocket**, for the earliest harvest. The larger tubers make excellent chips and early summer bakers Good disease resistance.

**T56497** (5 tubers) £4.49

**T56496** (20 tubers) £6.49 SAVE £11.47

**TZ56497** (5 tubers) *worth £4.49* Only 99p with 20 tubers or more of Potato Rocket

## 4. Rocket first early

**Uses:** New potato/boil

Possibly the **earliest early available,** producing large crops of attractive and uniform white-skinned and fleshed tubers for your **first crop of the season.** Good disease resistance.

**T14042** (5 tubers) £2.99

**T14008** (20 tubers) £4.99

**T99628P** (60 tubers) £12.99 SAVE £22.89

## Favourite variety Rocket now has a rival!

4

# ...ew & improved potatoes

**...ant:** from end February
**...arvest:** from 10 weeks
**...elivery:** from January until May 2015

## ...row Jazzy for ...igher yields and ...etter flavour than ...rusted favourite ...harlotte

...oil'em, steam'em, mash'em, ...ast'em! **There's not much you ...an't do with this new, mail order ...xclusive potato.** A must-have early ...opper for 2015!

MAIL ORDER Exclusive EXCLUSIVE

New

Harvest over 80 tubers from just a single 8 litre bag

Melt-in-the-mouth flavour

1

"We're delighted to be offering Jazzy to the home gardener - with yields this high and potatoes so tasty we know you'll never want to go back to Charlotte!"

Paul Hansord
Horticultural Director

### ... Jazzy second early

RHS AWARD OF GARDEN MERIT

**...ses:** Salad

...azzy is the all new small potato, that ...acks a big punch. It's **a waxy variety ...ursting with flavour** that lends itself to ...o many more uses than the standard ...oil and butter' method used with most ...ther salad varieties – though you can ...eep it simple if you want to! We've ...een amazed at the **high numbers of ...mall tubers** coming from Jazzy, both ...n container trials and our field growing. **...he harvests from our potato bags ...eed to be seen to be believed - we ...arvested over 80 tubers from just ...ne 8 litre grow bag!**

**...56501** (5 tubers) £4.99
**...56500** (20 tubers) £7.99 SAVE £11.97

## Customer favourite Charlotte now has a rival!

### 2. Charlotte second early

**Uses:** Salad

A very popular variety producing pear-shaped, yellow-skinned, waxy tubers with creamy yellow flesh. **Excellent eaten hot or cold.**

**T14069** (5 tubers) £2.99
**T14028** (20 tubers) £3.99
**T99614P** (60 tubers) £9.99 SAVE £25.89

**Organic Charlotte**
**T14039** (20 tubers) £6.99

SOIL ASSOCIATION ORGANIC STANDARD

2

**Special offer - buy any 4 packs of potatoes and get the 5th FREE**

Don't forget to add...
**Fruit Net**
**T14068**
(1 net) £16.99

Berries measure up to 4.5cm in length

## 6. Gooseberry Invicta

**Harvest:** June-July

One of the **heaviest cropping varieties available,** producing almost twice as much fruit as other varieties. **Wonderful flavoursome** fruits stay firm and retain their shape when cooked. Excellent mildew resistance.

**T40161** (1 bareroot) £12.99

**T14259P** (3 bareroots) £27.99

**Premium plant**
**T17093** (1 x 3 litre potted plant) £17.99

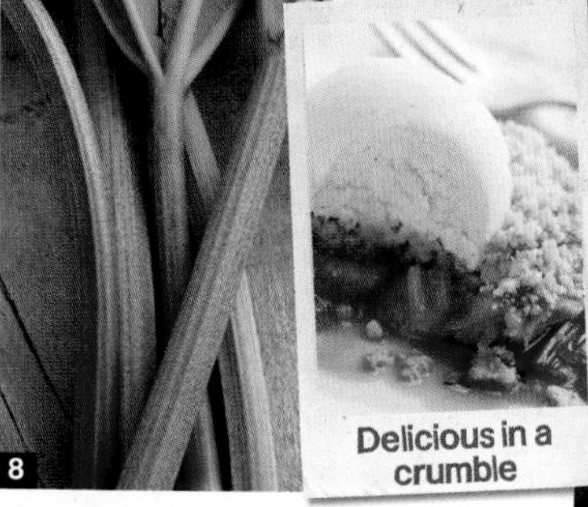


Delicious in a crumble

## 7. Blackcurrant Ebony

**Harvest:** July-August

**The sweetest-ever blackcurrant!** Produces large, firm currants - each one up to twice the size of a normal blackcurrant. **Outstanding dessert variety**, delicious eaten fresh or added to a tasty summer pudding.

**T14310** (1 bareroot) £11.99

**T14311P** (2 bareroots + 1 FREE) £23.98

**Premium plant**
**T46909** (1 x 3 litre potted plant) £16.99

## 8. Rhubarb Thompson's Terrifically Tasty

**Harvest:** March-June

Bred in Essex by a Mr. Thompson (no relation!), this is the earliest rhubarb we've ever found. Thick pink, flavoursome stalks tapering to green, are produced from March onwards, a whole month earlier than other rhubarb plants!

**T46918** (2 budded pieces) £10.99

## 9. Blackberry Reuben

**Harvest:** August-November

Measuring up to **4.5cm in length** and with an **average weight of up to 14g** per berry, this is the **largest-fruited blackberry available**. A fully mature plant can **yield up to 7 x 500g punnets of fruit.** Berries boast an **incredible level of sweetness.**

**T14223** (1 x 9cm pot-grown bush) £12.99

**Premium plant**
**T46919** (1 x 3 litre pot-grown bush) £17.99

## 10. Tayberry Buckingham

**Harvest:** July-August

**An easy-to-harvest, spineless** form of tayberry (a loganberry/ black raspberry cross). Produces delicious, 5cm (2in) long berries, **ideal eaten as a dessert**.

**T14271** (1 x 9cm pot-grown bush) £15.99

**Premium plant**
**T46906** (1 x 3 litre pot-grown bush) £19.99

Delicious eaten with fresh cream

# More fruit favourites

**Here at Thompson & Morgan, we pride ourselves on offering an extensive choice of interesting fruit varieties to our customers, but sometimes there's just not enough space to feature them all.**

Here we've pulled together a selection of 'must try' favourite varieties. Please visit our website to see the full Thompson & Morgan fruit offering: **www.thompson-morgan.com**

**Delivery:** November-December

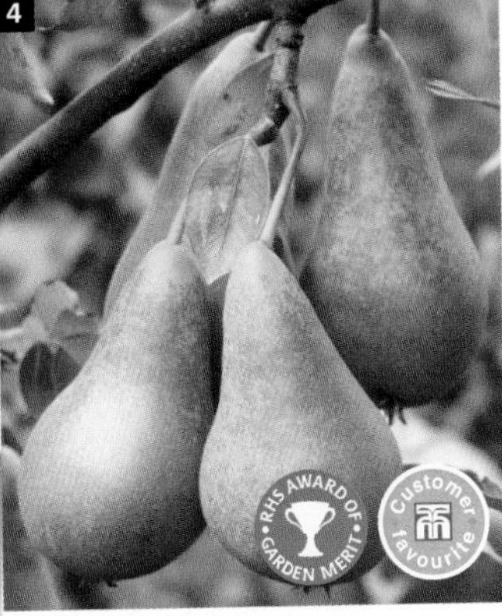


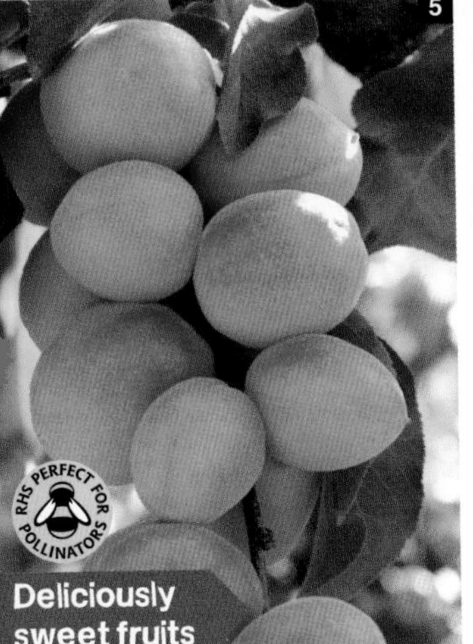


## 1. Cherry Stella

**Rootstock:** Gisella 6 **Harvest:** Jul-Aug

Britain's best-known dessert cherry, produces firm, dark red-fleshed fruits with a lovely sweet flavour. **Ideal for growing in small gardens**.

**T14248** (1 bareroot maiden) £28.99

## 2. Fig Brown Turkey

**Harvest:** August-September

Specially selected for the UK climate, Brown Turkey is **fully hardy** and can be grown very successfully outside, producing large crops of sweet and juicy figs. Looks stunning **fan-trained against a wall** or on the patio.

**T14277** (1 x 3 litre potted bush) £24.99

**Standard**

**T14302** (1 x 5 litre potted bush) £34.99

## 3. Nectarine Fantasia

**Rootstock:** Mont Clare **Harvest:** Sept

This easy to grow **mouth-watering nectarine** produces an **excellent crop** of fruits with juicy yellow flesh. Early harvests have a fresh tangy flavour, while later pickings taste rich and sweet.

**T14247** (1 bareroot tree) £32.99

## 4. Pear Conference

**Rootstock:** Quince A **Harvest:** Oct-Nov

The best known of all pears; excellent eaten as a dessert pear, but also exceptional when cooked. Long, bell-shaped fruits with firm flesh and a smooth and juicy flavour.

**T14276** (1 bareroot tree) £24.99

## 5. Apricot Flavourcot®

**Harvest:** October

**Rootstock:** Mont Clare

Specially bred to produce **huge crops** of egg-sized, **deliciously sweet fruits** in the UK climate. Excellent used cooked, preserved or eaten fresh.

**T14246**

(1 bareroot feathered maiden) £32.99

**Delivery:** November-December

5
New
T&M
Exclusive
EXCLUSIVE
First ever
edible weeping
peach tree
Weeping branches make
for easy picking


### 2. Apple Braeburn

**Harvest:** October **Type:** dessert
**Rootstock:** M9 **Store:** up to 4 months

**Britain's No.1 eating apple,** 'Braeburn'. This well-known variety earns its popularity by being easy to grow, early to crop from a young age and having excellent storage potential. An **excellent all-rounder,** producing bumper crops of delicious apples.

**T40205** (1 bareroot tree)
Last year's price ~~£19.99~~ NOW £14.99

### 3. Apple Bramley's Seedling

**Harvest:** October **Type:** cooking
**Rootstock:** M9 **Store:** up to 3 months

The **best-loved cooking apple.** Delicious in crumbles and pies. Will set a partial crop by themselves, but pollination will be improved by having another apple tree nearby – whether in your own garden or a neighbour's.

**T14274** (1 bareroot tree)
Last year's price ~~£24.99~~ NOW £19.99

**Patio tree T14130** (1 tree) £29.99
*M27 dwarf rootstock - perfect for the patio*

### 4. Plum Victoria

**Harvest:** August **Rootstock:** St Julien

**Britain's best-known plum**; delicious in pies and jams, but probably best eaten fresh from the tree in late August. The most reliable self-fertile garden variety, it will consistently produce a **heavy crop** of these distinctive, egg-shaped, medium-sized fruits.

**T14251** (1 bareroot maiden)
Last year's price ~~£19.99~~ NOW £14.99

**Patio Tree**
Specifically grafted onto a dwarf rootstock VVA1 enabling you to grow a patio tree of this **popular variety.** Approx. 1 metre tall in 3 years.

**T14169** (1 patio tree) £34.99

### 5. NEW Weeping Peach Lacrima

**Harvest:** August **Rootstock:** Mont Clare

Exclusive to Thompson & Morgan we are proud to offer the **world's first ever edible weeping peach tree**. Lacrima is a good cropper, starting to produce sweet and juicy fruit in the second year after planting. **A must have for those looking for the unusual.**

**T56490** (1 bareroot maiden tree) £29.99

# Raspberry

## The full season raspberry collection - 5 months of fruit

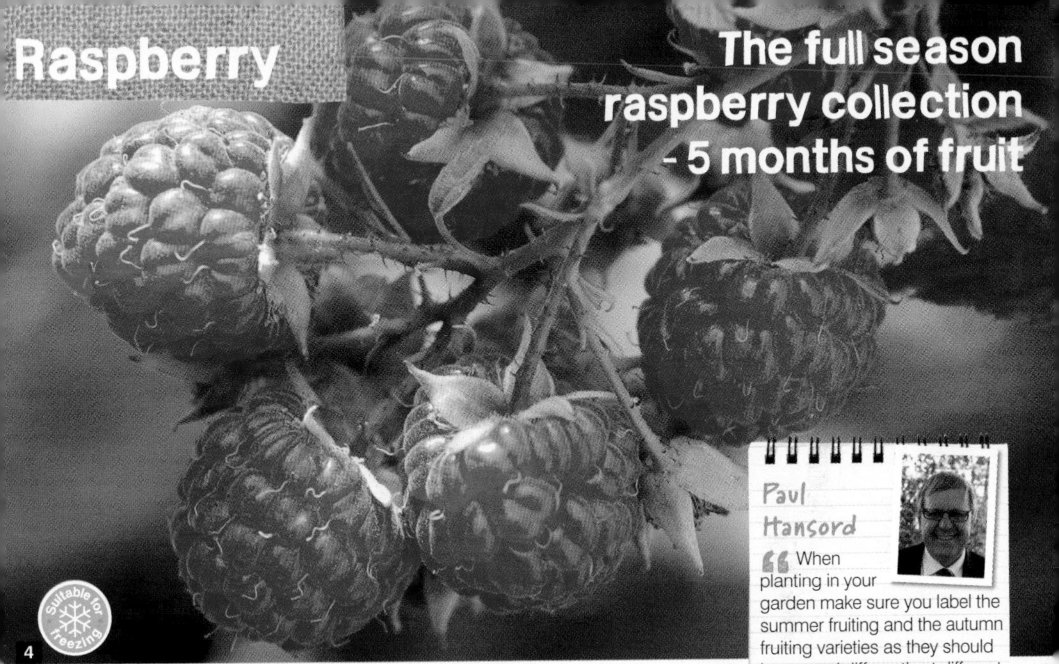

Suitable for freezing

4

**Paul Hansord**

"When planting in your garden make sure you label the summer fruiting and the autumn fruiting varieties as they should be pruned differently at different times of year."

## An easy-to-grow collection extending the harvest period from June to October

**Harvest:** June to October
**Delivery:** November-December

### 4. Raspberry Glen Moy
summer fruiting

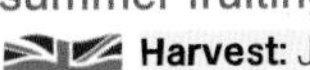

**Harvest:** June to mid July
We believe this to be the **best early-fruiting raspberry available**. Producing an abundance of sweet, juicy fruits from **spine-free canes**, makes harvesting a pleasure rather than a chore. Plants are resistant to virus-carrying aphids.

**T14261P** (6 canes) £14.99
**T14262P** (12 canes) £19.99

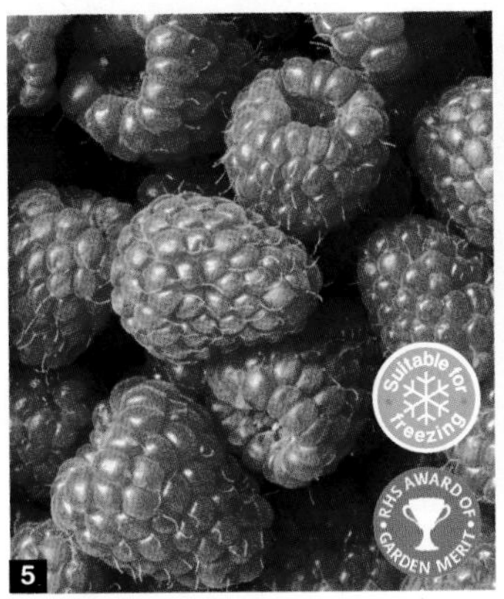


### 5. Raspberry Glen Ample
summer fruiting

**Harvest:** Mid June to July
Exceptionally high-yielding, mid-season variety producing large, deep-red, **succulent berries with a superb flavour.** Spine-free canes make picking easy and 12 canes can produce over 22kg (48lb) of fruit which holds well without spoiling and is excellent eaten fresh or from frozen.

**T14260P** (6 canes) £19.99
**T14249P** (12 canes) £28.99

### 6. Raspberry Joan J autumn

**Harvest:** July to October
An outstanding variety that **fruits in its first year**. Producing an abundance of **juicy and sweet-tasting** berries over a long cropping period. Berries are 30% larger than Autumn Bliss with a brighter colour and a superior flavour. **Ideal for picking daily** throughout the season.

**T14307P** (3 canes) £14.99
**T14308P** (6 canes) £19.99
**T14309P** (12 canes) £29.99

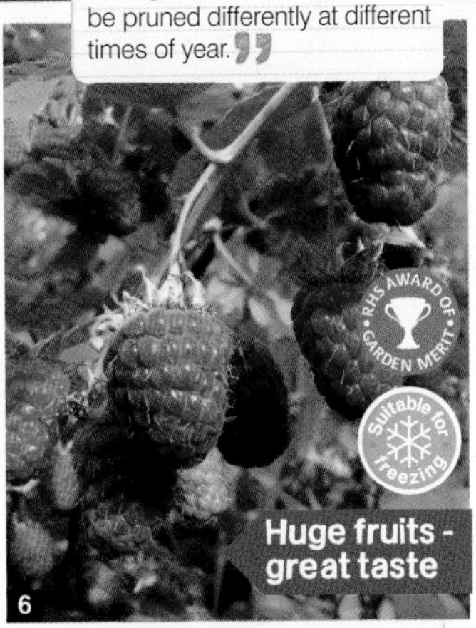

RHS AWARD OF GARDEN MERIT

Suitable for freezing

**Huge fruits - great taste**

6

### Full Season Raspberry Collection

**Fruits from June to October**
**Glen Ample, Glen Moy & Joan J**

(9 canes, 3 of each)
**T99667P £24.99**

(18 canes, 6 of each)
**T99666P** ~~£54.97~~ **ONLY £34.99**

**Save £19.98**

**What better way to evoke thoughts of summer and to set your taste buds tingling than a bowl of freshly-picked, sweet and juicy, home-grown strawberries?**

T&M's plants are raised by some of the country's leading soft fruit producers and are **graded by hand**. All plants supplied are the same **high quality** as those used by commercial growers and are raised from certified stock that is guaranteed to be **free from all pests and diseases**.

**Harvest:** June
**Delivery:** September-December

### 1. NEW Strawberry Sweetheart

**Harvest:** June

Our latest introduction combines **good old fashioned flavour** with modern plant breeding from the fruit experts at East Malling Research. The results? A fast cropper, beating Elsanta both on yield and early cropping. Sweetheart offers large, thin-skinned, cone-shaped fruit with the **perfect taste balance between sweet and acidic**.

**T56485P** (12 runners) £14.99

**Don't forget to add...**

Growing hints & tips

**Strawberry Fertiliser**

**T13104** (100g) £7.99

**T99554P** (10 sacks) £19.99

### 4. T&M's First Early

Customer favourite of recent years. These attractive brown-skinned bulbs will produce your **first crop of the season.**

**T46564** (75 sets) £3.99

**T46571C** (150 sets) £6.99 SAVE 99p

### 5. Tornado

INTRODUCED EXCLUSIVELY BY T&M

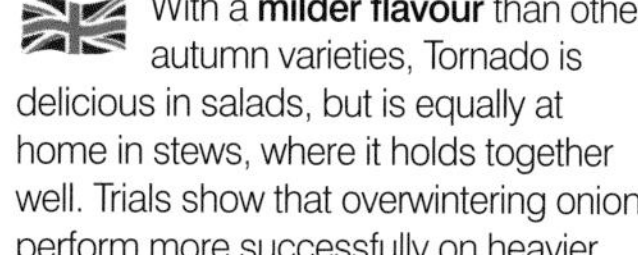

With a **milder flavour** than other autumn varieties, Tornado is delicious in salads, but is equally at home in stews, where it holds together well. Trials show that overwintering onions perform more successfully on heavier soils and are more **tolerant of water shortage** than spring-planted varieties. **Stores well for up to 8 weeks.**

**T46565** (75 sets) £4.99

**T46572C** (150 sets) £7.99 SAVE £1.99

# Shallots

**Plant:** from early September
**Harvest:** late June/early July
**Delivery:** from Sept until early Nov 2014

## Autumn is the best time to plant shallots...

Planting out your shallots in autumn gives them a longer growing season. Initial root establishment and early top growth occurs ahead of winter, establishing them ahead of cold weather. As spring warms up bulbs get off to a flying start. The result? Bigger bulbs for harvest.

### 6. Shallot Jermor

**Highly rated for flavour and increasingly sought after** for gourmet recipes due to a superbly sweet taste. A favourite with exhibitors as well as chefs. Jermor also has good storage potential.

**T46566** (20 bulbs) £9.99

The exhibitors' favourite

# and garlic

**Plant:** from early September
**Harvest:** from June-July
**Delivery:** from September until early February 2015

## Autumn planting gives the best quality and tastiest bulbs.

Hardneck varieties produce a stiff flower stem which can be removed or left to form 'scapes' (rocamboles), a delicacy in salads or stir-fries. Softneck varieties do not produce this flower stem, but have longer storage potential.

10

7

8

9

11

### 7. Early Purple Wight softneck

The earliest variety from autumn planting. Ready to harvest in May.

**T14197** (2 large bulbs) £6.99

### 8. NEW Vallelado softneck

A **Spanish softneck variety** with strong flavour, developed in the north of the country, making it **better suited to the UK climate** and growing conditions.

**T56513** (2 large bulbs) £6.99

### 9. Wight Cristo softneck

Pure white bulbs with an elegant bouquet for a wide range of dishes.

**T14198** (2 large bulbs) £6.99

### 10. Elephant hardneck

Not a true garlic, but a stem leek producing huge **bulbs which can grow to over 11cm in diameter** and weigh up to 450g! Produces large cloves (60-70g each) and are delicious roasted.

**T14538** (5 cloves) £8.99

**T14201** (12 cloves) £12.99

### 11. Provence Wight softneck

Provence can produce bulbs that approach Elephant Garlic size. The large, fat cloves are superb in aioli and bouillabaisse, but adds a 'taste of Provence' to all of your garlic recipes.

**T46859** (2 large bulbs) £6.99

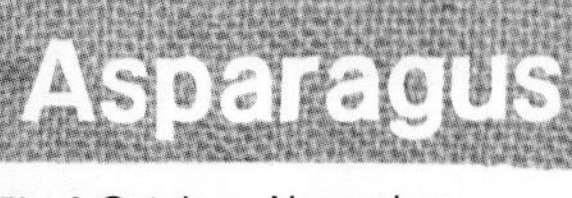


**Plant:** October - November
**Harvest:** late June/early July
**Delivery:** from October 2014 until late November 2014

## Fabulous varieties for autumn planting

This is an increasingly popular time for planting as the soil is warm for establishment prior to winter.

**Asparagus Collection**

(20 crowns, 5 each of Ariane, Mondeo, Pacific 2000, Purple Pacific)
**T99664P** ~~£47.96~~ £29.99
**Save £17.97**

(40 crowns, 10 each of Ariane, Mondeo, Pacific 2000, Purple Pacific)
**T99671P** ~~£71.96~~ **ONLY £44.99**
**Save £26.97**

### 1. NEW Amaro Montina

An ancient **rustic variety**, improved over time by Italian growers to produce **high quality, slender spears**. Shows **immunity to rust** and resistance to other fungal problems including fusarium.

**T56509** (10 crowns) £19.99
**T56510** (25 crowns) £36.99

### 2. Ariane

Heavy flush of large spears early in the season with significant yield and quality improvements over many varieties. Also produces 'fine' asparagus late in the year.

**T15055** (5 crowns) £11.99
**T15056** (10 crowns) £17.99
**T15057** (25 crowns) £34.99

### 3. Mondeo

Impressive **early yields** of great quality asparagus. The spears have tight tips throughout the season, as well as **excellent flavour** and good disease resistance. A real tough performer!

**T15058** (5 crowns) £11.99
**T15059** (10 crowns) £17.99
**T15060** (25 crowns) £34.99

### 4. Pacific 2000

Spears are **practically stringless** and super sweet, making them **delicious eaten raw** as well as lightly cooked.

**T15061** (5 crowns) £11.99
**T11294** (10 crowns) £17.99
**T11321** (25 crowns) £34.99

### 5. Purple Pacific

Keep the colour by steaming or simply **eat raw with dips** or in salads. Enjoy the flavour and benefit from the **anti-oxidants** that come with the purple colour.

**T15064** (5 crowns) £11.99
**T15065** (10 crowns) £17.99
**T15066** (25 crowns) £34.99

# Tubers

**Plant:** From March (artichoke)
From May (oca)
**Delivery:** from March until May 2015

## Try something different!

We've selected a great range of unusual edible tubers to test your taste buds! Visit **www.thompson-morgan.com** to see the full range.

6

### 6. Artichoke Originals

**Harvest:** October - December

For those gardeners who prefer the original, rounder, 'knobbly' tubers. Plants **make a useful windbreak** for the garden or allotment prior to harvesting.

**T46890** (10 tubers) £9.99
**T15088** (20 tubers) £14.99 SAVE £4.99

### 7. New Zealand Yam - Oca

**Harvest:** November - December

Unusual tubers with a zesty lemon flavour, that **can be boiled, baked, fried or eaten raw**. Attractive shamrock-like leaves can also be added to salads for a **refreshing citrus twist.**

**T15092** (5 tubers) £6.99
**T15091P** (10 tubers) £9.99 SAVE £3.99

7

# Gardening Equipment

## A few little extras to set you on the road to success

8 9 10 11 14

**3 for 2** on all Chempak®

## Chempak® feed & fertilisers

### 8. Potato Fertiliser
**T14173C** (1kg) £9.99

### 9. Onion Fertiliser
**T14176C** (1kg) £9.99

### 10. Fully Balanced No. 3
**T14369C** (800g) £9.99

### 11. High Potash Feed No. 4
**T13839C** (800g) £9.99

15

## Potato & Onion

13 12

Store your potatoes

### 12. Onion Bags
**T13880P** (10 bags) £13.99

### 13. Potato Sacks (paper)
**T46525P** (5 sacks) £9.99
**T46526P** (10 sacks) £16.99

### 14. Potato Sacks
**T13888P** (5 sacks) £12.99
**T99554P** (10 sacks) £19.99

### 15. Potato Scrubbing Gloves
**T13495** (1 pair) £5.99

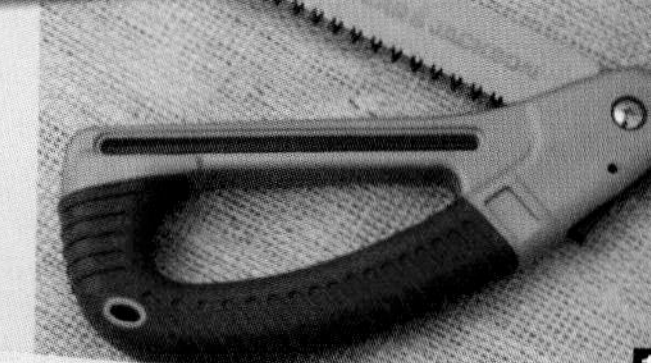

18

## Fruit

### 16. Fruit Net
**T14068** (1 net) £16.99

### 17. Hanging Strawberry Pouch
**T40108** (1 pouch) £6.99

### 18. Pruning saw
**T11551** (1 saw) £14.99

16 17

Protect your fruit

# Super Season of Spuds

## For a full season of your favourite potatoes

We've taken the hard work out of your potato crop planning for 2015 with our Super Season of Spuds Collection. Simply plant out the selected six varieties in one hit, for a steady supply of tubers right through the season. You can even store your Sárpo Mira for use right through winter.

**Plant:** from end February
**Harvest:** from 10 weeks
**Delivery:** from January until May 2015

MAIL ORDER Exclusive EXCLUSIVE

New

**Abbot** super salad **page 9**
**Faster and tastier than Rocket!**

New

**Jazzy** second early **page 8**
**Melt-in-the-mouth flavour**

**Sárpo Mira** maincrop **page 11**
**Exceptional blight resistance**

RHS AWARD OF GARDEN MERIT

**Pink Fir Apple** maincrop **page 11**
**Attractive, pink salad variety**

RHS AWARD OF GARDEN MERIT

**Desirée** early maincrop **page 11**
**The world's favourite red potato**

**Lady Christl** baby new **page 10**
**A dual purpose favourite, full of flavour**

### Super Season of Spuds Collection

For a full season of potatoes.

**Abbot** p9,
**Pink Fir Apple** p11,
**Lady Christl** p10,
**Sárpo Mira** p11,
**Jazzy** p8,
**Desiree** p11

(60 tubers, 10 of each variety listed) **T56514P** £16.99

(120 tubers, 20 of each variety listed) **T56515P** ~~£37.44~~ ONLY £19.99

**Save £17.45**

# Panna Cotta with Fresh Raspberries

**Any fresh summer fruit will work well here, especially berries, mangoes, peaches and cherries.**

**Serves 4**

**$1^1/_4$ gelatine leaves**
**370ml ($1^3/_4$ cups plus 2 tablespoons) milk**
**235ml (1 cup) single (light) cream**
**$^1/_2$ vanilla pod (vanilla bean), slit open and seeds scraped out**
**125g (generous $^1/_2$ cup) caster (superfine) sugar**
**110ml (scant $^1/_2$ cup) double (heavy) cream**
**fresh raspberries, to serve**

Cover the gelatine with a little warm water and leave to soften. Meanwhile, put the milk, single cream, vanilla pod and seeds and half the sugar in a pan and bring to the boil, stirring. Simmer gently for 1 minute. Remove from the heat and stir in the remaining sugar. Gently squeeze out excess moisture from the gelatine leaves and add them too. Strain through a fine sieve into a bowl and chill over ice.

Stir a little of the chilled mixture into the double cream to break it down, then add the double cream to the rest of the mixture. Strain again and divide between 4 moulds, such as dariole moulds or ramekins. Chill until set. Turn the panna cottas out on to plates and serve with fresh raspberries.

* **Roasted Garlic and Wild Mushroom Pizza**
* **Roasted Salmon Fillets with Red Wine Sauce and Mashed Potatoes**
* **Zesty Lemon Bars**

# Roasted Garlic and Wild Mushroom Pizza

**Serves 4**

**2 tablespoons olive oil**
**50g (1/2 cup) red onion, finely sliced**
**450g (1lb) mixed wild mushrooms, thickly sliced if large**
**1 tablespoon chopped oregano**
**225g (2 cups) fontina cheese, grated**
**225g (2 cups) mozzarella cheese, grated**
**semolina for dusting**
**sea salt and freshly ground black pepper**

**For the pizza dough:**
**2 1/2 teaspoons dried yeast**
**250ml (1 cup) warm water (40–45°C/105–115°F)**
**1 teaspoon honey**
**1 teaspoon extra virgin olive oil, plus extra for brushing**
**420g (3 cups) plain (all-purpose) flour**
**1 teaspoon salt**

**For the roasted garlic:**
**12 garlic cloves, peeled and trimmed**
**1 tablespoon olive oil**
**1/2 teaspoon red chilli flakes**

First make the pizza dough. In the bowl of a freestanding electric mixer, or in a large mixing bowl, dissolve the yeast in the water. Add the honey and stir together. Leave for 2–3 minutes or until the water is cloudy, then stir in the olive oil. If you are using an electric mixer, combine the flour and salt and add them to the yeast mixture all at once. Mix together using the paddle attachment, then change to the dough hook. Knead at low speed for 2 minutes, then increase to medium speed and knead for about 5 minutes, until the dough comes cleanly away from the sides of the bowl and clusters around the dough hook. Hold on to the machine if it bounces around. Turn the dough out on to a clean work surface and knead by hand for 2 or 3 minutes longer. It should be smooth and elastic. When you press it with your finger, it should slowly spring back, and it should not feel tacky.

If you are making the dough by hand, combine the flour and salt and fold the flour into the yeast and water mixture a third at a time using a large wooden spoon. As soon as you can scrape the dough out in one piece, scrape it on to a lightly floured work surface and knead for 10 minutes, adding flour as necessary, until the dough is smooth and elastic.
If you are using a food processor, mix the yeast, water, honey and olive oil together in a small bowl or a measuring jug. Place the flour and salt in a food processor fitted with the steel blade and pulse once or twice. Then, with the machine running, pour in the yeast mixture. Process until the dough forms a ball on the blade. Remove the dough from the processor and knead it on a lightly floured surface for a couple of minutes, adding flour as necessary, until it is smooth and elastic.

Transfer the dough to a clean, lightly oiled bowl, rounded side down first, then rounded side up. Cover the bowl tightly with cling film (plastic wrap) and leave it in a warm spot to rise for 30 minutes, or you can leave it for up to an hour. When the dough is ready, it will stretch as it is gently pulled.

Divide the dough into 2 or 4 equal balls, depending on how large you want your pizzas to be. Shape each ball by gently pulling down the sides of the dough and tucking each pull under the bottom of the ball, working round and round the ball 4 or 5 times. Then, on a smooth, unfloured surface, roll the ball around under your palm for about a minute, until it feels smooth and firm. Put the balls on a tray or platter, cover them with lightly oiled cling film or a damp towel and leave to rest for at least 30 minutes. At this point, the dough balls can be covered with cling film and refrigerated for 1–2 days. You will need to punch them down again when you are ready to roll out the pizzas.

For the roasted garlic, toss the garlic cloves with the olive oil and red chilli flakes in a small baking dish. Place the dish in an oven preheated to 190°C/375°F/Gas Mark 5 and roast the garlic, stirring occasionally, for 15–20 minutes, until the cloves are lightly browned. Watch the garlic as it browns because it takes on a bitter taste if it is roasted for too long. Remove from the oven and leave to cool. The garlic can be kept, covered, in the fridge until needed.

Make the mushroom topping while the pizza dough is resting. Heat a large sauté pan over a medium-high heat and add the olive oil. When it is hot, add the red onions and sauté for 2–3 minutes, until they begin to soften. Add the mushrooms and sauté for 5 minutes or until they are lightly browned. Add the oregano and roasted garlic and continue to cook, stirring, for about 5 minutes, until the mushrooms are tender and fragrant. Season to taste with salt and pepper and remove from the heat.

Preheat the oven to 250°C/500°F/Gas Mark 10, or as high as it will go, and place a pizza stone in it to heat. In the meantime, press out the dough. Place a ball of dough on a lightly floured surface. While turning the dough, press down on its centre with the heel of your hand, gradually spreading it out to a circle 18–20cm ($7^1/4$–8 inches) in diameter for small pizzas, 30–35cm (12–14 inches) for larger ones. Alternatively, use a rolling pin to get an even circle. With your fingers, form a slightly thicker raised rim around the edge of the circle. Brush everything but the rim with a little olive oil, then sprinkle on the fontina and mozzarella cheeses. Sprinkle the sautéed mushrooms over the cheese, then top the pizzas as you like. Dust a pizza paddle (also called a baker's peel) or a rimless flat baking tray with semolina and slip it under a pizza. Slide the pizza on to the hot baking stone or into a pizza pan, or place the pizza pan on the stone – the heat from the stone will help it achieve a crisp crust. Bake for about 10 minutes, until the cheese topping is bubbling and the rim of the crust is a deep golden brown. Remember that the oven is very hot and be careful as you put the pizza in and again as you remove it from the oven.

Use the pizza paddle to slide the pizza out of the oven and on to a cutting board. Repeat with the remaining pizzas. Use a pizza cutter or a sharp knife to cut the pizza into slices and serve immediately.

**Variations**

Depending on your taste, you could spread the dough with tomato sauce or pesto sauce, about 2 tablespoons for small pizzas, 4–6 tablespoons for larger ones. If you don't have sauce, a can of tomatoes, drained, chopped and seasoned with salt and chopped sautéed garlic, will do. Top with the shredded or grated cheeses of your choice. (I like a mixture of mozzarella and fontina, as above.) Add thinly sliced vegetables such as tomatoes, red peppers or red onions; sautéed sliced vegetables such as mushrooms, aubergine (eggplant), courgettes (zucchini) or artichoke hearts; thinly sliced cured meats such as pepperoni or prosciutto; or pitted olives, prawns (shrimp) or small pieces of lightly cooked chicken. Add a light sprinkling of grated Parmesan, crumbled goat's cheese or blue cheese and some finely chopped fresh herbs such as basil or oregano or dried herbs such as thyme, oregano or herbes de Provence.

# Roasted Salmon Fillets with Red Wine Sauce and Mashed Potatoes

**Serves 4**

- **75g ($^3/_4$ stick) unsalted butter**
- **4 x 175g (6-oz) salmon fillets**
- **1 tablespoon coarsely ground black pepper**
- **1 tablespoon finely chopped fresh ginger**
- **1 tablespoon extra virgin olive oil**
- **600g ($1^1/_4$lb) baking potatoes, peeled and cut into 5cm (2-inch) chunks**
- **175ml ($^3/_4$ cup) double (heavy) cream**
- **a pinch of freshly grated nutmeg**
- **sea salt and freshly ground white pepper**
- **finely sliced spring onions (scallions), to serve**

**For the red wine sauce:**

- **115g (1 stick) unsalted butter**
- **3 shallots, very finely chopped**
- **2 garlic cloves, very finely chopped**
- **1 plum tomato, peeled, deseeded and chopped**
- **500ml (2 cups) red wine, such as Pinot Noir or Merlot**
- **1 tablespoon balsamic vinegar**
- **1 tablespoon good-quality bottled barbecue sauce**
- **freshly ground black pepper**

Melt 25g (2 tablespoons) of the butter. Cut the remaining butter into small pieces and set aside. Brush the salmon fillets on both sides with some of the melted butter, then sprinkle on both sides with the black pepper, ginger and some salt, gently pressing the seasonings on to the fillets. Use the olive oil to brush the bottom of a baking dish large enough to hold the fillets. Place the salmon in the dish and drizzle over the remaining melted butter. Refrigerate while you make the mashed potatoes and the sauce.

Put the potatoes in a saucepan filled with enough lightly salted cold water to cover them well. Bring to the boil, then simmer briskly until the potatoes are tender. Meanwhile, gently heat the cream in a small saucepan. Drain the potatoes well, return them to the pan, cover tightly and leave for 5–10 minutes. Pass them through a food mill set over the saucepan, or just mash them in the pan with a potato masher until smooth. Add the warm cream and the diced butter and stir over a low heat with a wooden spoon until thoroughly blended. Season to taste with salt, white pepper and nutmeg. Cover and keep warm, or you can reheat them in a microwave just before serving.

For the sauce, heat half the butter in a medium saucepan over a medium heat until foamy. Add the shallots and garlic and sauté briefly, just until glossy and aromatic. Stir in the tomato and sauté for 2 minutes more. Stir in the wine, raise the heat slightly and bring to the boil. Simmer briskly for 10–15 minutes, until reduced to about 120ml ($^1/_2$ cup). Stir in the vinegar and barbecue sauce, then pour the sauce through a fine sieve into a clean saucepan. Over a low heat, whisk in the remaining butter a little bit at a time. Season to taste with a little salt and pepper, then cover and keep warm while you roast the salmon.

Place the salmon in an oven preheated to 250°C/500°F/Gas Mark 10, or as high as your oven will go. Roast for about 10 minutes, until the salmon is cooked through but still moist and slightly shiny pink in the centre when its flakes are separated with the tip of a small, sharp knife.

To serve, mound the potatoes in the centre of 4 hot serving plates and place a roasted salmon fillet on top. Spoon the sauce over the salmon and around the potatoes. Garnish with spring onions and serve.

# Zesty Lemon Bars

**Serves 4**

**4 eggs**
**200g (1 cup) granulated sugar**
**35g ($^1/_4$ cup) plain (all-purpose) flour**
**a pinch of salt**
**175ml ($^3/_4$ cup) lemon juice**
**60ml ($^1/_4$ cup) milk**
**1 tablespoon finely grated lemon zest**
**icing (confectioners') sugar for dusting**

**For the base:**
**210g ($1^1/_2$ cups) plain (all-purpose) flour**
**90g ($^3/_4$ cup) icing (confectioners') sugar**
**3 tablespoons cornflour (cornstarch)**
**a pinch of salt**
**1 tablespoon finely grated lemon zest**
**175g ($1^1/_2$ sticks) unsalted butter, cut into 1cm ($^1/_2$-inch) pieces**

Line a 23 x 30cm (9- x 12-inch) baking tin (pan) with baking parchment. To make the base, put the flour, icing sugar, cornflour, salt and lemon zest in a food processor and pulse several times to combine them. With the machine running, gradually drop in the pieces of butter through the feed tube and continue to process until you have a slightly crumbly dough. Transfer the mixture to the prepared baking tin and, with your fingers, press it over the base to form an even layer. Bake in the lower third of an oven preheated to 180°C/350°F/Gas Mark 4 for 25–30 minutes, until light golden. Remove from the oven and leave to cool. Turn the oven down to 160°C/325°F/Gas Mark 3 and adjust the rack to the middle.

For the topping, whisk the eggs together until smooth. Combine the sugar, flour and salt in a bowl, then whisk this mixture into the eggs. Stir in the lemon juice, milk and lemon zest.

Pour the topping mixture over the base. Return the tin to the oven and bake for about 30 minutes, until the custard is set, jiggling only slightly when the tin is moved. Remove from the oven and leave to cool completely. Cover the tin with cling film (plastic wrap) and chill for at least 2 hours.

Use a sharp knife to cut the mixture into rectangular bars. Arrange the bars on a platter and dust with icing sugar just before serving.

# thirty

# GORDON RAMSAY

## Gordon Ramsay

**Gordon Ramsay started his culinary career at Marco Pierre White's first restaurant, Harvey's, then moved to Le Gavroche. This was followed by three years in France, working for Guy Savoy and Joël Robuchon. In 1993 he was awarded two Michelin stars at London's newly opened Aubergine. Five years later he set up his own eponymous restaurant in Chelsea where he was awarded three Michelin stars. Gordon Ramsay Holdings owns several restaurants, including the Savoy Grill, Gordon Ramsay at Claridge's, Angela Hartnett at the Connaught and Pétrus. Gordon Ramsay is the author of several books and has presented two major television series.**

**What are your favourite foods/tastes/flavours?**
I love the classic combinations of ingredients, that's my style, but recently I have become a big fan of spices, particularly Asian food. There is a whole different culture and technique to this style of food, which most Europeans don't understand, and that's what makes it more interesting.

**What is your favourite utensil?**
The Bamix hand mixer. It reminds me of the first expensive piece of equipment that I could afford when I opened Aubergine. I was heavily influenced by Guy Savoy and his light style of cooking and I used this to aerate my soups and sauces.

**What is your most useful piece of kitchen equipment?**
A good non-stick pan. Roasting fish and scallops to perfection is impossible without one.

**What is your favourite season?**
Spring, with the start of the new-season lamb, the fresh peas and broad (fava) beans. The food is light and feminine. It's a very pretty season.

**What is your favourite meal?**
Being what they call a 'fine dining' chef, I like to eat very simple, straightforward food, without any fuss or frills. To be honest, there's nothing better than a late supper of my wife Tana's shepherd's pie, with loads of ketchup.

**How do you decide what to cook?**
I tend to cook according to my mood and, of course, keeping seasonal, but I have a preference for cooking fish and shellfish as they're so versatile.

**What inspires you?**
Inspiration comes at strange times. I eat out as much as I can to see how other chefs put their slant on ingredients. You can be inspired by even the smallest of ideas.

When I was young, my inspiration came from my passion to build a strong business. These days my driving force is my family. I have four young children and I want them to have a good life.

**What is your favourite drink?**
On the odd occasion I treat myself to a nice Batard Montrachet, but that is indeed a very special occasion! Otherwise it's the odd Southern Comfort, but I don't really get time to drink that often.

**What are your likes and dislikes?**
I like to be busy! I thrive on the pressure and the more challenging the better. I hate being bored – that's when I tend to get into trouble!

**How can you inspire others to enjoy great food and cooking?**
The way to inspire people is to be a strong leader and, with that, to lead by example. You have to be hands on and show your staff that you can do what you

are expecting them to do. Teach people to have standards and not to forget them!

**What are your top ten ingredients?**
Sea bass, scallops, pig's trotters, new-season lamb, La Ratte potatoes, salsify, foie gras, white truffles, caviar and broad beans.

**What are your kitchen secrets?**
The secret of a good kitchen is consistency. Maintaining standards at any level is vital and this comes from thorough checking and good-quality produce.

**What are your top tips?**
To run a successful business is hard work! There are lots of tips I could give but the most important is to be organized. It makes the chaos a little easier.

**Do you ever eat junk food?**
I don't really eat junk food, but I am a little partial to a takeaway curry! I have to say, though, that my local Indian restaurant is certainly not junk.

**How do you feel about cooking for children?**
Food for children is vital, both at home and in restaurants. I try to cook for my kids at least once a week at home and it usually consists of a big stew from the leftovers of my numerous photo shoots. I don't really think you should force fine dining on to a small child. Their palate has not advanced enough to understand what they are eating!

**Can you give one piece of advice for the domestic cook?**
My advice would be to search for top-quality produce. Let the food speak for you and this means you don't have to make the food too fussy.

* Warm Salad of Smoked Eel and New Potatoes with Horseradish Cream
* Calf's Liver with a Sweet and Sour Mushroom and Rocket Marmalade
* Coffee Panna Cotta

## Warm Salad of Smoked Eel and New Potatoes with Horseradish Cream

**Serves 4**

**200ml (7oz) crème fraîche**
**1 heaped teaspoon horseradish relish**
**12 Charlotte potatoes**
**2 tablespoons olive oil**
**50g (2oz) streaky bacon, cut into lardons**
**300g (10oz) smoked eel fillets, broken into chunks**
**3 tablespoons vinaigrette**
**100g (3½oz) baby spinach leaves**
**sea salt and freshly ground black pepper**

Mix the crème fraîche and horseradish together and season well, then set aside.

Cook the potatoes in boiling salted water until tender, then drain and leave to cool. Slice thickly. Heat the olive oil in a large frying pan (skillet), add the potatoes and sauté until crisp and golden. Set aside. Fry the bacon lardons until they are crisp and their fat has rendered.

Gently mix the potatoes, lardons and eel together in a large bowl. Season and mix with just enough of the vinaigrette to coat lightly.

Toss the spinach with the remaining vinaigrette and arrange on 4 warm plates. Divide the potato mixture between them and top with a large scoop of the horseradish cream.

# Calf's Liver with a Sweet and Sour Mushroom and Rocket Marmalade

**Serves 4**

**olive oil and butter for frying**
**4 large banana shallots, finely chopped**
**a sprig of thyme**
**1 tablespoon demerara (light brown) sugar**
**2 tablespoons sherry vinegar**
**150g (2 cups) button mushrooms, chopped**
**balsamic vinegar**
**100g ($3^1/2$oz) rocket (arugula)**
**4 x 100g ($3^1/2$-oz) pieces of calf's liver, trimmed**
**salt and freshly ground black pepper**
***pommes purée* and classic vinaigrette, to serve**

Heat 2 tablespoons of olive oil in a large pan, add the shallots and sauté until they brown slightly. Add the thyme and sugar and cook until the shallots have caramelized to a golden brown. Deglaze the pan by pouring in the sherry vinegar and stirring well, then simmer until reduced.

In a separate pan, heat 2 tablespoons of olive oil, add the mushrooms and sauté until all the moisture has evaporated. Remove from the heat and mix with the shallots. Season well and add a few drops of balsamic vinegar. Stir in the rocket and set aside.

Heat a large non-stick pan and sauté the liver in it in a little oil and butter for about 5 minutes, until medium rare. Remove from the heat and leave to rest for a few minutes, then cut each piece into 5 nice slices.

Serve the liver fanned out over some *pommes purée* on each plate, topped with a good spoonful of the mushroom mixture and drizzled with a little vinaigrette.

# Coffee Panna Cotta

**Serves 4**

**2 tablespoons liquid glucose**
**150g ($\frac{3}{4}$ cup) caster (superfine) sugar**
**300ml ($1\frac{1}{4}$ cups) double (heavy) cream**
**5 tablespoons milk**
**$1\frac{1}{2}$ tablespoons strong espresso coffee**
**1 tablespoon Tia Maria**
**$1\frac{1}{2}$ gelatine leaves**
**fresh raspberries, to serve**

Put the liquid glucose, half the sugar and 2 tablespoons of water into a heavy-based saucepan. Heat slowly until dissolved, then turn up the heat and simmer until it turns into a pale golden brown caramel. Spoon a little of the caramel into 4 dariole moulds, just to coat the base of each one, and leave to set.

Put the double cream and milk in a pan and bring to the boil, then reduce the heat and simmer for 5 minutes. Add the remaining sugar and stir until dissolved, then mix in the coffee and Tia Maria. Remove from the heat.

Soak the gelatine leaves in cold water for about 5 minutes, until soft, then gently squeeze out excess liquid. Add the gelatine to the hot cream and stir until dissolved, then pass through a fine sieve to be sure there are no lumps. Cool slightly, then divide between the moulds. Chill until set.

To serve, pull the sides of the panna cotta away from the top of each mould with your fingers and upend on to a small plate. Surround with fresh raspberries and trickle over the remaining caramel.

# thirty one

# GARY RHODES

## Rhodes Twenty Four

**Gary Rhodes has become a household name in the UK as a result of his numerous cookery books and television series. He won his first Michelin star at the Castle Hotel, Taunton, at the age of twenty-six. It was during his time there that he developed a passion for British food and started refining traditional dishes into modern British classics. After a stint as head chef at the prestigious Greenhouse restaurant in London, he opened a string of highly acclaimed establishments, including City Rhodes and Rhodes in the Square. In 2004 he opened another City restaurant, Rhodes Twenty Four, and his first restaurant outside the UK at the stunning Calabash Hotel in Grenada.**

It is over thirty years since I first began to feel inspired by the idea of working with food. One of the most exciting elements for me was the ease with which you could discover the true flavour of ingredients, and the almost unlimited variety of combinations that could then be tried. However, the exact moment I decided to become a chef occured when I was serving the simplest of dishes. Marguerite Patten has become a culinary institution, writing and sharing more recipes than one can remember. I was cooking Sunday lunch and, to follow the classic roast, I'd stirred, creamed and bound Marguerite's recipe for steamed lemon sponge with lemon sauce. As I turned the pudding out of its basin, the air began to fill with a sweet, citrus bite. This became stronger and fuller as the lemon sauce was poured over the top and trickled down the sides. Looking around the table, I watched my family's expressions change. Their faces told me that their taste buds were alive and eager, waiting to tuck in. This was the moment my mind was made up. I'd cooked many dishes before but none had provoked such a reaction. I wanted to become a chef.

For me, this is what cooking is all about – creating dishes to please others. After all, the dinner table is the greatest social meeting point in the world, drawing families and friends together on a regular basis.

I've found that what people want to eat tends to be determined by their mood. Sometimes, we'll set the family table with plates of charcuterie, a bowl of salad and a platter of cheese. Other times it might be risotto or pasta dishes, home-made soups, or British classics such as stews, casseroles and pot roasts. My inspiration comes not only from the professional kitchen but also from books and magazines. I love collecting cookery books, discovering other chefs' personalities, how they think, feel and work with food. This inspires me to create new dishes, providing perhaps just a small spark that sets the mind alive, leading on to a totally different dish that carries my own personality.

I like simplicity in food. This doesn't necessarily mean it has to be easy to prepare and cook but it does mean never masking flavours, allowing room for all the ingredients, each complementing the other. My main dislike is overdressed plates, where people have thought more about presenting a picture than creating something good to eat. Keeping things simple eases stress in the kitchen and from that you feel inspired to cook more and more at home. This has the knock-on effect of your children becoming aware of what they are eating and then wanting to cook it with you.

I enjoy all the seasons. Each presents something fresh and new to add to our repertoire. The recipes below take advantage of summer ingredients. All three dishes are easy to follow. To start, there is a warm tomato salad dressed with melting Gorgonzola, olive oil and rocket (arugula) leaves. Parma ham (prosciutto) can also be added to this, either left natural or quickly seared to a crisp finish. The main course might appear to have an autumn/winter feel but I serve it in a very summery mode, the pork replacing cold ham slices, served warm and juicy with a new potato salad and smoked-bacon green beans. An alternative is to serve the beans cold and bound in a dressing (French beans in particular eat well as a salad).

To finish, it's ice cream. This one is a little different, using sloe gin and orange curd. Although the gin reads very generously, it's balanced by the strength of the orange curd and mellowed with the crème fraîche and yoghurt. Blackberries take you into late summer, but most other summer fruits, especially raspberries and strawberries, will go equally well with the sloe orange ice. Many biscuits (cookies) – tuiles, brandy snaps, shortbreads and small madeleine sponges – are readily available to buy and serve with the dish, or search through your collection of cookery books and make them yourself.

Many chefs are asked, 'What are your top ten ingredients?' Well, I have many more than ten – closer to a hundred, in fact. However, I've listed ten here, in no particular order, but all with a reason:

- Asparagus – served crisp with a hollandaise sauce, it's hard to match.
- Scallops – seared for a bitter-sweet edge, yet still maintaining an almost translucent centre.
- Cheese – Cheddar, Gorgonzola and Parmesan in particular for cooking. Any for eating!
- Potatoes – so versatile; my favourite is mash.
- Oxtail – braised slowly until it falls off the bone.
- Fish – virtually all, but especially Dover sole, sea bass and wild salmon.
- Mussels – cooked quickly and served with crusty bread to mop up their juices.
- Duck – whether cooked pink or slow-roasted.
- Tomatoes – in soups or salads, roast or semi-dried.
- Summer fruits – raspberries, strawberries, blackberries, to name but a few.
- Finally, there are some luxury extras I adore that I thought I'd share with you: foie gras, caviar, langoustines and lobsters, truffles, wild mushrooms.

# Toasted Tomato Salad with Melting Gorgonzola and Rocket Leaves

**Serves 4**

**6 medium-large (or 12 small) plum tomatoes, cut lengthways in half**
**olive oil for drizzling**
**100–175g ($3^1/_2$–6oz) Gorgonzola cheese, crumbled**
**a large handful of rocket (arugula) leaves**
**Maldon sea salt**
**a twist of black pepper**

Put the tomato halves cut-side up on an oiled and seasoned baking tray. Season each with a sprinkling of salt flakes and a twist of black pepper. Drizzle with a little olive oil and place under a preheated grill (broiler). Cook for 5–6 minutes, until beginning to soften. At this point, sprinkle the crumbled Gorgonzola over the tomatoes and return to the grill. As the cheese warms, it will begin to melt and bubble, topping the tomatoes in a rustic fashion.

Arrange the softened, toasted tomatoes on individual plates, scatter the rocket leaves over and drizzle with olive oil. The simple warm salad is ready to serve.

**Note**

There are endless variations on this 'salad', so here are a few to consider:

- Basil pesto can be bound with natural yoghurt, soured cream or crème fraîche and spooned over and around.
- A few drops of aged balsamic vinegar can be whisked into some olive oil to finish.
- If you're not a blue cheese fan, Brie, Parmesan, Gruyère, Gouda and many more cheeses will melt and eat equally well.
- Finely shredded spring onions (scallions) can be mixed with the rocket or sprinkled over the cooked tomatoes.
- Walnut or hazelnut oil can be substituted for olive oil.
- Warm butter- or olive-oil-brushed toasted bread makes a good base for the salad portions.

# Slow-roast Pork Belly with Warm New Potato Salad and Smoked Bacon Runner Beans

**Serves 4**

**1kg (2¹/4lb) boned pork belly, rind left on and scored**
**1 tablespoon olive oil**
**Maldon sea salt**
**a twist of black pepper**

For the potato salad:
**675g (1¹/2lb) new potatoes**
**3 tablespoons olive oil**
**1–2 tablespoons lemon juice**
**4 spring onions (scallions), finely shredded, or 1 heaped tablespoon chopped chives, or both**
**150ml (²/3 cup) crème fraîche**

For the runner beans:
**450g (1lb) runner beans, finely sliced**
**100g (²/3 cup) pancetta, diced**
**1 tablespoon Dijon or wholegrain mustard**
**50g (3¹/2 tablespoons) unsalted butter, diced**

Season the meat side of the pork with salt and pepper. Turn the belly joint, brush with the olive oil and season with a generous sprinkling of salt. Place the belly, rind-side up, on a wire rack sitting over a baking tray. Place in an oven preheated to 160°C/325°F/Gas Mark 3 and roast for 3 hours. During this time, the melting fat will baste the meat. When cooked, the joint should be crisp on top with a super-succulent texture beneath, so soft it will carve with a spoon. Remove the pork from the oven and leave to rest until just warm.

Meanwhile, cook the new potatoes in boiling salted water until just tender. Drain well, cut each potato in half and season with salt and pepper. Stir together the olive oil and lemon juice, sprinkle this mixture over the potatoes and spoon through to ensure all are coated. Cover and keep warm.

The sliced runner beans can be cooked at the last moment. Simply plunge them into boiling salted water and simmer until tender. Depending on their thickness, this can take anything from 1 to 5 minutes. Drain well and set aside. The pancetta can be crisped in advance. Heat a frying pan (skillet) and, once warm, add the pancetta and fry over a medium heat. The fat will be released, the pancetta slowly becoming crisp. Drain and add to the runner beans.

Just before serving, mix the shredded spring onions or chives and the crème fraîche with the warm potatoes. To finish the runner beans, heat a few tablespoons of water in a small saucepan with the mustard. Once simmering, whisk in the butter until emulsified, to create a loose mustard butter sauce. Season with a pinch of salt and a twist of pepper.

Divide the pork belly into 4 strips, placing each on a plate with the runner beans and pancetta. Drizzle the beans with the mustard butter sauce and offer the potato salad separately.

**Note**

- Smoked bacon can be used instead of pancetta, creating a richer contrast of pork flavours.
- The roast belly eats equally well at room temperature with apple sauce, a tossed leaf salad and the warm new potatoes.

# Sloe Gin and Orange Curd Ice Cream with Soft Blackberries

**Serves 4**

**325g (11oz) orange curd**
**300ml (1¼ cups) crème fraîche**
**300g (1¼ cups) natural (plain) yoghurt**
**150ml (⅔ cup) sloe gin**
**225g (8oz) blackberries**
**50g (½ cup) icing (confectioners') sugar**

Whisk together the orange curd, crème fraîche, yoghurt and sloe gin, then churn in an ice-cream maker until thick and creamy, ready to freeze for a firmer finish. If you don't have an ice-cream maker, place the mixture in the freezer, whisking from time to time, until almost frozen. Then turn out, blitz in a food processor and refreeze until firm.

Meanwhile, put the blackberries in a large saucepan or frying pan (skillet). Add 2 tablespoons of water and sprinkle over the icing sugar. Place over a moderate heat to dissolve the sugar, while gently warming and stirring the fruit. Once the blackberries are beginning to soften, remove from the heat and leave to cool to room temperature.

To serve, spoon the fruit into 4 glasses, drizzling it with the blackberry syrup. Scoop the ice cream into balls and place on top, offering any extra separately. Alternatively, spoon the ice cream into bowls and offer the blackberries separately, while still warm.

# thirty two

# MICHEL RICHARD

## Citronelle

**Considered a pioneer in creating the revolutionary French/Californian cuisine that is now so prevalent, Michel Richard believes the right spirits and fresh ingredients are integral parts of his menu. He dazzles the culinary world with his innovative combinations and witty presentation, while always infusing his light, fresh and intelligent style with an element of texture.**

**What are your favourite foods/tastes/flavours?**
Black truffles and roasted garlic.

**What is your favourite utensil?**
A knife. If you don't have a knife, you don't cook.

**What is your most useful piece of kitchen equipment?**
A stove. Because we are not sushi chefs.

**What is your favourite season?**
Winter. It is a warm feeling. I love snow, and our guests eat and drink more. We are closer to each other.

**What is your favourite mealtime?**
Dinner, because I love wine and it is a relaxing time. There is a lot of time ahead of us before we work again.

**How do you decide what to cook?**
It is based on what I find in the market, availability, and who I am cooking for.

**What inspires you?**
The quality of the ingredients.

**What is your favourite drink?**
Wine, Côtes du Rhone especially. Or any good wine. *Vive le champagne!*

**What are your likes and dislikes?**
No coriander! No bad food! Ban white truffle oil!

**How can you inspire others to enjoy great food and cooking?**
By offering great food in a great setting. Make a reservation at Citronelle.

**How did you become a chef?**
Still working on it.

**What are your top ten ingredients?**
Potatoes, flour, butter, salt, beef, chicken, onion, garlic, fresh herbs, LOVE.

**What are your kitchen secrets?**
No secrets.

**What are your top tips?**
Fresh, fresh.

**What is your favourite junk food?**
Hot dogs.

**How do you feel about cooking for children?**
I love it. I am the father of six kids. *Vive la pasta et la pizza.*

**Can you give one piece of advice for the domestic cook?**
Don't try to be a grand chef. Keep it simple. It's easier for us, we have thirty chefs to help us and you don't. And, you have to do the dishes and I don't.

* Salmon Rillettes
* Aubergine with Scallops and Goat's Cheese
* Egg Soufflé

## Salmon Rillettes

**Serves 4**

**150g (5oz) salmon fillet**
**100g (1/2 cup) cream cheese**
**2 anchovy fillets, chopped**
**1/2 onion, finely diced**
**1 teaspoon red wine vinegar**
**salt and freshly ground black pepper**

Season the salmon with salt and pepper and wrap in foil. Bake for 20 minutes in an oven preheated to 150°C/300°F/Gas Mark 2. Using a fork, mix the salmon with the cream cheese, anchovies, onion and vinegar. Place in a dish and serve with slices of toasted brioche or baguette.

# Aubergine with Scallops and Goat's Cheese

**1 large aubergine (eggplant), about 675g (1$^1/_2$lb), peeled and cut lengthways into slices 5mm ($^1/_4$ inch) thick**
**about 5 tablespoons olive oil**
**2 tablespoons balsamic vinegar**
**salt and freshly ground black pepper**

For the scallops:
**2 tablespoons olive oil**
**2 large garlic cloves, crushed**
**8 large scallops, halved horizontally and patted dry**

For the goat's cheese sauce:
**60g (2oz) goat's cheese**
**250ml (1 cup) milk**
**1 tablespoon chopped chives**
**a generous pinch of ground cumin**

Arrange the aubergine slices in a single layer on a large baking sheet. Brush both sides with the olive oil and bake in an oven preheated to 200°C/400°F/Gas Mark 6 for 15–20 minutes, until tender and easily pierced with a knife. Brush the top of the aubergine slices with the balsamic vinegar and season with salt and pepper; this can all be done in advance.

For the scallops, line a baking sheet with kitchen paper towels. Heat the oil and garlic in a large, heavy, non-stick frying pan (skillet) over a medium-high heat. Add the scallops and cook for about 3 minutes, until barely opaque, turning with tongs halfway through. Transfer to the prepared baking sheet and blot the scallops. Season with salt and pepper.

To make the sauce, put the goat's cheese and milk in a small, heavy-based saucepan and whisk over a medium-low heat for 4–5 minutes, until they form a thick, smooth paste. Stir in the chives and cumin and season with salt and pepper. You may add a bit more milk, if needed, until the sauce has the consistency of ketchup (catsup).

To assemble, oil a 23 x 30cm (9- x 12-inch) baking dish. Arrange half the aubergine slices side by side in the dish, overlapping and trimming to give an even layer. Arrange the scallops on top of the aubergine and spoon over half the sauce. Cover with the remaining aubergine, trimming as necessary, and the remaining sauce. This can be prepared ahead, covered and set aside at room temperature or in the fridge. Remove from the fridge 1 hour before serving.

To serve, place the dish about 8cm (3$^1/_4$ inches) below a hot grill (broiler) and leave for 3–4 minutes, until browned and heated through. Serve immediately.

# Egg Soufflé

**This is a wonderful little dessert. Kids love it, too. It's a surprise. When you find the 'yolk', it is lemon!**

**Serves 4**

**8 eggs**
**juice of 3 large lemons**
**325g (1½ cups plus 2½ tablespooons) caster (superfine or granulated) sugar**
**40g (2½ tablespoons) unsalted butter**

Using an egg cutter, cut the tops off the eggs. Discard the tops, keeping only the bottom section of the shell for presentation. Separate the yolks and whites of 4 eggs. The remaining 4 eggs can be used for an omelette the next day.

Make a lemon curd by placing the egg yolks, lemon juice, 100g (½ cup) of the sugar and the butter in a microwave-safe bowl and microwaving them for 5 minutes, pulling out to whisk every minute. Cover with cling film (plastic wrap) and leave to cool. It will thicken as it cools. The lemon curd can be made the day before and kept refrigerated.

Whisk the egg whites, adding half the remaining sugar little by little, until they form soft peaks. Fold in the remaining sugar with a spatula.

Place the 8 eggshells in eggcups. Put the meringue in a piping bag and half fill each shell with meringue. Put the lemon curd in another piping bag and pipe about a teaspoonful into each eggshell. Add more meringue to the top to make it look like a soufflé. Place in the microwave for 5 seconds before serving. If you have a blowtorch, you could burn the top for a few seconds, or they can be put under a hot grill (broiler) for a few seconds.

# thirty three

# ALAIN ROUX

## Waterside Inn

Alain Roux is chef-patron of the Waterside Inn in Bray, Berkshire. He has been working alongside his father, Michel Roux, since 1992, and although Michel continues to offer advice and guidance it is Alain who is in charge. Alain's training started in pastry at Millet in Paris. He then continued his culinary career at many illustrious establishments in France, including La Côte St Jacques in Joigny, Restaurant Pic in Valence, La Bonne Etape at Châteaux-Arnoux and Château de Montreuil at Montreuil-sur-Mer. He is also a Master Pâtissier of the International Association 'Relais Desserts'.

**What are your favourite foods/tastes/flavours?**
Black pudding (a blood sausage), black truffles, sticky toffee pudding, offal.

**What is your favourite utensil?**
A palette knife (a long, slim metal spatula).

**What is your most useful piece of kitchen equipment?**
A cooker.

**What is your favourite season?**
All the seasons; I respect them all.

**What is your favourite meal?**
Breakfast: bavette à l'échalote.
Lunch: horse steak.
Tea: scones with clotted cream.
Dinner: andouillette.

**How do you decide what to cook?**
Seasonal market – ingredients.

**What inspires you?**
The look and smell of ingredients. My Dad.

**What is your favourite drink?**
Champagne.

**What are your likes and dislikes?**
I like the heat in my kitchen in winter.
I dislike fruit and vegetables wrapped in cellophane.

**How can you inspire others to enjoy great food and cooking?**
By telling them that cooking is easy and you get great pleasure from producing a dish.

**How did you become a chef?**
I started as a pastry chef in Paris.

**What are your top ten ingredients?**
Truffles, vanilla, potatoes, eggs, chestnuts, chocolate, lemon, black grapes, ceps (porcini), scallops.

**What are your kitchen secrets?**
Learn from your mistakes or disasters.

**What are your top tips?**
Always work with a sharp knife.

**Do you have any favourite junk food?**
Danish hot dogs.

**How do you feel about cooking for children?**
This is the best fun ever and an essential part of their education.

**Can you give one piece of advice for the domestic cook?**
Never follow a recipe from A–Z (certainly not one of my Dad's!).

# Parsnip Soup with Ceps

**I love root vegetables and find soup very comforting in winter. A little touch of ginger spices up the sweetness of the parsnips. Ceps, one of my favourite mushrooms, work beautifully as a garnish.**

**Serves 4**

**45g (3 tablespoons) butter**
**700g (4 1/2 cups) parsnips, chopped**
**200g (generous 1 cup) leeks, chopped**
**2 pinches of ground ginger**
**150ml (2/3 cup) dry white wine**
**1.5 litres (6 cups) water, or chicken or vegetable stock**
**2 tablespoons olive oil**
**200g (7oz) fresh ceps (porcini), sliced**
**2 tablespoons snipped flat-leaf parsley**
**4–6 tablespoons double (heavy) cream, optional**
**salt and freshly ground black pepper**

Melt the butter in a large saucepan, stir in the parsnips, leeks and ginger, then cover and cook gently for 10 minutes. Pour in the wine and water or stock. Bring to the boil, then lower the heat and simmer gently for about 20 minutes, until the parsnips are tender. Blend in a food processor until smooth, then pass through a fine sieve into a clean pan. Adjust the consistency with a little additional water or stock, if necessary. Season to taste with salt, pepper, and more ginger if needed. Keep warm.

Heat the olive oil in a frying pan (skillet), add the ceps and cook until lightly golden. Stir in the parsley and season with salt and pepper.

Put the mushrooms into a large, hot tureen and pour over the hot soup. Serve immediately. If you wish, serve the cream in a sauceboat and spoon it into each bowl at the table.

# Pot-roast Pheasant Flavoured with Orange, Served with Potato and Chestnut Purée

**This is one of the simplest and most attractive ways of cooking pheasant. As my Dad [Michel Roux] often goes shooting, I regularly have the chance to cook the pheasants he brings back. In this winter menu, the flavour of sprouts and the sweetness and aroma of orange give a unique tang to the dish.**

**Serves 4**

**2 plump, oven-ready pheasants, weighing about 750g (1lb 10oz) each**
**75g (5 tablespoons) butter**
**juice of 2 oranges**
**400g (14oz) Brussels sprouts, trimmed**
**grated zest of 1 orange**
**salt and freshly ground black pepper**

**For the potato and chestnut purée:**

**300g (10oz) Desiree or other floury potatoes, peeled and cut into chunks**
**45g (3 tablespoons) butter**
**150ml (2/3 cup) warm milk**
**100g (2/3 cup) peeled cooked chestnuts, chopped**

For the potato and chestnut purée, cook the potatoes in lightly salted boiling water until tender, then drain. Pass through a potato ricer into a clean pan, or mash thoroughly with a potato masher. Add the butter and mix in with a wooden spoon. Add the warm milk and chestnuts and correct the seasoning with salt. Keep warm.

Season the pheasants with salt and pepper, then heat 30g (2 tablespoons) of the butter in a large casserole and brown the pheasants in it on all sides. Add the orange juice, cover the casserole with the lid and transfer to an oven preheated to 180°C/350°F/Gas Mark 4. Cook for 20–25 minutes.

Meanwhile, cook the Brussels sprouts in lightly salted boiling water for 2 minutes, then drain and refresh in cold water. Drain well again and shred the sprouts with a chopping knife. Finish cooking them in a pan with the grated orange zest, the remaining butter and some salt and pepper to taste. Keep warm.

When the pheasants are done, take them out of the casserole, cover with foil and leave to rest for 5–10 minutes. Strain the cooking juices from the casserole through a fine sieve. Adjust the seasoning with salt and pepper to taste and keep warm.

To serve, cut the legs off the pheasants, then take the breasts off the bone and cut each one into 3. Divide the Brussels sprouts between 4 plates, place the pheasant on top and put the potato purée on the side. Spoon the cooking juices over the pheasant and serve.

# Warm Toblerone Soufflé

**I am very fond of chocolate and, since I come from a family that specializes in pâtisserie, and particularly in warm soufflés, I wanted to have a bit of fun with this kind of chocolate dish. It needs very few ingredients and is straightforward to make. I am sure that everyone will enjoy eating it. I normally have to buy an enormous bar of Toblerone ...**

**Serves 4**

**a little softened butter**
**75g (6½ tablespoons) caster (superfine) sugar, plus 30g (2½ tablespoons) for coating**
**200g (7oz) Toblerone, chopped**
**2 teaspoons plain (all-purpose) flour**
**7 egg whites**

Brush the insides of four 8cm (3¼-inch) ramekins, 3.5cm (1½ inches) deep, with softened butter. Put the 30g (2½ tablespoons) of caster sugar in one of the dishes and rotate it to coat the inside thoroughly. Tip the excess sugar into the next dish and repeat, coating them all with sugar in this way.

Put 140g (5oz) of the Toblerone in a bowl and place it over a pan of simmering water, making sure the water isn't touching the base of the bowl. When it has melted, remove from the heat and stir in the flour.

Beat the egg whites with the 75g (6½ tablespoons) of sugar until they form semi-firm peaks. Using a whisk, mix one-third of the whites into the melted Toblerone, then delicately fold in the rest with a spatula or a large metal spoon. Scatter the remaining chopped Toblerone over the surface and mix gently. Divide the mixture between the ramekin dishes. Smooth the surface with a palette knife (metal spatula) and use the tip of the knife to ease the mixture away from the edge of the dishes. Place on a baking tray and bake for 10–12 minutes in an oven preheated to 200°C/400°F/Gas Mark 6. Serve immediately.

thirty four

# ALBERT ROUX

## Le Gavroche

Founder member of the Académie Culinaire UK, Albert Roux was the youngest chef to be elected Maître Cuisinier de France in 1968. Co-founder of the renowned Le Gavroche in London, which has been awarded several Michelin stars since it opened in 1967, Albert has won many awards in recognition of his culinary achievements. This includes the OBE in 2003 and his most recent award, the Légion d'Honneur of France.

**What are your favourite foods/tastes/flavours?**
I love vegetables. I try to eat only seasonal food, which I find has much more flavour.

**What is your favourite utensil?**
A whisk.

**What is your most useful piece of kitchen equipment?**
A stove.

**What is your favourite season?**
Spring.

**What is your favourite mealtime?**
Dinner.

**How do you decide what to cook?**
It depends how I feel on the day.

**What inspires you?**
Going to the market early in the morning.

**What is your favourite drink?**
Champagne.

**What are your likes and dislikes?**
I don't like pumpkin and I love chips (french fries).

**How can you inspire others to enjoy great food and cooking?**
By sharing my favourite meal with them.

**How did you become a chef?**
It was my destiny.

**What are your top ingredients?**
Vinegar, butter and salt.

**What are your kitchen secrets?**
I have no secrets.

**What are your top tips?**
Be happy.

**Do you have any favourite junk food?**
A Big Mac.

**How do you feel about cooking for children?**
I love it.

**Can you give one piece of advice for the domestic cook?**
Don't overstretch yourself; keep it simple.

WINNING JUST GOT EASIER...
vcbet.co.uk
08000 978794

* Mackerel Tartare with Poached Quail's Egg, Peppercorn Dressing and Black Pepper Tuiles
* Cassoulet of Guinea Fowl with Garlic
* Mixed Berries with Lemon Custard and Shortbread

## Mackerel Tartare with Poached Quail's Egg, Peppercorn Dressing and Black Pepper Tuiles

**Serves 4**

**2 very fresh mackerel, filleted and skinned**
**1 teaspoon lemon juice**
**a pinch of salt**
**4 quail's eggs, soft boiled and shelled**

For the black pepper tuiles:
**120g (1 stick) butter**
**100g (2/3 cup) plain (all-purpose) flour**
**1 teaspoon salt**
**1 tablespoon sugar**
**2 egg whites**
**1 teaspoon cracked black pepper**

For the peppercorn dressing:
**1 egg yolk**
**2 teaspoons Dijon mustard**
**2 teaspoons white wine vinegar**
**100ml (7 tablespoons) groundnut (peanut) oil**
**20g (4 teaspoons) green peppercorns**
**salt**

For the garnishes:
**1/2 tablespoon superfine capers**
**1/2 tablespoon chopped parsley**
**1/2 tablespoon finely chopped gherkin**
**1/2 tablespoon finely chopped shallot**

First make the tuiles. Beat the butter until light and fluffy. In a separate bowl, mix the flour, salt and sugar together. Whisk the egg whites into the dry ingredients, then whisk in the butter and black pepper. Allow the mixture to rest in the fridge for at least 1 hour.

Cut a triangle from the centre of the lid of a plastic ice-cream tub. Put the lid on a non-stick baking sheet and spread some of the tuile mixture into the triangular hole, using a palette knife (metal spatula). Lift off the lid and repeat with the remaining mixture. Bake the tuiles in an oven preheated to 200°C/400°F/Gas Mark 6 for 4–6 minutes, until just turning golden. Immediately lift the tuiles off the baking sheet with a palette knife and gently curve them over a rolling pin. Leave until cool.

For the dressing, whisk the egg yolk, mustard and vinegar together, then gradually whisk in the oil. Add some warm water, if necessary, to obtain the consistency of double (heavy) cream. Purée the peppercorns in a blender or food processor and add to the dressing. Season with salt to taste.

Remove any bones from the mackerel fillets and cut the fillets into 4mm (slightly smaller than 1/4-inch) dice. Mix with the lemon juice and salt. Press the mixture into four 7cm (2 3/4-inch) square pastry cutters.

Mix all the garnishes together and arrange a thin, circular layer of them in the centre of each serving plate. Place the mackerel tartare on top, then lift off the cutter. Spoon a small amount of the dressing on either side and garnish the tartare with a triangular pepper tuile and a quail's egg.

# Cassoulet of Guinea Fowl with Garlic

**Serves 4**

**120g ($^2/_3$ cup) dried haricot (navy) beans, preferably Lingot beans**
**750ml ($3^1/_3$ cups) chicken stock**
**1 bouquet garni**
**120g ($^3/_4$ cup) carrots, sliced**
**1 small onion, peeled and stuck with 1 clove**
**1 large guinea fowl**
**1 teaspoon paprika**
**4 tablespoons olive oil**
**8 garlic cloves**
**150ml ($^2/_3$ cup) white wine**
**40g ($1^1/_2$oz) sun-dried tomatoes, sliced**
**1 tablespoon chopped parsley**
**salt**

Cover the beans with cold water and leave to soak for at least 4 hours. Drain and rinse the beans and put them in a pan with the chicken stock, bouquet garni, carrots and onion. Set over a low heat, bring to the boil and cook gently for 1 hour, skimming any foam from the surface when necessary. Remove from the heat and leave to cool.

Remove the breasts, legs and thighs from the guinea fowl. Sprinkle the legs and thighs with most of the paprika and some salt and fry in half the olive oil with the unpeeled garlic cloves until they turn a deep brick colour. Pour off the fat, then add the wine and simmer until reduced by half. Add the beans and their cooking liquid and return to the boil, skimming the surface again. Cover, transfer to an oven preheated to 180°C/350°F/Gas Mark 4 and cook for 45 minutes.

Dust the guinea fowl breasts with the remaining paprika and some salt and sauté in the remaining olive oil until a deep brick colour. Cut in half and stir into the bean mixture, then return to the oven for 10–12 minutes. Remove from the oven and stir in the sun-dried tomatoes. Sprinkle with the parsley and serve.

# Mixed Berries with Lemon Custard and Shortbread

**Serves 4**

**800g ($1^3/_4$lb) mixed red berries**
**zest of 1 lemon, pared in long, thin strips**
**130g (generous $^1/_2$ cup) caster (superfine) sugar**
**2 teaspoons crème de menthe**

For the shortbread:

**250g ($1^3/_4$ cup) plain (all-purpose) flour**
**a pinch of salt**
**250g ($2^1/_4$ sticks) softened unsalted butter, cut into cubes**
**2 egg yolks**
**100g ($^1/_2$ cup) caster (superfine) sugar, plus extra for sprinkling**
**1 tablespoon crème fraîche**
**2 teaspoons vanilla extract**

For the lemon custard:

**6 egg yolks**
**70g (6 tablespoons) caster (superfine) sugar**
**240ml (1 cup plus 1 tablespoon) single (light) cream**
**240ml (1 cup plus 1 tablespoon) lemon juice**

To make the shortbread, sift the flour and salt into a bowl, make a well in the centre and add the soft butter, egg yolks, sugar, crème fraîche and vanilla. Mix them together with your fingertips, then slowly draw in the flour without overworking the mixture. Form the dough into a sausage shape, wrap in cling film (plastic wrap) and chill for at least 2 hours.

On a lightly floured work surface, roll out the dough to 4mm (slightly less than $^1/_4$ inch) thick and cut it into 4cm ($1^3/_4$-inch) rounds. Sprinkle with caster sugar and place on baking sheets lined with baking parchment paper. Bake in an oven preheated to 180°C/350°F/Gas Mark 4 for 15–18 minutes, until pale golden. Leave to cool slightly, then transfer to a wire rack to cool completely.

For the lemon custard, whisk the egg yolks and 40g ($3^1/_2$ tablespoons) of the sugar together until the mixture is very thick and pale. Put the cream, lemon juice and the remaining sugar in a saucepan and bring to the boil, then pour the boiling cream on to the egg yolk mixture, whisking all the time. Return to the pan and cook very gently, stirring all the time, until the custard thickens. Do not let it boil. Pass through a sieve and leave to cool, then cover with cling film and chill.

Wash, hull or stone the fruit as necessary and chill. Put the lemon zest in a pan with just enough water to cover and bring to the boil. Drain and refresh in cold water, then drain again. Return to the pan with the sugar, crème de menthe and 2 tablespoons of water. Boil until all the water has evaporated. Using a fork, spread the candied zest on to greaseproof paper and allow to cool.

Put the berries into chilled bowls and pour over the chilled custard. Sprinkle with the lemon zest and serve with the shortbread.

# thirty five

# MICHEL ROUX

## Waterside Inn

One of the most renowned and highly regarded figures in the culinary world, Michel Roux has been the owner of the three-Michelin-starred Waterside Inn in Bray, Berkshire, for the past 30 years. He holds countless culinary honours, in addition to having received the OBE and the Chevalier de la Légion d'Honneur. The conception and creation of recipes is his great passion, and the ability to share these wonderful creations with his clients is, he says, one of the most satisfying feelings anyone can have.

**What are your favourite foods/tastes/flavours?**
Favourite foods – stew and fish.
Favourite flavours – Mediterranean.

**What are your favourite utensils?**
A whisk and a knife.

**What is your most useful piece of kitchen equipment?**
Steamers and a blast deep-freezer.

**What is your favourite season?**
Spring.

**What is your favourite meal?**
Breakfast: full English (fried eggs, bacon, sausage, baked beans, broiled tomatoes, toast).
Lunch: a bowl of soup.
Tea: scones with clotted cream and home-made jam.
Dinner: lightly grilled (broiled) lobster.

**How do you decide what to cook?**
I visit the local market and decide on seasonal produce, and the weather.

**Who inspires you?**
Carême and, more recently, Michel Guérard.

**What is your favourite drink?**
Champagne.

**What are your likes and dislikes?**
I like young people with positive attitudes. I dislike short cuts.

**How can you inspire others to enjoy great food and cooking?**
By sharing experiences.

**How did you become a chef?**
Natural instinct.

**What are your top ten ingredients?**
Lemon, olive oil, vanilla, basil, flat-leaf parsley, eggs, cream, mushrooms, tomatoes, peaches.

**What are your kitchen secrets?**
My secrets are not secrets for long, as I pass them on to others!

**What are your top tips?**
Good organization, a tidy environment and buying the best ingredients.

**Do you have any favourite junk food?**
Crisps (potato chips).

**How do you feel about cooking for children?**
I just love it!

**Can you give one piece of advice for the domestic cook?**
Keep it simple.

## Pan-fried Red Mullet on Spinach Salad with Sauce Vierge

**Serves 4**

**8 very fresh red mullet, weighing 100–140g ($3^1/_2$–5oz) each**
**$3^1/_2$ tablespoons olive oil**
**200g (7oz) young spinach leaves**
**a pinch of caster (superfine) sugar**
**1 tablespoon balsamic vinegar**
**1 teaspoon strong Dijon mustard**
**5 tablespoons sunflower oil**
**zest and juice of $^1/_2$ lemon**
**salt and freshly ground black pepper**

For the sauce vierge:

**150ml ($^2/_3$ cup) olive oil**
**60g ($^1/_3$ cup) tomatoes, peeled, deseeded and finely diced**
**juice of 1 lemon**
**1 tablespoon snipped chervil**
**$^1/_2$ small garlic clove, finely chopped**
**4 coriander seeds, crushed**
**2 tablespoons snipped basil leaves**

Scrape off the scales from the red mullet with the back of a knife, then rinse the fish in very cold water and sponge dry. With a very sharp filleting knife, cut off the heads, then, starting from the back, lift the fillets off the backbone, without separating them at the belly. Pull out the backbones and the guts. Carefully sponge the insides of the boned fish, making sure you have removed all the bones (use tweezers to pull out any that remain). Open them out flat, lay them in a deep dish and season lightly with salt and pepper. Pour over 3 tablespoons of the olive oil and set aside.

Wash the spinach in cold water, then drain and gently pat dry. In a bowl, whisk together the sugar, a little salt and pepper, the vinegar, mustard, sunflower oil and lemon zest and juice. Keep this vinaigrette at room temperature.

For the sauce vierge, combine all the ingredients in a small pan, mix gently and season with salt and pepper.

To cook the red mullet, heat the remaining olive oil in a non-stick frying pan (skillet), then add the fish, skin-side down, and cook over a high heat for 1 minute. Turn and cook for about a minute longer, until just cooked through.

Warm the sauce vierge to about 30–40°C/86–104°F. Mix the spinach with the vinaigrette and place on a large plate or oval dish. Arrange the red mullet like sunrays, with their tails pointing inwards and the fattest part of the fillets towards the edge of the plate. Drizzle some of the sauce vierge on to the mullet and serve the rest separately.

# Chicken Cooked in a Sealed Cocotte with Riesling and Wild Mushrooms

**A light version of a casserole or stew, this is one of my favourite dishes. A few small boiled new potatoes sprinkled with snipped flat-leaf parsley would make a nice accompaniment.**

**Serves 4**

**1 very plump free-range chicken, weighing about 1.6kg ($3^1/_2$lb), cut into 8 pieces**
**60g (4 tablespoons) clarified butter**
**16 baby white onions, peeled**
**300g (2 cups) carrots, cut into chunky sticks**
**1 bottle of dry Riesling wine**
**80g ($6^1/_2$ tablespoons) butter**
**750g ($1^2/_3$lb) wild mushrooms, such as girolles and trompettes de la mort, cleaned**
**150g (1 cup) plain (all-purpose) flour, to seal the lid**
**salt and freshly ground black pepper**

Season the chicken pieces with salt and pepper. Put the clarified butter in a cast-iron casserole and set over a medium heat. When the butter is hot, add the chicken pieces and cook, turning them over after a few minutes, until they are evenly coloured all over.

Remove the chicken breast pieces and set aside. Add the onions to the casserole and cook with the leg pieces for about 7 minutes. Remove the leg pieces, pour off most of the fat from the casserole, then add the carrots and Riesling. Cook gently until the liquid has reduced by three-quarters.

Heat the butter in a large frying pan (skillet) over a medium heat, add the wild mushrooms and cook until they render their liquid. Tip them into a colander, drain well, then season lightly with salt. Return all the chicken pieces to the casserole, add the mushrooms and put on the lid.

Put the flour in a bowl and add a little cold water, stirring with a spoon to make a softish paste. Use the spoon to spread this paste between the edge of the lid and the outside top edge of the casserole to create a hermetic seal. Place in an oven preheated to 180°C/350°F/Gas Mark 4 and cook for 20 minutes.

To serve, bring the casserole to the table, break the seal and lift off the lid so that the aromas of this marvellous chicken dish waft out for the pleasure of your guests.

# White Peaches Baked with Honey and Lavender

**I love to eat peaches throughout the summer and this dish is to die for. If white peaches are unavailable, use yellow ones.**

**Serves 4**

**150g (scant 1/2 cup) lavender honey**
**150ml (2/3 cup) water**
**6 stalks of lavender, with flowers**
**4 very ripe white peaches, skinned and drizzled with the juice of 1 lemon**
**4 macaroons**
**8 small stems of redcurrants**
**4 'tips' of mint leaves**

Put the honey and water in a pan with 2 stalks of lavender. Bring slowly to the boil, stirring constantly, then remove from the heat. Place the peaches in a small roasting tin (pan), pour the honey syrup over them and bake in an oven preheated to 180°C/350°F/Gas Mark 4 for about 10 minutes, basting a couple of times.

Remove the peaches from the pan with a slotted spoon, place on a plate and leave to cool. Pour the cooking liquid from the roasting tin through a sieve into a pan and simmer for a few seconds, then leave to cool.

When the peaches are almost cold, carefully make a small incision with a knife at the side of each one and remove the stone (pit). Replace with a macaroon. Place the peaches on 4 serving plates and pour the cooled cooking liquid over them. Arrange 2 stems of redcurrants and a sprig of lavender on each plate, then place the mint on top of each peach. A sorbet of red berries will complement this dessert beautifully.

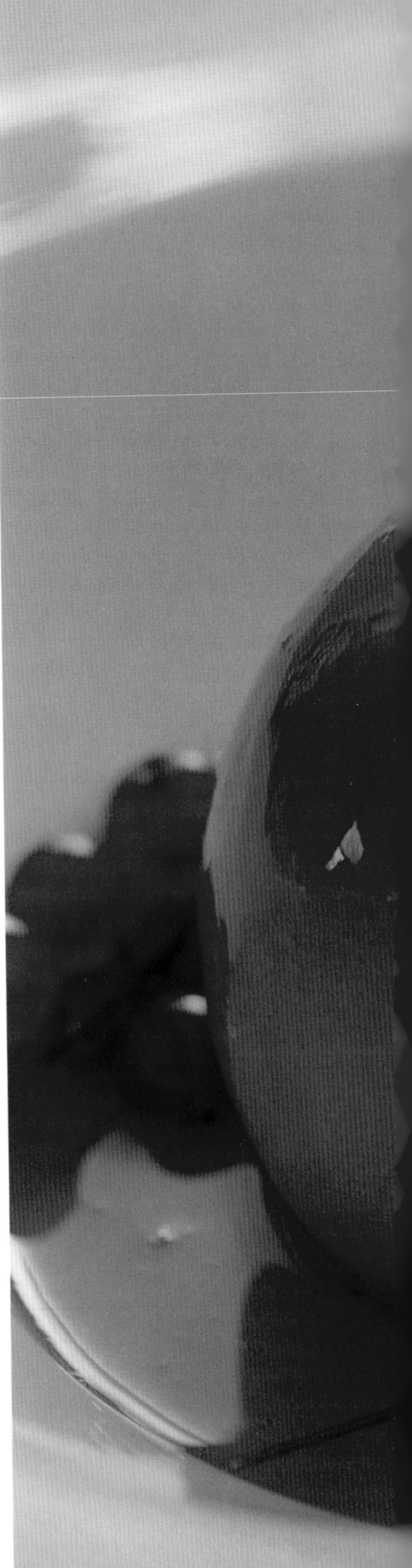

# thirty six

# MICHEL ROUX Jr

## Le Gavroche

Michel Roux Jr is one of London's most respected chefs and his restaurant, Le Gavroche, continues to receive recommendations for excellence from a variety of sources. He spent his culinary education under the tutelage of some of the world's greatest chefs, including a two-year spell with Alain Chapel. Michel's training, coupled with the love and respect for fine ingredients that he inherited from his father, Albert Roux, results in a unique flair and a passion for great food – encompassing the simplest to the most lavish of dishes.

**What are your favourite foods/tastes/flavours?**
Summer, because of the sunshine and the beautiful assortment of luscious fruit and vegetables it brings.

**What is your favourite utensil?**
I always need a classic braising pot in the kitchen, such as Le Creuset.

**What inspires you?**
Walking through the markets in France is always an inspiration.

**What is your favourite mealtime?**
I have no favourite mealtime as long as I can sit down and enjoy what I am eating with good company, especially my wife and daughter, Gisele and Emily.

**Who inspires you?**
Alain Chapel will always be an inspiration for me, not only for his style and taste but also because of his way of life and his eye for perfection.

**What is your favourite drink?**
It has to be vintage champagne. There are so many great houses but Krug is always special. Otherwise, being a marathon runner, I must say that I consume vast quantities of water, especially Evian.

**Do you ever eat junk food?**
I hate junk food and all it stands for. Pre-prepared convenience foods are no better. Something has to be done to address this problem soon before all the hospitals become full of obese patients or people with health problems due to poor diet.

**What are your top ten ingredients?**
In no special order, Maldon sea salt, caviar, raspberries, Victoria plums, white tuna, pure dark chocolate, Poilâne bread or similar, wild salmon, 48-month Iberico ham and unpasteurized cheese.

**How do you feel about cooking for children?**
It's important to teach children how to eat properly and how to enjoy sitting at the table. And get them used to eating in restaurants, like they do in France.

**Can you give one piece of advice for the domestic cook?**
When cooking at home for a party or for friends, keep it simple and seasonal.

* Parmesan Palmiers
* Roast Poulet de Bresse
* Raspberry Yoghurt

## Parmesan Palmiers

**Serves 4**

**280g (9–10oz) puff pastry**
**80g (3oz) parmigiano reggiano (Parmesan cheese), freshly grated**
**flour for dusting**

Lightly dust a work surface with flour and roll out the puff pastry to an approximate 35cm (14-inch) square. Sprinkle with some of the grated Parmesan and then bring in 2 sides to the centre of the square. Sprinkle more cheese on top and lightly roll with the rolling pin to seal. Repeat this process once more, sprinkling generously with cheese. Press down firmly with the rolling pin and leave to rest in the fridge for at least an hour.

When ready to cook, take the pastry out of the fridge and place on a board scattered with a little grated cheese. Cut into pieces 6mm (a little over 1/4 inch) thick and lay these on a non-stick baking sheet at least 6cm (2 1/2 inches) apart. Pinch each palmier in the middle to help shape it into a heart. Bake in an oven preheated to 190°C/375°F/Gas Mark 5 for 7–8 minutes, then flip them over using a palette knife (metal spatula). Return to the oven until golden. Leave on a wire rack to cool, if you can! Perfect with an old bottle of Bollinger.

## Roast Poulet de Bresse

**Serves 4**

**1 Bresse chicken, or other good traditional free-range chicken, weighing 1.3–1.6kg ($2^3/4$–$3^1/2$lb)**
**4 tablespoons olive oil**
**a sprig of rosemary**
**2 tablespoons crème fraîche**
**8 Charlotte potatoes, peeled**
**2 tablespoons butter**
**8 small shallots, peeled**
**8 garlic cloves**
**125ml ($^1/2$ cup) dry white wine**
**$3^1/2$ tablespoons water**
**salt and freshly ground black pepper**

Rub the chicken with a little of the olive oil, plus some salt and pepper, then season the cavity. Place the rosemary and crème fraiche in the cavity.

Cook the potatoes in boiling salted water for 3-4 minutes, then drain and set aside.

Put the chicken in a hot roasting tin (pan) with the rest of the oil and place on the hob (stovetop). Colour evenly on all sides, then transfer to an oven preheated to 200°C/400°F/Gas Mark 6. Roast the bird on its side for 10 minutes, then turn it on to the other side and cook for a further 10 minutes. After this, turn the bird on to its back and add the butter, potatoes, peeled shallots and the garlic cloves in their skins. Reduce the oven temperature to 180°C/350°F/Gas Mark 4 and roast for 30 minutes, shaking the tin occasionally to turn the vegetables over.

Transfer the chicken to a serving plate and tip out all the juices from its cavity into the roasting tin. Gently take out the vegetables and set them around the chicken. Cover and keep warm.

Place the roasting tin over a high heat and pour in the wine and water. Boil for 4–5 minutes, scraping the base of the tin with a wooden spoon to lift the roasting sugars. Serve this gravy with the bird. We would normally serve the chicken with a big green salad and pour some of the roasting juices on to it.

## Raspberry Yoghurt

**Serves 4**

**600g (18 oz) raspberries**
**4 tablespoons icing (confectioners') sugar**
**juice of 1 lemon**
**500g ($2^1/4$ cups) Greek (thick plain) yoghurt**
**8 digestive biscuits (graham crackers)**
**2 tablespoons raspberry jam**

Purée half the raspberries with the icing sugar and lemon juice to make a coulis. Pass through a fine sieve and then chill.

Take 4 large cocktail glasses or tumblers and put a few raspberries in each, followed by enough yoghurt to cover. Then break up the biscuits and sprinkle them over the yoghurt. Follow this with the jam, more yoghurt and finally the remaining fresh raspberries. Pour the coulis on top and serve.

# thirty seven

# MARK SARGEANT

## Gordon Ramsay at Claridge's

Mark won the much-acclaimed Young Chef of the Year award in 1996 and joined Gordon Ramsay at Aubergine restaurant shortly afterwards. He then moved to the Gordon Ramsay restaurant, where he was an integral part of the team from its opening through to the award of its highly prized third Michelin star. In 2001 he opened Gordon Ramsay at Claridge's, winning his first Michelin star a year later. He has subsequently won the Chef of the Year award, ten years after his mentor, Gordon. Mark has also co-written Gordon Ramsay's last four cookery books.

**What are your favourite foods/tastes/flavours?**
I love really simple, comforting foods with a good depth of flavour but not too rich. For me, the perfect main course would be a good piece of beef with fries and loads of béarnaise sauce. I'm not a big fan of so-called luxury ingredients but I would kill for a good white truffle! They are truly amazing. As for puddings, it has to be lemon tart.

**What are your favourite utensils?**
My knives. Other than that, a good, sharp Japanese mandoline.

**What is your most useful piece of kitchen equipment?**
This may seem a strange answer but, for all the technology and gadgets around these days, a kitchen would be nowhere without cling film (plastic wrap). It's without doubt the best thing ever invented!

**What is your favourite season?**
As I suspect most chefs will reply, my favourite season is autumn. All the seasonal vegetables and game and wild mushrooms are in abundance and chefs are in their element at this time of year. Spring would be a close second.

**What is your favourite mealtime?**
I go to Clarke's every Saturday for brunch and they do the best fry-up in town. Home-made pork sausages, crispy pancetta, flat mushrooms, fried egg, toast and mustard, all washed down with a glass of peach Prosecco.

**How do you decide what to cook?**
I generally cook what I would like to eat. When I go to restaurants, I try to visualize how the dishes will look and taste when they come out, and I am usually wrong. I don't think food should be too complicated, and the simplicity of good ingredients should speak for itself.

**What inspires you?**
Inspiration can come at very strange times. You can be all poetic about it and say it's the seasons or the smell of your summer holiday in Provence, but I usually get ideas halfway through service when I'm in the shit and my brain is working overtime! It's more about how to evolve a dish or an idea into something better.

**What is your favourite drink?**
I'm quite partial to a gin and tonic but I'm discovering the delights of Californian Chardonnay at the moment, which I find delicious. Also, I love chocolate milk.

**What are your likes and dislikes?**
I like most things and people – life is too short not to. I even like vegetarians, but my main dislike really is vegans. I mean, a joke's a joke! Especially when they want my Menu Prestige!

**How can you inspire others to enjoy great food and cooking?**
I think to inspire other people to enjoy good food you need to take the fear factor out of cooking. It should be something they enjoy and find that it's within their boundaries. Don't confuse them with jargon or science, just teach them about good ingredients and cooking techniques.

**How did you become a chef?**
For some insane reason I wanted to be a chef at eight years old. No one in my family had anything to do with the industry. I would prefer to be winning the Superbike season, of course, but that's life!

**What are your top ten ingredients?**
English asparagus, white truffles, broccoli, mackerel, salted butter, good rib-eye beef, La Ratte potatoes, rhubarb, ginger, coriander (cilantro).

**What are your kitchen secrets?**
There are far too many little secrets to list but the main ones to running a successful kitchen are keep your eyes and ears open and respect your customers. There's no point being an arrogant chef with an empty restaurant.

**Do you ever eat junk food?**
I don't eat junk food at all, ever ... but I had a Double Whopper the other day and it was amazing!

**How do you feel about cooking for children?**
I really think children should be encouraged to eat well. Don't be too adventurous but at the same time don't let them get too fussy – my friend's mother used to cook five different meals a day because her kids had got too demanding. Let them know where the food comes from and don't force them to be vegetarians. That is the biggest crime ever! They should be able to decide for themselves when the time comes.

**Can you give one piece of advice for the domestic cook?**
DON'T PANIC! If it goes wrong, don't worry, you aren't being judged by paying customers or Michelin inspectors. Take your time and don't bite off more than you can chew.

# Soused Mackerel Fillets with Warm Sourdough

**Serves 4**

**4 large mackerel fillets, pin bones removed**
**4–5 tablespoons sea salt**
**olive oil for drizzling**
**4 thin slices of sourdough bread**
**leaves from 1 sprig of thyme**

For the marinade:
**10 banana shallots, sliced into rings**
**600ml (2 1/2 cups) white wine vinegar**
**250g (1 1/4 cup) caster (superfine) sugar**
**1 cinnamon stick**
**20 coriander seeds**
**20 white peppercorns**

Place all the ingredients for the marinade in a large pan and bring to the boil. Remove from the heat and leave to infuse.

Season the fish generously with the sea salt and place in the fridge for 3–4 hours. Remove from the fridge and rinse under cold water for about 30 minutes (to do this, put the fish in a container full of water in the sink and leave under a slow running tap). Pat the fish dry and place in a dish that is large enough to hold the fillets in a single layer without too much space around them. Pour the marinade, which should be at room temperature, over the fish and leave in the fridge for 12 hours or overnight.

To serve, remove the fish from the marinade and pat dry. Drizzle over a little olive oil and rub it into the skin to give it a shine. Place some of the shallot rings from the marinade on serving plates and put the fish on top.

Drizzle one side of the sourdough bread with olive oil, then scatter over some sea salt and the thyme leaves. Toast on both sides. Serve the fish with the sourdough toast and a mixed salad.

# Braised Neck of Lamb with Cabbage and Carrots

**Serves 4**

**750g (1$^{2}/_{3}$lb) lamb neck fillet (tenderloin), cut into large pieces**
**1 tablespoon plain (all-purpose) flour**
**2–3 tablespoons olive oil**
**3 tablespoons tomato purée (paste)**
**1 garlic clove, lightly crushed**
**1 bay leaf**
**2 sprigs of thyme**
**1 litre (1 quart) good-quality chicken stock**
**1 large Savoy cabbage**
**1 onion, sliced**
**25g (2 tablespoons) butter, plus an extra knob of butter**
**2 bunches of young carrots**
**salt and freshly ground black pepper**

Season the lamb pieces and dust them with the flour. Brown the lamb in the olive oil in a large casserole, then remove and set aside. Add the tomato purée, garlic, bay leaf and a thyme sprig to the casserole and cook until the purée has browned slightly. Return the lamb to the casserole and cook, stirring, for 2 minutes, so it is nicely coated with the purée. Add the stock and bring to the boil, then reduce the heat and simmer for 1–2 hours, until the lamb is tender.

Meanwhile, remove the large, outer leaves from the cabbage, blanch them in boiling salted water for 3–4 minutes, until tender, then drain well. Refresh in cold water and drain again.

Cut out the core from each leaf and lay out the leaves, overlapping slightly, in a rectangle on a large sheet of cling film (plastic wrap).

Finely slice the middle of the cabbage. Sweat the onion in the 25g (2 tablespoons) of butter with the remaining thyme sprig until softened, then add the sliced cabbage and 1–2 tablespoons of water and cook until tender. Season well, then gently squeeze out excess moisture from the cabbage. Spread the cooked cabbage mixture all over the cabbage leaves in an even layer. Roll up like a Swiss roll (jelly roll), using the cling film to roll it tightly – if necessary, roll it again in a second sheet of cling film to give a good shape. Twist the ends of the cling film to seal. Chill the cabbage roll for 1 hour. Scrub the carrots and put them in a pan with just enough salted water to cover. Add the knob of butter and cook, uncovered, until the carrots are tender and most of the liquid has evaporated to form a light glaze.

To serve, slice the cabbage roll into 4 and reheat in a steamer for 5–6 minutes. Remove the pieces of lamb from the cooking liquor with a slotted spoon, then strain the liquid. If it is too thin, pour it into a clean pan and simmer until reduced to a sauce consistency. Place the cabbage in a bowl with the lamb on top and scatter the carrots around. Pour the braising juices over the meat and vegetables.

# Rhubarb and Vanilla Cheesecake

**Serves 4**

**250g (9oz) HobNob biscuits (cookies)**
**75g (5 tablespoons) unsalted butter**
**2 tablespoons clear honey**
**100g (7 tablespoons) cream cheese**
**100ml ($3^1/_2$oz) crème fraîche**
**1 vanilla pod (vanilla bean), split open lengthways**
**200ml (7oz) double (heavy) cream**
**juice and grated zest of 1 lemon**
**3–4 tablespoons caster (superfine) sugar**

For the rhubarb:

**200g (1 cup) caster (superfine) sugar**
**100ml (7 tablespoons) water**
**400g (14 oz) young rhubarb, trimmed and cut into 4cm ($1^3/_4$-inch) batons**

Put the HobNobs in a plastic bag and crush them to crumbs with a rolling pin. Melt the butter in a saucepan and stir in the biscuit crumbs and honey. Press this mixture into 4 ring moulds, about 7–8cm (3–$3^1/_2$-inch) in diameter, and place in the fridge to set.

Mix the cream cheese and crème fraîche together until smooth, then scrape in the seeds from the vanilla pod. Lightly whip the cream and fold it into the cream cheese mixture, together with the lemon zest and juice. Sweeten with caster sugar to taste, then divide the mixture between the moulds and smooth the top. Return to the fridge.

To cook the rhubarb, put the sugar and water in a pan and bring gently to the boil, stirring occasionally so the sugar dissolves. Simmer for a few minutes, then add the rhubarb. When the mixture comes back to a simmer, remove from the heat. Let the rhubarb cool in the syrup (it will continue to cook as it cools).

To serve, place the cheesecakes on 4 plates and remove the ring moulds. Place the rhubarb on top and pour any juices around.

# thirty eight

# JULIAN SERRANO

## Picasso

**Julian Serrano is executive chef of Picasso restaurant at Bellagio's in Las Vegas. Although Spanish, he has an affinity for French cuisine. He completed most of his training in France and travels there once a year in search of new inspirations. He has earned the prestigious James Beard Foundation Award twice, as 'Best Chef in the Southwest 2002' and 'Best Chef of California 1998', and is regarded as one of the finest culinary talents in the nation.**

**What are your favourite foods/flavours?**
Provençal with herbs, vegetables and fresh fish.

**What is your favourite utensil?**
A chef's knife.

**What is your most useful piece of kitchen equipment?**
A sorbet machine.

**What is your favourite season?**
Winter.

**What is your favourite mealtime?**
Dinner.

**How do you decide what to cook?**
I go to the market to see what is fresh.

**What inspires you?**
Predominantly places – especially the market.

**What is your favourite drink?**
Cuba Libre.

**What are your likes and dislikes?**
I like everything except sea urchin.

**How can you inspire others to enjoy great food and cooking?**
Through education. I love to show people how to cook and to excite them about what they can do on their own.

**How did you become a chef?**
I had a tremendous desire to travel and felt that a culinary career would afford me this opportunity. So I enrolled in school ... and here I am today.

**What are your top ten ingredients?**
Salt, pepper, olive oil, vinegar, butter, curry, paprika, saffron, tomato, herbs.

**What are your kitchen secrets?**
I don't have any secrets.

**What is your favourite junk food?**
Potato crisps and Spanish roasted almonds.

**How do you feel about cooking for children?**
I think it is extremely important for kids and is an excellent practice. Children are honest and will always tell you what they feel.

**Can you give one piece of advice for the domestic cook?**
I encourage people to taste. The more they taste, the more refined their palate will become. And I always tell people to cook what THEY like to eat.

# Warm Lobster Salad with Panaché of Tropical Fruit and Citrus Vinaigrette

**Serves 4**

**4 x 450g (1lb) lobsters**
**1 small head of celeriac (celery root)**
**1 mâche (corn salad) lettuce**
**1 red oakleaf lettuce**
**1 curly endive lettuce**
**2 heads of chicory (Belgian endive)**
**1 head of Treviso**
**1 papaya, peeled, deseeded and finely diced**
**1 mango, peeled, stoned (seeded) and finely diced**
**1 kiwi fruit, peeled and finely diced**
**chervil leaves and pink peppercorns, to garnish**

**For the citrus vinaigrette:**

**2 tablespoons blood orange juice**
**2 tablespoons pineapple juice**
**2 tablespoons lemon juice**
**2 tablespoons lime juice**
**250ml (1 cup) extra virgin olive oil**
**1 tablespoon port**
**125ml (1/2 cup) sherry vinegar**
**2 tablespoons truffle jus (optional)**
**1 tablespoon honey**
**salt and freshly ground black pepper**

Tie each lobster to a wooden stick to keep the tail straight after cooking. Put the lobsters in a very large pot of boiling water and poach for 2 minutes. Remove the lobsters from the water and leave to cool. Remove the tails and cut each one into 4 or 5 medallions, holding them together to retain the tail shape. Set aside.

To prepare the vinaigrette, simmer the blood orange and pineapple juice separately for 30 seconds over a medium heat. Simmer the lemon and lime juice together for 1 minute. Combine all the juices in a mixing bowl and whisk in the olive oil, port, sherry vinegar, truffle jus, if using, and honey. Season with salt and pepper to taste.

Peel the celeriac and cut it into fine matchsticks. Toss it with just enough of the citrus vinaigrette to coat. Create a bed of salad on large individual serving plates for the lobster-shaped presentation. For the head, place some mâche leaves in a semi-circle at the top of the plate and on top of that another semi-circle of oakleaf lettuce, topped with curly endive. In the centre, place a spoonful of the celeriac. This will make a bed for the lobster medallions. Fan out some Belgian endive leaves at the bottom of the plate, creating a tail, and then place a Treviso leaf in the centre of the endive.

Put the lobster tail meat in a sauté pan with 4 tablespoons of the dressing and warm through gently. Place the lobster medallions on the bed of lettuce in the shape of a lobster. Place the claws on either side of the head section of the salad. Spoon the warmed dressing over the entire salad and garnish with chervil leaves and pink peppercorns. Mix together all the diced fruit and place a spoonful on top of each portion of lobster.

# Loin of Lamb with Crust of Truffles au Jus and Parmesan Potatoes

**2 x 8-bone racks (best ends) of lamb, ask your butcher to bone out the lamb and give you the bones and trimmings**
**2 egg yolks, lightly beaten**
**1 fresh black truffle, chopped**
**½ bunch of parsley, chopped**
**2 tablespoons truffle oil**
**12 baby carrots**

For the lamb stock:

**2 tablespoons olive oil**
**the bones and meaty trimmings from the lamb**
**2 celery sticks, diced**
**1 onion, diced**
**1 leek, diced**
**2 garlic cloves, chopped**
**a few sprigs of thyme**
**1 tablespoon tomato purée (paste)**

For the sauce:

**2 tablespoons olive oil**
**4 shallots, finely diced**
**500ml (2¼ cups) Merlot wine**
**1 tablespoon chopped truffles (optional)**
**salt and freshly ground black pepper**

For the Parmesan potatoes:

**30g (2 tablespoons) butter**
**4 medium-sized red potatoes, peeled and cut into slices 3mm (⅛ inch) thick**
**250ml (1¼ cups) chicken stock**
**4 tablespoons freshly grated Parmesan cheese**

First make the lamb stock. Heat the olive oil in a roasting tin (pan) on the hob (stovetop), add the bones and trimmings and cook until beginning to colour. Transfer to an oven preheated to 180°C/350°F/Gas Mark 4 and roast until the bones are a good golden colour, turning them regularly. Drain off the fat and put the meat and bones in a large pan. Add all the diced vegetables and the thyme and tomato purée and cover with water. Bring to the boil, then reduce the heat and simmer for 50 minutes. Strain through a fine sieve and set aside.

For the sauce, heat the olive oil in a pan, add the shallots and sweat for about 10 minutes, until softened. Add the Merlot and simmer until almost completely evaporated. Pour in the lamb stock and simmer until reduced by half. Season with salt and pepper to taste, then stir in the chopped truffles, if using. Set aside.

Brush the lamb lightly with the beaten egg yolks, then roll it in the chopped truffle and parsley. Heat the truffle oil in a roasting tin on the hob, add the lamb and cook over a medium heat until lightly browned on all sides. Do not allow the truffle crust to become crispy. Transfer to an oven preheated to 150°C/300°F/Gas Mark 2 and cook for 15 minutes or until the lamb is done to your liking.

Meanwhile, prepare the potatoes. Use the butter to grease a baking dish, then layer the potatoes in it, seasoning between the layers. Pour over the chicken stock, sprinkle with the Parmesan and bake in an oven preheated to 200°C/400°F/Gas Mark 6 for about 45 minutes, until the potatoes are tender. Cook the baby carrots in boiling salted water until tender, then drain.

To serve, divide the potatoes and carrots between 4 plates. Slice each piece of lamb in half and place on the plates, cut-side up. Pour the sauce around.

# Mascarpone Cheesecake with Lemon Curd and Blueberry Sauce

450g (1lb) cream cheese, at room temperature
175g (3/4 cup plus 2 tablespoons) caster (superfine) sugar
1 1/2 vanilla pods (vanilla beans)
200g (3/4 cup plus 2 tablespoons) mascarpone cheese, at room temperature
1 egg, at room temperature

**For the shortbread base:**

250g (1 2/3 cups) plain (all-purpose) flour
250g (2 3/4 cups) ground almonds (very finely ground blanched almonds)
250g (1 1/4 cups) caster (superfine or granulated) sugar
250g(2 1/4) sticks butter, cut into small dice
1 egg
1/2 teaspoon vanilla extract

**For the lemon curd:**

150ml (2/3 cup) lemon juice, from Meyer lemons or good organic lemons
120g (heaped 1/2 cup) caster (superfine or granulated) sugar
1 tablespoon finely grated lemon zest
4 eggs
175g (1 1/2 sticks) butter, diced

**For the blueberry sauce:**

550g (18oz) blueberries, plus a few extra to decorate
115g (heaped 1/2 cup) caster (superfine or granulated) sugar
2 teaspoons vanilla extract
4 tablespoons water

First make the shortbread base. Sift the dry ingredients into the bowl of a food mixer. Add the butter and mix on a low speed until the mixture resembles coarse cornmeal. Add the egg and vanilla and mix until the ingredients come together to form a dough. Shape into a ball, wrap in cling film (plastic wrap) and chill for 30 minutes. On a lightly floured surface, roll out the dough to 3mm (1/8 inch) thick and cut into rounds with a 4cm (1 3/4-inch) pastry cutter, or to fit whichever ring moulds you plan to use for the cheesecake. Place them about 3cm (1 1/4 inches) apart on a baking sheet lined with baking parchment and bake in an oven preheated to 160°C/325°F/Gas Mark 3 until golden around the edges. Remove from the oven and leave to cool on a wire rack. You will only need 4 shortbread biscuits (cookies) for the cheesecake but the rest will keep well in an airtight tin.

Next make the lemon curd. Put everything except the butter in a bowl set over a pan of simmering water, making sure the water does not touch the base of the bowl. Cook, stirring, until the mixture is thick enough to coat the back of the spoon. Remove from the heat, whisk in the butter and then strain the curd through a fine sieve (strainer). Leave to cool, then chill.

To make the cheesecake, put the cream cheese and sugar in a bowl. Split the vanilla pods open, scrape out the seeds into the bowl and beat the mixture until no lumps remain. Add the mascarpone and beat again until smooth. Finally, mix in the egg.

Gently press a shortbread biscuit into the bottom of each of 4 ring moulds, 4cm (1 3/4 inches) in diameter and 5cm/2 inches deep. Place on a baking sheet. Fill each mould about two-thirds full with the cheesecake mixture and bake in an oven preheated to 120°C/250°F/Gas Mark 1/2 for 8 minutes. Turn the cheesecakes front to back and bake for another 8 minutes. Remove from the oven and leave to cool, then chill until set. Fill up the rings with the lemon curd, smoothing it over with a spatula to ensure the top is flat. Place in an oven preheated to 120°C/250°F/Gas Mark 1/2 for 8 minutes, then turn and cook for another 8 minutes. Remove from the oven and leave to cool, then chill until the curd is firm.

Meanwhile, make the blueberry sauce. Combine all the ingredients in a small saucepan and cook over a very low heat until the berries have collapsed. Crush them gently with a fork, then carefully strain off the liquid, discarding the berries, and leave to cool. Refrigerate until needed.

To serve, divide the blueberry sauce between 4 plates. Wrap each cheesecake mould in a hot, damp towel for a few seconds, then run a knife around the edge and remove the ring mould. Place the cheesecakes on top of the blueberry sauce and decorate with a few blueberries.

# DELIA SMITH

**Delia Smith is Britain's best-selling cookery author, whose books have sold over 16 million copies. She is also a director of Norwich City Football Club, where she is in charge of Canary Catering, several restaurants and a regular series of food and wine workshops. She is married to the writer and editor, Michael Wynn Jones, and they live in Suffolk.**

**What are your favourite foods/tastes/flavours?**
Home cooking and traditional British and Italian.

**What is your favourite utensil?**
A small, flat-sided skewer to test when things are done.

**What is your most useful piece of kitchen equipment?**
A well-designed oven.

**What is your favourite season?**
Winter, with log fires and slow-cooked food.

**What is your favourite mealtime?**
Traditional Sunday lunch.

**How do you decide what to cook?**
Whatever happens to be at its best in season.

**What inspires you?**
People, travel, magazines and cookery books.

**What is your favourite drink?**
Red, white and rosé.

**What are your likes and dislikes?**
Don't like 'poncy' food in any shape or form but perfection in simplicity.

**How can you inspire others to enjoy great food and cooking?**
That is what I have spent my life trying to do.

**How did you become a chef/cookery writer?**
Working my way up from being a kitchen assistant in a small, French, London restaurant.

**What are your top ten ingredients?**
Really good, well-hung meat, fresh fish caught in British waters, home-grown vegetables and salads, fresh herbs, good butter, olive oil, crème fraîche, spanking-fresh free-range eggs, lots of lovely cheeses, artisan dried pasta.

**What are your kitchen secrets?**
I have revealed all!

**What are your top tips?**
Use a reliable recipe.

**What is your favourite junk food?**
Hamburgers.

**How do you feel about cooking for children?**
Great. The BBC Complete Cookery Course has been used in school broadcasts.

**Can you give one piece of advice for the domestic cook?**
Use my books.

* **Baked Eggs in Wild Mushroom Tartlets**
* **Roast Gammon with Blackened Crackling and Citrus, Rum and Raisin Sauce**
  **Potatoes Boulangère with Rosemary**
* **Chocolate Mascarpone Cheesecake with Fruit and Nuts, served with Crème Fraîche**

# Baked Eggs in Wild Mushroom Tartlets

**For a long time now, I haven't made a quiche or tart for entertaining. I really feel that serving them individually is prettier, more practical and people really seem to enjoy them. The following recipe contains a base of a very concentrated mixture of fresh mushrooms and dried porcini, and this coupled with a light, softly baked egg and crisp pastry is a delight.**

**Serves 6**

For the pastry:

**75g (5 tablespoons) soft butter, plus a little extra for greasing**
**175g (1¼ cups) plain (all-purpose) flour, sifted**
**40g (1½oz) Parmesan, finely grated**

For the filling:

**6 large (extra-large) eggs**
**25g (1oz) dried porcini**
**175g (6oz) chestnut (cremini) mushrooms**
**175g (6oz) open-cap mushrooms**
**75g (5 tablespoons) butter**
**2 small red onions, peeled and finely chopped**
**2 cloves garlic, peeled and chopped**
**2 teaspoons lemon juice**
**1 heaped tablespoon chopped fresh parsley**
**25g (2 tablespoons) Parmesan, finely grated**
**salt and freshly milled black pepper**

You will also need six 1cm (½-inch) deep quiche tins (pans) with a base diameter of 10cm (4 inches), greased, a 14cm (5½-inch) plain cutter and a solid baking sheet.

Begin by placing the porcini in a bowl. Pour 200ml (7oz) boiling water over them and leave to soak for 30 minutes. Now make the pastry. This can be done in a processor, or by rubbing the butter into the flour and stirring in the grated Parmesan and sufficient cold water (about 3 tablespoons) to mix to a soft but firm dough. Place it in a plastic bag and leave in the fridge for 30 minutes. This pastry will need a little more water than usual, as the cheese absorbs some of it.

For the filling, melt 50g (3½ tablespoons) of the butter in a heavy-based frying pan (skillet), add the onions and garlic and fry until they are soft and almost transparent, about 15 minutes. Meanwhile, finely chop the chestnut and open-cap mushrooms. When the porcini have had their soaking, place a sieve over a bowl and strain them into it, pressing to release the moisture. (You can freeze the liquid for stocks or sauces.) Then chop the porcini finely and transfer them with the other mushrooms to the pan containing the onions. Add the remaining butter, season and cook till the juices of the mushrooms run, then add the lemon juice and parsley. Raise the heat slightly and cook the mushrooms without a lid, stirring from time to time, until all the liquid has evaporated and the mixture is of a spreadable consistency. This will take about 25 minutes.

Meanwhile, preheat the oven to 200°C/400°F/Gas Mark 6. Now roll out the pastry to a thickness of 3mm (about ⅛ inch) and cut out 6 rounds, re-rolling if necessary. Line the tart tins with the pastry, pushing it down from the top so it will not shrink while cooking. Trim any surplus from the top and prick the base with a fork. Now leave them in the fridge for a few minutes until the oven is up to temperature.

Next, place the tins on the baking sheet and bake on the middle shelf of the oven for 15–20 minutes or until the pastry is golden. Remove them from the oven and reduce the temperature to 180°C/350°F/Gas Mark 4. Divide the filling between the tarts, making a well in the centre with the back of a spoon. Then break an egg into a saucer, slip it into a tart and scatter a little Parmesan over. Repeat with the other 5 tarts and now return them to the oven for 12–15 minutes, until they are just set. Serve straight away.

# Roast Gammon with Blackened Crackling

**At the moment there is some superb-quality gammon in-store. Modern curing methods have eliminated the need for pre-soaking, which makes it a perfect joint for roasting. If you leave the skin on, score it and paint it with black treacle, it turns into superb crackling during the cooking. It's then a very easy joint to carve, and serving it with citrus, rum and raisin sauce is a heavenly combination.**
**The rum and raisin sauce is sweet-sharp. If possible, make it the day before you need it, so the raisins have plenty of time to absorb all the flavours and become nice and plump.**
**Potatoes boulangère are crisp and golden on the top, soft and creamy within. They are absolutely perfect for entertaining, as they sit happily in the oven without needing any attention.**

**Serves 6**

For the gammon:

**2.25kg (5lb) prime British gammon joint (boneless ham, but with the skin remaining), smoked or unsmoked**
**1 level tablespoon black treacle (molasses)**
**sea salt**

For the sauce:

**1 large, juicy orange, preferably unwaxed**
**1 lime**
**5 tablespoons dark rum**
**75g (1/2 cup) raisins**
**110g (1/2 cup) dark brown sugar**
**1 slightly rounded teaspoon arrowroot**

For the potatoes:

**1.1kg (2 1/2lb) potatoes, such as Desiree or Romano**
**15g (1/2oz) rosemary**
**2 medium onions, about 350g (12 oz)**
**284ml tub (1 1/4 cups) of chicken stock**
**150ml (2/3 cup) milk**
**40g (3 tablespoons) butter**
**sea salt and freshly milled black pepper**

As soon as you buy the gammon, remove all the wrapping paper and dry the skin really well with kitchen paper towels. After that, ease the string away from the skin. Then, using a very sharp pointed knife, score the skin in a criss-cross pattern, making little 1cm (1/2-inch) diamonds. This is quite easy to do if you insert the tip of the knife only, then, holding the skin taut with one hand, drag the tip of the knife down in long movements. When you've done this, replace the string and put the gammon on a plate. Store it, uncovered, at the bottom of the fridge, if possible 2 or 3 days before you need it. This means the skin will go on drying, which makes better crackling. To cook the gammon, preheat the oven to 240°C/475°F/Gas 9. Place the gammon in a roasting tin (pan), skin-side upright – if it won't stand up straight, use a couple of wedges of foil to keep it in position. If the treacle is very cold, warm it slightly, then, using a pastry brush or a wodge of paper, lightly coat all the little diamonds of skin. After that, sprinkle the skin lightly with salt, pressing in well.

Now place the roasting tin in the oven. After 25 minutes, turn the heat down to 180°C/350°F/Gas Mark 4. Then continue to let the gammon cook for 1 3/4 hours; it should feel tender all the way through when tested with a skewer. After it comes out of the oven, give it at least 30 minutes' resting time, covered with foil, in a warm place.

**For the sauce**

All you do is remove the outer zest from the orange, using a potato peeler so that you don't get any of the pith. Then pile the little strips on top of one another and, with a very sharp knife, cut them into really thin, needle-sized strips. If you've got the orange peel piled up and your knife is sharp, this is a lot easier than it sounds.

Next remove the zest from the lime, this time using a fine grater, and squeeze the juice from the lime and orange. Place all the ingredients in a saucepan. Whisk the arrowroot into the mixture and place the pan on a gentle heat, whisking all the time until it starts to simmer. As soon as this happens, it will change from opaque to clear, so then remove it from the heat. When it is cool enough, pour it into a serving dish, cover with cling film (plastic wrap) and chill until needed.

**For the potatoes**

You will need an ovenproof dish, 28 x 20 x 5cm (11¼ x 8 x 2 inches), greased. Preheat the oven to 180°C/350°F/Gas Mark 4.

Begin by preparing the rosemary, which should be stripped from the stalks, then bruised in a pestle and mortar. After that, take two-thirds of the rosemary leaves and chop them finely. Now peel the potatoes and the onions. Cut the onions in half and then the halves into the thinnest slices possible. The potatoes should be sliced, but not too thinly. All you do is arrange a layer of potato over the base of the dish, followed by a layer of onion and a scattering of rosemary and season with salt and pepper. Then continue layering, finishing with a layer of potatoes, slightly overlapping one another.

Now mix the stock and milk together and pour that all over the potatoes. Season the top layer, then scatter the unchopped rosemary leaves all over the top. Now put little flecks of butter all over the surface of the potatoes and place on the highest shelf of the oven for 45–60 minutes, or until the top layer of potatoes is crisp and golden and the underneath is tender.

# Chocolate Mascarpone Cheesecake with Fruit and Nuts, served with Crème Fraîche

**This is quite simply a chocolate cheesecake to die for. If you like chocolate, if you like dark chocolate with fruit and nuts, and if you like luscious, velvet-textured mascarpone – need I say more?**

**Before embarking on a baked cheesecake, remember that, to prevent cracking, it's best cooled slowly in a switched-off oven. So you will need to make it well ahead.**

**Serves 6**

**For the filling:**

**95g ($3^1/_2$oz) dark chocolate with 70–75 per cent cocoa solids**

**250g (9oz) mascarpone, at room temperature**

**50g ($^1/_3$ cup) raisins**

**110g (1 cup) whole hazelnuts**

**200g (7oz) 8-per-cent-fat fromage frais (fromage blanc), at room temperature**

**2 large (extra-large) eggs, at room temperature, lightly beaten**

**40g ($2^2/_3$ tablespoons) golden caster (superfine) sugar**

**For the base:**

**50g ($^1/_3$ cup) whole hazelnuts**

**110g ($3^1/_2$oz) sweet oat biscuits (cookies)**

**25g (2 tablespoons) butter, melted**

**To decorate:**

**95g ($3^1/_2$oz) dark chocolate with 70–75 per cent cocoa solids for the chocolate curls**

**1 teaspoon (unsweetened) cocoa powder**

**To serve:**

**crème fraîche or pouring cream**

You will also need an 18cm ($7^1/_4$-inch) cake tin (pan), preferably springform, 7.5cm (3 inches deep); if shallower than this, line the sides with baking parchment paper.

Preheat the oven to 200°C/400°F/Gas Mark 6.
First of all, place all the hazelnuts for the base and the filling in the oven and toast to a golden brown; use a timer and have a look after 5 minutes, giving them extra if they need it. Then remove them from the hot tray to cool. Set aside 110g (1 cup) for the filling. Meanwhile, make the base of the cheesecake by crushing the biscuits in a polythene (plastic) bag with a rolling pin – not too finely, though, as it's nice to have a fairly uneven texture. Then chop the remaining 50g (scant $^1/_2$ cup) toasted hazelnuts. Now tip all the crushed biscuit crumbs into a bowl, add the chopped nuts and melted butter and mix everything very thoroughly before packing it into the base of the cake tin, pressing it very firmly all over. Now place the tin in the oven and pre-bake the crust for 20 minutes. Then remove it and let it cool while you make the filling. Reduce the oven temperature to 150°C/300°F/Gas Mark 2.

To make the filling, first break the chocolate into small squares. Next, place them in a small, heatproof bowl, which should be sitting over a saucepan of barely simmering water, making sure the base of the bowl doesn't touch the water. Then, keeping the heat at its lowest, allow the chocolate to melt slowly – it should take about 3 minutes to melt and become smooth and glossy. Then remove it from the heat.

Now spoon the mascarpone and fromage frais into a large bowl and whisk them together until smooth, preferably with an electric hand whisk. Then add the eggs and sugar and give it another good whisking before adding the melted chocolate – use a rubber spatula so that you get every last bit of chocolate from the basin – and then lightly fold the chocolate into the egg mixture. Finally, add the raisins and toasted hazelnuts. Now pour the mixture into the tin, smoothing it out with the back of a spoon, then place it on the centre shelf of the oven and bake for $1^1/_4$ hours. After that, turn the oven off but leave the cheesecake inside until it's completely cold.

To make the chocolate curls, melt the chocolate in a heatproof bowl set over a saucepan of barely simmering water (make sure the base of the bowl doesn't touch the water). When the chocolate has melted, pour it on to a flat, smooth surface. It should be about 5mm ($^1/_4$ inch) thick. If you don't have a flat, smooth surface, the underside of a large plate will do. Leave the chocolate to set – what you want is for the chocolate to be set hard enough so that if you press the surface of the chocolate, it doesn't leave an indentation. If you use a plate, you can set the chocolate by placing it in the fridge to chill for 45 minutes.

Now use a cheese slicer to make the chocolate curls, or a knife will do if you hold the blade in both hands. Just pull it all along the chocolate towards you and it should curl up. What is very important to know here is that if it doesn't curl and you end up with a pile of chocolate shavings they'll look just as nice. Either way, place them in a rigid plastic container and then put this in the fridge until you need them.

To serve the cheesecake, sprinkle the surface with chocolate curls, dust with a sprinkling of cocoa powder and serve in slices, with crème fraîche or cream handed round separately.

# CHRIS STAINES

## Foliage

**Chris Staines began his career at the Michelin-starred Llangoed Hall in Wales. Training with Nico Ladenis and Marco Pierre White in their three-Michelin-starred restaurants followed, providing invaluable experience and tutelage. Currently head chef of Foliage restaurant in the Mandarin Oriental Hyde Park Hotel, London, he takes great pride in the produce that he uses, appreciating that the key to fabulous food rests in the quality of ingredients, working simply with the product and understanding how food combinations work.**

**What are your favourite foods/tastes/flavours?**

There are too many to name. The reason I became a chef was that I found the whole thing so fascinating. I learned to love the flavours, textures and smells of the kitchen, things as diverse as freshly baked bread, raw meat, freshly picked herbs, vanilla, the smell as you roast a piece of foie gras, the anticipation of braising oxtail.

Really anything that has 'kick ass' flavour.

**What are your favourite utensils?**

A set of sharp knives, without which nothing we do in the kitchen would be possible, and of course my tasting spoon, without which my job would not be half the pleasure and fun that it is!

**What is your most useful piece of equipment?**

An electric blender. How people got by without them, I can only guess. Things such as mousses, purées, soups and sauces take on a whole new life when made with a blender.

**What is your favourite season?**

It's a very difficult question for any chef who is passionate about what they do. For me, every season holds a new and completely different appeal, each as exciting as the last. I can only compare it to an artist being given different colours at different times of the year, only with food we get different colours, textures and flavours depending on the season: in spring, the abundance of green vegetables, fresh peas and salads; in summer, the reds of summer fruits; autumn brings the diversity of root vegetables and wild mushrooms; winter the rich reds and browns of the game season.

**What is your favourite meal?**

Breakfast: I won't lie, it has to be a good old-fashioned fry-up. The works – bacon, eggs, sausage, tomatoes, mushrooms, black pudding and, of course, fried bread, all with lashings of a well-known red sauce!

Lunch: something a little less heavy – fresh crusty bread with cheese, pickles, cured meats and salad and, of course, a nice glass of red wine to wash it all down.

Dinner: something simple, such as a nice steak (entrecôte for preference) with garlic and frites.

**How do you decide what to cook?**

The biggest influence on what I cook or put on the menu is the seasons. I think anyone who cooks for a living would be silly not to take advantage of the best produce at any given time of year. It makes a lot more sense to offer produce that is at its peak of quality, as you have less to do to it in order to get the best results. Unfortunately, due to intensive farming methods, the miniaturization of the global market and force growing, many ingredients are available all year round. The thing that suffers at the end of the day is the quality and flavour of the product, so you need to have a basic knowledge of what's good and when.

**What inspires you?**

Lots of things inspire me, whether it be a smell, a flavour, a picture or even the weather. But most of all I would say that

people inspire me both professionally and personally. When you see what some people have achieved against all the odds, it makes you think, 'Hold on, things aren't that bad after all ... get on with it.'

**What is your favourite drink?**
Stella Artois, Dom Perignon and red wine.

**What are your likes and dislikes?**
Likes: eating out, sunshine, good company.
Dislikes: rudeness, public transport, bad personal hygiene.

**How can you inspire others to enjoy great food and cooking?**
I would like to think that what I do on a daily basis has inspired at least one person, or at least given them pause for thought, by sourcing the best ingredients, showcasing the flavours and textures and presenting them in interesting and different ways. Also by reminding every one of my staff that this is FUN, that the reason we are working as chefs is because we enjoy it and that we shouldn't take it too seriously.

**How did you become a chef?**
I can clearly remember watching Michel and Albert Roux on television when I was younger and being spellbound not only by what they were doing but by their bickering and the obvious pleasure they derived from their work. I would try to recreate the things they cooked with my Mum. Then, years later, I got a job washing up in a local hotel and used to help the chefs preparing and serving the food for the restaurant. By this stage I was well and truly hooked.

**What are your top ten ingredients?**
In no particular order, fleur de sel, oil, herbs, butter, alcohol, gelatine, foie gras, water, love, sugar.

**What are your kitchen secrets?**

- There are no rules.
- Even when something goes wrong, pretend that is how it was meant to turn out.
- Always go for the best ingredients you can afford, as it's a lot easier to get a good result from a good-quality product.

**What are your top tips?**
Never be afraid to try something out and don't be too concerned if it goes wrong. Some of the greatest culinary triumphs, which endure as classics to this day, were accidents.

**Do you have any favourite junk food?**
Chips (French fries).

**How do you feel about cooking for children?**
I really don't have a problem cooking for children, and I believe that if you treat them with respect and are a bit careful, they will try anything you put in front of them. If they are taught to respect what they eat from an early age, then they will have a much better understanding of food, which can only be a good thing.

**Can you give one piece of advice for the domestic cook?**
Use recipes as mere guidelines. The more you cook, the more confident you will become and the more ideas you will have of your own. Don't be afraid, for example, to substitute one type of fish for another, or add more or less of something, or even add something that is not listed. It won't always work out but the more you experiment the more confident you will become. And if it doesn't work out, what the hell ... cooking is supposed to be fun!

* Warm Goat's Cheese and Tomato Tarts with Rocket and Aged Balsamic Dressing
* Slow-roast Belly of Pork with Yorkshire Pudding, Roast Potatoes and Shallot Purée
* Spicy Roast Pineapple with Vanilla Ice Cream and Black Pepper

# Warm Goat's Cheese and Tomato Tarts with Rocket and Aged Balsamic Dressing

**Serves 4**

**250g (9oz) puff pastry**
**100g (3½oz) rocket (arugula)**
**8 ripe tomatoes**
**100g (7 tablespoons) pesto**
**6 tablespoons olive oil**
**4 crottin de Chavignol cheeses, cut horizontally in half, or 8 slices from a goat's cheese log**
**12 basil leaves, torn**
**2 tablespoons aged balsamic vinegar**
**fleur de sel (sea salt) and freshly ground black pepper**

Roll out the puff pastry thinly, turning it frequently to maintain an even shape. Place on a greased and floured baking tray (or a tray covered with greaseproof or waxed paper) and leave in the fridge for 1 hour to rest.

In the meantime, pick any large stalks from the rocket, wash it under cold running water and set aside. Slice the tomatoes as thinly as possible, going from the top to the bottom.

Cut the puff pastry into 4 rectangles, about 12 x 8cm (5 x 3¼ inches), or whatever size and shape you like, and prick them evenly with a fork, which helps the pastry rise evenly and prevents air bubbles. Spread a liberal layer of pesto over the pastry bases, then arrange the tomatoes on top, leaving a 1cm (½-inch) border all round. Season well with fleur de sel and pepper, drizzle with 4 tablespoons of the olive oil and place in an oven preheated to 200°C/400°F/Gas Mark 6 for 10–12 minutes, until the pastry is golden brown and crisp. Place the goat's cheese on top and return briefly to the oven to soften (the idea is not to melt the cheese but just to heat it through slowly until soft).

Place the tarts on 4 plates and sprinkle a liberal amount of the rocket and torn basil over them. Whisk the balsamic vinegar with the remaining olive oil and some salt and pepper. Drizzle this dressing liberally over the salad and serve.

## Slow-roast Belly of Pork with Yorkshire Pudding, Roast Potatoes and Shallot Purée

**Serves 4**

**1kg (2 1/4lb) pork belly**
**100g (1/3 cup) fleur de sel (sea salt)**
**a handful of mixed thyme and rosemary sprigs**
**beef or bacon dripping**
**1kg (2 1/4lb) small shallots**
**4 large baking potatoes, peeled and cut into 2cm (3/4-inch) cubes**
**2 heads of garlic, broken into individual cloves**
**500g (18oz) button mushrooms, cut in half**
**salt and freshly ground black pepper**

For the Yorkshire pudding:

**2 eggs**
**150ml (2/3 cup) whole milk**
**3/4 teaspoon salt**
**85g (2/3 cup) plain (all-purpose) flour, sifted**

For the caramelized apples:

**caster (superfine) sugar for sprinkling**
**2 apples, cut in half**
**50g (3 1/2 tablespoons) butter**

About 24 hours before you want to serve the pork belly, cut it into 4 portions and cover liberally with the sea salt, thyme and rosemary. Cover and refrigerate.

The next day, wash off the salt and herbs and pat the pork belly dry. Heat some dripping in a frying pan (skillet) over a medium heat, add the pork belly and seal on all sides. Place skin-side down on a baking tray, place in an oven preheated to 140°C/275°F/Gas Mark 1 and cook for 2 hours. Remove from the oven and leave to rest in a warm place.

Meanwhile, peel the shallots and slice them roughly (they are easier to peel if you cover them with boiling water first). Heat some dripping in a heavy-based pan, add the shallots, season with salt and pepper and cook over a low heat, stirring occasionally, until the shallots colour lightly as the natural sugar starts to caramelize. When they are completely soft, purée in a food processor or with a hand-held blender and adjust the seasoning. Keep warm.

Heat some dripping in a large, ovenproof frying pan and add the potatoes. Cook, moving them around occasionally, until coloured on all sides, then add the unpeeled garlic cloves and cook for a further 2–3 minutes. Finally add the button mushrooms, season liberally with salt and pepper and place in an oven preheated to 180°C/350°F/Gas Mark 4. Cook for 20–30 minutes, until a knife inserted in the potatoes doesn't meet any resistance. Meanwhile, mix the eggs, milk, salt and some pepper together for the Yorkshire puddings. Leave to stand for 10 minutes, then whisk in the sifted flour. Put a generous amount of dripping in a 4-cup Yorkshire pudding tin (or use a 6-hole muffin pan, putting a few tablespoons water in the unfilled molds) and place in an oven preheated to 200°C/400°F/Gas Mark 6 for about 10 minutes, until the fat is smoking hot. Pour the pudding batter into the hot fat and return to the oven for 10–20 minutes, until golden, crisp and well risen.

For the apples, sprinkle a thin layer of caster sugar in a heavy-based frying pan and place over a fairly high heat. Add the apple halves, cut-side down, and cook until well coloured underneath, adding a touch of water if necessary to prevent burning. Turn and colour the other side, then add the butter and set aside. When the Yorkshire puddings are ready, place half an apple in each one.

Serve with the pork, roast potatoes and shallot purée.

# Spicy Roast Pineapple with Vanilla Ice Cream and Black Pepper

**Serves 4**

**600g (3 cups) caster (superfine) sugar**
**4 vanilla pods (vanilla beans)**
**2 bananas, sliced**
**1 dried chilli**
**90g (3oz) fresh ginger, chopped**
**$5^{1}/_{2}$ tablespoons dark rum**
**1 litre (1 quart) water**
**1 pineapple**
**vanilla ice cream, to serve**
**sprigs of mint, to decorate**
**freshly ground black pepper**

The syrup for the pineapple is best made 24 hours in advance to allow the flavours to infuse, but it can be made the same day if you don't have the time.

First place the sugar in a large, heavy-based pan over a medium heat and let it melt, stirring occasionally so it melts evenly. Continue to cook until it turns to a light brown caramel, or 165°C/329°F on a sugar (candy) thermometer. Slit the vanilla pods (vanilla beans) open lengthways, scrape out the seeds, and add both pods and seeds to the caramel. Then add the bananas, chilli and ginger, turn the heat down low and let the caramel penetrate these ingredients. Add the rum and water and bring back to the boil.

Ideally leave to cool, then refrigerate overnight. Blend in a liquidizer (blender), then strain through a sieve, leaving you with a smooth syrup.

Peel the pineapple and cut it into slices 1-1.5cm ($^{1}/_{2}$-$^{3}/_{4}$ inch) thick, trimming around the edges to give uniform circles. Cut out the hard centre using a small pastry cutter, then place the pineapple slices in a baking dish. Cover with the syrup and place in an oven preheated to 180°C/350°F/Gas Mark 4. Cook for 15-20 minutes, until the pineapple rings are soft, spooning the syrup over them occasionally to keep them moist. (The pineapple can be cooked in advance if you prefer, and then reheated gently.)

Place the pineapple rings on individual plates or a large platter. Put a scoop of ice cream on each pineapple ring and decorate with a sprig of mint. Turn the top of your pepper mill to the loosest setting and mill one even twist of pepper over each ball of ice cream. Drizzle a small amount of syrup over and around each pineapple ring and serve.

forty one

# RICK STEIN

## Seafood Restaurant

Somewhat misleadingly labelled a 'celebrity chef', Rick Stein runs four restaurants, a delicatessen, a pâtisserie, a seafood cookery school and a hotel in the small fishing port of Padstow, Cornwall. He has developed these over the last 30 years into a destination attraction, which means that the Seafood Restaurant is booked for many months in advance. He has attributed his success to a simple observation: 'Nothing is more exhilarating than fresh fish simply cooked'. Rick still lives in Padstow for part of the year, though he now has a house in Sydney, too.

**What are your favourite foods/tastes/flavours?**
Fish and shellfish/Asian.

**What are your favourite utensils?**
A good set of knives.

**What is your most useful piece of kitchen design and equipment?**
A good worktop with plenty of space, and a mortar and pestle.

**What is your favourite season?**
Summer.

**What is your favourite meal?**
Breakfast: wok-fried duck eggs with spring onions, chilli, coriander (cilantro) and oyster sauce.
Lunch: hake with butterbeans and sauce verte.
Tea: Darjeeling tea and cucumber sandwiches.
Dinner: grilled Dover sole and minted new potatoes.

**What is your favourite drink?**
White Burgundy.

**How do you decide what to cook?**
I go to the fish market.

**What inspires you?**
The sight of very fresh fish.

**What are your likes and dislikes?**
Likes – Australia.
Dislikes – questionnaires.

**How can you inspire others to enjoy great food and cooking?**
By having a tremendous enthusiasm for and love of cooking myself.

**How did you become a chef?**
I wanted a night club and it went wrong, so I ended up cooking by default.

**What are your top ten ingredients?**
Fish, shellfish, chilli, tarragon, fish sauce, coriander, soy sauce, garlic, ginger, olive oil.

**What are your kitchen secrets?**
Give yourself plenty of time.

**What are your top tips?**
Relax – cooking shouldn't be difficult and you should enjoy it.
Keep it simple.

**Do you have any favourite junk food?**
Australian meat pies with Roselle's tomato ketchup (catsup).

**How do you feel about cooking for children?**
Love it! They're so enthusiastic.

**Can you give one piece of advice for the domestic cook?**
Mistrust all recipes written by chefs.

* Marinated Tuna with Passion Fruit, Lime and Coriander
* Grilled John Dory Fillets on Aïoli Potatoes
* Banana Pavlovas with Custard and Cream

## Marinated Tuna with Passion Fruit, Lime and Coriander

**Chefs generally agree that tuna is best served extremely rare. Here I've taken the idea of the South American ceviche and added some Australian flavours, but not marinated the fish in the passion fruit and lime dressing for any more than 10 minutes. It makes a perfect first course but is also endlessly popular at drinks parties. And by the way, the more wrinkly the passion fruit, the more ripe and therefore juicy they will be.**

**Serves 4**

**a 3cm (1¼-inch) thick piece of tuna loin fillet, weighing about 400g (14oz)**

**2 small, ripe and wrinkly passion fruit, weighing about 35g (1½oz) each**
**1 tablespoon lime juice**
**3 tablespoons sunflower oil**
**1 medium-hot green chilli, deseeded and finely chopped**

**1 teaspoon caster (superfine) sugar**
**1½ tablespoons finely chopped coriander (cilantro)**
**½ teaspoon salt**
**5 turns of the black pepper mill**

Put the piece of tuna on a board and cut it across into very thin slices. Lay the slices, side by side but butted close up together, on four 25cm (10-inch) plates. Cover each one with cling film (plastic wrap) and set aside in the fridge for at least an hour or until you are ready to serve.

Shortly before serving, make the dressing. Cut the passion fruit in half and scoop the pulp into a sieve set over a bowl. Rub the pulp through the sieve to extract the juice, then discard the seeds. There should be about 1 tablespoon of juice. Stir in the lime juice, sunflower oil, green chilli, sugar, coriander, salt and pepper.

To serve, uncover the tuna, spoon over the dressing and spread it over the fish with the back of the spoon. Leave for 10 minutes before serving.

# Grilled John Dory Fillets on Aïoli Potatoes

**I've chosen to grill the John Dory, one of my favourite fish, because frying it would add more oil to the delicious aïoli potatoes. This is an example of what I would call simple fish cookery. Too often with restaurant cooking, I find there's just too much going on on the plate with delicate fish like John Dory.**

**May I suggest a chilled bottle of Domaine de Tempiers Bandol Rosé to go with this? Not easy to find but well worth the effort. The recipe for the aïoli will make more than you need here but it is difficult to prepare in smaller quantities. Store in a screw-top jar in the fridge and use within 1 week.**

**Serves 4**

**500g (18oz) new potatoes, such as Jersey Royals or Belle de Fontenay, scraped clean**
**4 x 150–175g (5–6oz) fillets of John Dory**
**a little olive oil for brushing**
**1 tablespoon chopped flat-leaf parsley**
**salt and freshly ground black pepper**

**For the aïoli:**
**4 garlic cloves, peeled**
**1/2 teaspoon salt**
**1 medium (large) egg yolk**
**2 teaspoons lemon juice**
**180ml (3/4 cup) extra virgin olive oil**

**For the salad:**
**1 teaspoon white wine vinegar**
**1/4 teaspoon Dijon mustard**
**a good pinch of caster (superfine) sugar**
**4 teaspoons extra virgin olive oil**
**50g (2oz) curly endive (frisée)**

First make the aïoli. Put the garlic cloves on a chopping board and crush them under the blade of a large knife. Sprinkle them with the salt and then work with the knife blade into a smooth paste. Transfer the paste to a bowl, add the egg yolk and lemon juice and whisk everything together. Very gradually whisk in the olive oil to make a thick, mayonnaise-like mixture.

For the salad, whisk together the vinegar, mustard and sugar and then slowly whisk in the olive oil. Season to taste with salt and pepper and set aside.

Put the potatoes into a pan of well-salted cold water (i. e. 1 teaspoon of salt per 600ml (2 1/2 cups) water), bring to the boil and cook for 12–15 minutes, until just tender. Drain, return them to the pan, cover and keep warm.

Preheat the grill (broiler) to high. Brush the John Dory fillets on both sides with olive oil and season lightly with salt and pepper. Place them skin-side up on a lightly oiled grilling tray or the rack of the grill pan. Grill the John Dory for 5–6 minutes, until just cooked through.

Meanwhile, thickly slice the potatoes into a bowl and stir in 3 tablespoons of the aïoli, the chopped parsley and some seasoning to taste. Toss the curly endive with enough of the salad dressing to coat all the leaves lightly.

Put the fish on 4 warmed plates and serve with the aïoli potatoes and salad.

# Banana Pavlovas with Custard and Cream

**I've always loved banana custard so I just had to combine it with the other sweet I enjoy enormously, pavlova. This complements the tuna and John Dory perfectly for a light meal with an Australian feel.**

**Serves 4**

**3 egg whites**
**a small pinch of salt**
**175g (3/4 cup plus 2 tablespoons) caster (superfine) sugar**
**1 teaspoon cornflour (cornstarch)**
**1/2 teaspoon white wine vinegar**

**To serve:**
**2 ripe passion fruit**
**2 small, ripe but firm bananas**
**8 tablespoons thick custard or crème anglaise**
**8 tablespoons extra thick double (heavy) cream**

Line a baking sheet with baking parchment paper. In a large bowl, whisk the egg whites with the pinch of salt until they form stiff peaks. Gradually whisk in the sugar to make a very stiff and shiny meringue. Whisk in the cornflour and vinegar.

Drop 4 large spoonfuls of the mixture on to the lined baking sheet, spread each one into a 10cm (4-inch) round and then make a slight dip in the centre with the back of a spoon. Bake in an oven preheated to 140°C/275°F/Gas Mark 1 for 45 minutes or until pale in colour and marshmallow-like in the centre. Turn off the oven, leave the door ajar and leave them to cool.

To serve, halve the passion fruit and scoop out the pulp with a teaspoon. Peel and slice the bananas and fold them into the custard. Put the mixture in the centre of each pavlova and spoon the cream on top. Spoon the passion fruit pulp over the cream and serve within 5 minutes.

# forty two

# NORIYUKI SUGIE

Asiate

Nori's introduction to the culinary world began at an American-style restaurant in Tokyo, when he was a fifteen-year-old guitarist in a rock band. When culinary arts eclipsed music as his passion, he joined the prestigious Tsuji Culinary School in Osaka and continued his studies at Château de l'Eclair. He honed his talents at three Michelin-starred restaurants in France, opened his own restaurant in Australia, and then moved to Chicago as Charlie Trotter's chef de partie. In December 2003 Nori made his New York debut as chef de cuisine of Asiate, in the new Mandarin Oriental Hotel. He has since become one of Gotham's hottest chefs, delighting guests with his distinctive French- and Japanese-influenced cuisine.

**What are your favourite foods/tastes/flavours?**
Asian foods with clean tastes and simplicity of flavour.

**What is your favourite utensil?**
A long spoon for its versatility.

**What is your most essential piece of kitchen equipment?**
A steamer.

**What is your favourite season?**
Autumn, because of the quality and abundance of the foods available.

**What is your favourite meal?**
Breakfast: pain au chocolat, croissants, yoghurt and coffee.
Lunch: Japanese noodles.
Dinner: Rice hotpots, sushi, crudo.

**How do you decide what to cook?**
At home, I always incorporate vegetables in my cooking, and choose the meat and cooking method to match my mood.

**What inspires you?**
Images – the visual impact of contrasting colours and balance of space are my first inspiration in creating new dishes.

**What is your favourite drink?**
Burgundian wines.

**What are your likes and dislikes?**
Likes – liquids such as soup.
Dislikes – too much spice.

**How can you inspire others to enjoy great food and cooking?**
I try to inspire others by creating exciting dishes that make a statement. From the moment it's conceived, to the presentation on the table, to the very last bite, my aim is to delight the senses and imagination.

**How did you become a chef/cookery writer?**
Writing a cookbook was a natural step for me to take as I strive to emulate the chefs who have taught me.

**What are your top ten ingredients?**
Seasonal vegetables, soy sauce, seafood, sake, pork, mirin, extra virgin olive oil, fish sauce, potatoes, dashi.

**What are your kitchen secrets?**
Slow cooking overnight for the most tender and flavourful meats.

**What are your top tips?**
Always taste the food you make throughout the entire cooking process.

**Do you have any favourite junk food?**
Instant noodles.

**How do you feel about cooking for children?**
I really enjoy cooking for children, especially since I feel it's very important to share the expansive world of different flavours and textures with them.

**Can you give one piece of advice for the domestic cook?**
The most important thing to remember is balance. Not only should good food taste great in your mouth but it should also excite your mind and be good for your body.

* Sake-steamed Clams with Chorizo and Asian spices
* Rice Hotpot with Salmon, Caviar and Nori
* Peach Crêpes en Papillote with Star-anise-infused Maple Syrup

# Sake-steamed Clams with Chorizo and Asian spices

**Serves 4**

**2kg ($4^1/_2$lb) carpet-shell clams (*palourdes*)**
**40g ($1^1/_2$-oz) piece of chorizo sausage, cut into slices 1cm ($^1/_2$ inch) thick**
**400ml ($1^3/_4$ cups) sake**
**250ml (1 cups) water**
**2 lemongrass sticks, bruised and cut into 3cm ($1^1/_4$-inch) lengths**
**2 tablespoons finely shredded fresh ginger**
**1 bunch of spring onions (scallions), cut into 3cm ($1^1/_4$-inch) lengths**
**120g (1 stick) butter**
**2 tablespoons finely shredded red chillies**
**4 limes**
**4 tablespoons coriander (cilantro) leaves**
**2 tablespoons Thai basil leaves**

Wash the clams under cold running water until the water runs clear. Discard any open ones that do not close when tapped lightly.

Sauté the chorizo in a large pan over a medium heat for a few minutes. Add the sake, water, lemongrass and ginger and bring to the boil. Add the clams, spring onions and butter, then cover and cook, shaking the pan occasionally, for 2–3 minutes, until the clam shells open.

Arrange the clams in the centre of 4 deep plates and spoon the chorizo and sake juice around them. Sprinkle the shredded chillies over the plates and squeeze over the lime juice. Garnish with the coriander and basil leaves and serve.

# Rice Hotpot with Salmon, Caviar and Nori

**Serves 4**

**720g (3$^2/_3$ cups) Japanese rice**
**360ml (1$^1/_2$ cups) water**
**200ml (7oz) soy sauce**
**2 tablespoons dashi powder**
**360g (12oz) salmon fillet, cut into 12 pieces, about 5 x 3cm (2 x 1$^1/_4$ inches)**
**4 tablespoons salmon roe caviar**
**4 shiso leaves, cut into thin strips**
**2 sheets of nori, cut into thin strips**
**2 tablespoons chopped chives**
**2 tablespoons white sesame seeds**
**4 egg yolks**

Wash the rice under cold running water until the water runs clear, then set aside. Combine the water and soy sauce in a casserole and bring to a simmer. Add the dashi powder, then remove from the heat and cool to room temperature.

Add the rice to the liquid and bring to the boil. Remove from the heat and arrange the salmon pieces on top of the rice. Cover the pan and place in an oven preheated to 220°C/425°F/Gas Mark 7 for 15–20 minutes, until the rice is cooked.

Divide between 4 plates, spoon the salmon roe on top of each piece of salmon and sprinkle the shiso leaves, nori, chives and white sesame seeds on top. Place an egg yolk in the centre of each portion, between the 3 salmon pieces, then serve.

# Peach Crêpes en Papillote with Star-anise-infused Maple Syrup

**Serves 4**

**4 peaches**
**1 tablespoon maple syrup**
**8 star anise**
**4 cinnamon sticks**
**3 vanilla pods (vanilla beans)**
**zest of 1 orange**
**a handful of roasted almonds**

For the crêpes:
**75g (1/2 cup) plain (all-purpose) flour**
**1 1/2 teaspoons sugar**
**1/2 teaspoon salt**
**200ml (7oz) milk**
**1 egg**
**1 egg yolk**
**1 tablespoon beer**
**25g (2 tablespoons) butter, melted**

Stone (pit) the peaches and slice them into eighths. Put the peach slices in a saucepan with the maple syrup, star anise, cinnamon sticks, vanilla pods and orange zest. Cook over a medium heat until the peach slices are tender.

To make the crêpes, sift the flour, sugar and salt into a bowl. Mix together the milk, egg, egg yolk and beer. Gradually whisk this mixture into the flour until just incorporated.

Place a crêpe pan or non-stick frying pan (skillet) over a medium heat and brush with a little of the melted butter. Use the batter to make 4 thin crêpes, brushing the pan with more butter as necessary.

Place 4 peach slices in each crêpe, then fold in the sides and roll up. Place each filled crêpe in the centre of a sheet of baking parchment. Arrange the remaining peach slices, vanilla pods, star anise, orange zest and roasted almonds around each crêpe, then tie or twist together the ends of the baking parchment to make a closed bundle. Place in an oven preheated to 180°C/350°F/Gas Mark 4 for about 8 minutes, until the paper is golden brown. Cut each parcel open at the table to serve.

# forty three

# CHARLIE TROTTER

## Charlie Trotter

Charlie Trotter's is regarded as one of the finest restaurants in the world. Since its inception in 1987, it has dedicated itself to excellence in the culinary arts and has received numerous awards. Charlie Trotter was given an award at the White House by President Bush and Colin Powell for his work with the Charlie Trotter Culinary Education Foundation, and was named one of only five 'heroes' to be honoured by Colin Powell's charity, America's Promise. In 2004 he received the Humanitarian of the Year award from the International Association of Culinary Professionals.

**What are your favourite foods/tastes/flavours?**
A favourite I don't have ... how can I? I am obsessed with all foods. But anything in season, prepared simply and served amongst friends – you can't beat that.

**What are your favourite utensils?**
A perfectly honed knife, a brand new S peeler, a well-used mortar and pestle, a hand blender and a wasabi grater – to name a few.

**What is your most useful piece of kitchen equipment?**
A kyrovac machine for sous-vide. It also aids us when we travel to do charity dinners out of state. We take all the food with us (including the salt!) and pack it neatly in the kyrovac bags. It makes preparing a ten-course dégustation menu quite feasible on the road.

**What is your favourite season?**
Spring. It gets my mouth watering for fiddlehead ferns, morel mushrooms and ramps [wild leeks]. It is the time of year when the soil is exploding with young vegetables.

**What is your favourite mealtime?**
I would say the time between lunch and dinner. This is when I get to sit down with my son, Dylan, and enjoy a great after-school snack.

**How do you decide what to cook?**
By looking at what ingredients are available. If you start with fresh, pristine, organic foodstuffs, you are already on your way to creating something truly spectacular.

**What inspires you?**
Music, literature, family and true love.

**What is your favourite drink?**
It depends on the time of day and what I am doing. If I have just finished a ten-mile run along the lake, an icy-cold Lemon-Lime Gatorade hits the spot, but if it is the end of a night's service, I may reach for a glass of La Landonne.

**What are your likes and dislikes?**
I dislike laziness, people who don't recycle, dishonesty, and simpleminded thinkers. I love being challenged intellectually, thinking way outside the box, and pleasing others, but above all else I love my son and my mother.

**How can you inspire others to enjoy great food and cooking?**
By showing them how gratifying it is to explore cooking. My favourite memories are of conversations that occurred around the dinner table with people who are important in my life. Everyone should have memories like that.

Restaurant Magazine/Laurie Fletcher

**How did you become a chef?**
I loved cooking for my roommates in college, and it all just evolved from there. You could say I got a late start, but once I found my passion there was no stopping me. I am still at my happiest in the kitchen.

**What are your top ten ingredients?**
Yuzu citron juice, Alba white truffles, Mani extra virgin olive oil, duck eggs, Velvet Rose Cheese from Sweet Grass Farms, Giuseppe Giusti balsamic vinegar (they have been making it for over 500 years), Brandywine or red and yellow currant heirloom tomatoes (especially when they are incredibly ripe), ramps, veal cheeks, kaffir lime leaves.

**What are your kitchen secrets?**
I really don't have any kitchen secrets; I love to share everything I know with others. But I guess one thing that not all chefs have is the amazing team of fifty-five totally dedicated members of staff that I have on my side. They are the secret to my success!

**What are your top tips?**
Chop your herbs at the very last second. This will release their aromatic oils, allowing them to explode with flavour.
Taste and season your food several times throughout the cooking process. It just kills me when I see young cooks not tasting the food they are preparing. You have to taste a sauce several times throughout the evening. It is not the sauce you began with, it is constantly changing.

**Do you have any favourite junk food?**
Gummy Bears.

**How do you feel about cooking for children?**
Love it, as long as it isn't Mac and Cheese from a box. But seriously, kids love to cook and explore in the kitchen. My thirteen-year-old son can make a pretty serious maki roll!

**Can you give one piece of advice for the domestic cook?**
Be organized and do as much prep as you can in advance. That way, you can be relaxed and ready when your guests arrive.

* Yukon Gold Potato Soup with Poached Oysters and Crispy Potatoes
* Buttermilk-poached Pheasant Breasts with Blue Hubbard Squash–strewn Quinoa
* Crêpes with Explorateur Cheese and Red Wine Dates

## Yukon Gold Potato Soup with Poached Oysters and Crispy Potatoes

**Serves 4**

**6 small Yukon Gold potatoes, or other waxy potatoes, peeled and diced**
**1 litre (1 quart) water**
**1 bay leaf**
**125ml (1/2 cup) crème fraîche**
**juice of 1/2 lemon**
**salt and freshly ground black pepper**

For the garnish:

**100g (1 cup) bacon lardons**
**1 leek, cut into 5mm (1/4-inch) rings**
**1 garlic clove, crushed**
**1 tablespoon chopped parsley**
**2 tablespoons chopped herbs**

For the poached oysters:

**24 small oysters, shucked, juices reserved and strained**
**3 tablespoons lemon juice**
**1 tablespoon chopped parsley**
**1 tablespoon grated lemon zest**
**2 tablespoons finely diced shallot**
**125ml (1/2 cup) extra virgin olive oil**

For the crispy potatoes:

**1 small baking potato, peeled and cut into fine strips**
**2 tablespoons plain (all-purpose) flour**
**250ml (1 cup) grapeseed oil**

To prepare the soup, put the potatoes, water and bay leaf in a large saucepan and season with salt. Bring to a simmer and cook for about 10 minutes, until the potatoes are tender. Remove the bay leaf and purée the potatoes and water in a food processor until smooth. Whisk in the crème fraîche and lemon juice.

To prepare the garnish, cook the bacon lardons in a sauté pan over a medium heat for about 5 minutes, until the fat runs. Add the leek and garlic and cook for about 5 minutes longer, until the leek is tender and the bacon is crisp. Add the parsley and season with pepper.

To prepare the oysters, place the strained oyster juices in a saucepan and add the oysters. Leave over a medium heat until the oysters are just warm and beginning to firm up. Remove the oysters from the liquid. Whisk the lemon juice, parsley, lemon zest, shallot and olive oil into the oyster juice, then season to taste with salt and pepper. Return the oysters to the saucepan and reheat just before serving, if necessary.

To prepare the crispy potatoes, lightly dredge the potato in the flour and season with salt and pepper. Shape the potato into small discs, 5cm (2 inches) in diameter. Heat the grapeseed oil in a sauté pan, add the potatoes and fry for 3-4 minutes on each side, until golden brown and crisp. Transfer the potato discs to kitchen paper towels and blot. Season with salt. Select the 4 best discs and set aside; reserve any leftover ones for snacking.

To serve, season the soup to taste with salt and pepper and warm over a medium heat. Divide the bacon mixture between 4 shallow soup bowls and carefully balance a crispy potato disc on top. Arrange 2 of the oysters on top of the potato and 4 more in the bowl. Ladle the soup around the oysters, being careful not to cover the crispy potato, then sprinkle with the chopped herbs.

# Buttermilk-poached Pheasant Breasts with Blue Hubbard Squash–strewn Quinoa

**Serves 4**

**2 pheasant breasts, skinned**
**1 garlic clove, crushed**
**1 bay leaf**
**3 sprigs of thyme**
**450ml (2 cups) buttermilk**
**1 tablespoon extra virgin olive oil**
**1 tablespoon chopped micro tatsoi sprouts or flat-leaf parsley**
**salt and freshly ground black pepper**

For the spiced pepitas:

**100g (3/4 cup) pepitas (pumpkinseeds)**
**1/4 teaspoon chilli powder**
**1/4 teaspoon Hungarian sweet paprika**
**1 teaspoon sugar**
**1 1/2 tablespoons extra virgin olive oil**

For the squash:

**1 blue Hubbard squash, halved, deseeded and cut into 2.5cm (1-inch) wedges**
**25g (2 tablespoons) butter**
**1/2 teaspoon chilli powder**
**1 teaspoon thyme leaves**
**350ml (1 1/2 cups) vegetable stock or water**

For the quinoa:

**2 teaspoons extra virgin olive oil**
**1 teaspoon finely chopped fresh ginger**
**40g (1/4 cup) shallots, very finely diced**
**350g (2 cups) cooked quinoa**
**4 tablespoons chopped dried sweet cherries**
**2 tablespoons chopped chives**
**1 tablespoon pumpkinseed oil**
**1 tablespoon balsamic vinegar**

To garnish:

**4 teaspoons pumpkinseed oil**
**2 tablespoons micro tatsoi sprouts or chopped herbs**

To prepare the pepitas, combine the pumpkinseeds, chilli powder, paprika, sugar and olive oil in a bowl and season with salt and pepper. Spread them out on a baking sheet lined with baking parchment and bake in an oven preheated to 200°C/400°F/Gas Mark 6 for 7 minutes or until toasted. Set aside.

To prepare the squash, place it in a large sauté pan with the butter and cook over a medium heat for 10 minutes. Add the chilli powder and thyme and continue to cook for about 5 minutes, until the squash is caramelized and tender. Set aside about 40 squash wedges. Purée the remaining squash in a blender with the stock or water until smooth, then pass through a fine sieve. Warm the squash purée in a small saucepan and season to taste with salt and pepper.

To prepare the pheasant, place the pheasant breasts, garlic, bay leaf, thyme and buttermilk in a shallow saucepan and bring to a slow simmer. Simmer for 20 minutes or until the pheasant is just cooked through. Remove the pheasant from the buttermilk and let it rest for 3 minutes, then cut it into slices about 8mm (1/3 inch) thick. Gently toss the slices with the olive oil and chopped tatsoi sprouts or parsley, then season to taste with salt and pepper.

To prepare the quinoa, place the olive oil, ginger and shallots in a sauté pan and cook over a medium heat for about 5 minutes, until the shallots are translucent. Add the quinoa, cherries, about two-thirds of the spiced pepitas and half the reserved squash wedges. Mix well, then add the chives, pumpkinseed oil and balsamic vinegar. Season to taste with salt and pepper.
To serve, reheat the reserved squash wedges, if necessary. Put the quinoa mixture in the centre of 4 serving plates and arrange the sliced pheasant on top. Spoon the squash purée around the quinoa and arrange the reserved squash wedges around the sauce. Sprinkle the remaining pepitas around the plate and drizzle the pumpkinseed oil around the squash purée. Garnish with the micro tatsoi sprouts or chopped herbs.

# Crêpes with Explorateur Cheese and Red Wine Dates

**Serves 4**

**245g ($1^{3}/_{4}$ cups) plain (pastry) flour**
**1 tablespoon sugar**
**$^{1}/_{2}$ teaspoon salt**
**450ml (2 cups) milk**
**5 medium (large) eggs**
**5 tablespoons melted butter**
**4 tablespoons clarified butter**
**225g (8oz) Explorateur cheese, rind removed, cut into 8 pieces, 7.5cm x 1cm x 5mm (3 x $^{1}/_{2}$ x $^{1}/_{4}$ inches)**

For the dried fruit sauce:

**2 tablespoons sugar**
**2 teaspoons water**
**15g (1 tablespoon) butter**
**35g ($^{1}/_{3}$ cup) almonds, sliced**
**1 tablespoon currants**
**1 tablespoon chopped dried sweet cherries**
**1 tablespoon chopped dried cranberries**
**125ml ($^{1}/_{2}$ cup) Red Wine Reduction (see Note below)**
**$^{1}/_{2}$ teaspoon freshly ground black pepper**

For the red wine dates:

**12 dates, pitted and chopped**
**125ml ($^{1}/_{2}$ cup) Red Wine Reduction (see Note below)**
**2 teaspoons chopped rosemary**

For the almond sauce:

**70g ($^{1}/_{2}$ cup) almonds, soaked in water overnight and then drained**
**125ml ($^{1}/_{2}$ cup) water**
**1 tablespoon extra virgin olive oil**
**1 teaspoon sugar**
**salt and freshly ground black pepper**

To garnish:

**4 teaspoons extra virgin olive oil**
**1 tablespoon 2.5cm (1 inch) long pieces of chive, cut on the diagonal**
**2 teaspoons rosemary leaves**
**freshly ground black pepper**

To prepare the dried fruit sauce, combine the sugar and water in a small, heavy-based sauté pan and cook over a medium heat without stirring for 5-8 minutes, until it becomes a golden brown caramel. Swirl the pan as necessary to distribute the caramel. Add the butter and almonds and cook for 2 minutes, stirring to combine. Add the dried fruits, wine reduction and pepper and stir well, then set aside.

To prepare the dates, place the dates, wine reduction and rosemary in a saucepan and cook over a medium-low heat for 5 minutes, until the flavours have combined. Set aside.

For the almond sauce, purée the almonds, water, olive oil and sugar in a blender until smooth, then season to taste with salt and pepper. Warm over a medium heat just before serving.
To make the crêpes, put the flour, sugar, salt, milk, eggs and melted butter in a mixing bowl and mix thoroughly with a whisk. Heat a crêpe pan over a medium-high heat and brush it with just enough of the clarified butter to coat the base. Using a ladle, add 60ml (4 tablespoons) of the batter to the pan and cook the crêpe for 2 minutes or until the edges begin to harden. Carefully flip the crêpe over and cook for 30 seconds on the other side. Remove the crêpe from the pan and lay it flat on a baking sheet. Repeat with the remaining clarified butter and crêpe batter to make 8 crêpes all together. Put a piece of cheese in each one, then roll the crêpe up and trim the edges. Just before serving, warm the crêpes in an oven preheated to 180°C/350°F/Gas Mark 4 for 2 minutes.

To serve, spoon some of the almond sauce in the centre of each plate and place 2 crêpes, one overlapping the other, on top. Place a spoonful of the date mixture in front of the crêpes and spoon the dried fruit sauce around the plate. Drizzle the olive oil around the crêpes and sprinkle with the chives and rosemary. Top with some freshly ground black pepper.

**Note**

For the Red Wine Reduction, chop 175g (1 cup) Spanish onion, 75g ($^{1}/_{2}$ cup) carrot and 1 leek (white part only). Place in a large saucepan with 1 tablespoon of grapeseed oil and sauté over a high heat for 10 minutes, until golden brown and caramelized. Add 1 chopped Granny Smith apple, 1.5 litres (6 cups) Merlot wine and 750ml (3 cups) port and simmer, uncovered, over a medium heat for 1 hour. Strain through a fine sieve and return to the saucepan. Simmer for 30-40 minutes or until reduced in volume to 250ml (1 cup). The reduction will keep in the refrigerator for 4 days or in the freezer for 2 months.

**Opposite: Top, Buttermilk-poached Pheasant Breasts with Blue Hubbard Squash-strewn Quinoa; bottom, Crêpes with Explorateur Cheese and Red Wine Dates**

# forty four

# BRIAN TURNER

## Brian Turner Mayfair

Brian Turner can only be characterised as a typical no-nonsense Yorkshireman. During the heyday of the great hotels, he trained at the Savoy and Claridges in London and the Beau Rivage in Lausanne, Switzerland. In the early 1970s he was awarded a Michelin star at the Capital Hotel in London. In 1986 he opened his first restaurant, Turner's of Walton Street, to critical acclaim. Having been awarded a CBE, Brian Turner now concentrates on the training of young people for the industry, in addition to his restaurant and thriving television career.

**What are your favourite foods/tastes/flavours?**
Seasonal, fresh and simple – roast meats, perhaps.

**What are your favourite utensils?**
A chopping board and a large knife.

**What is your favourite season?**
Winter.

**What is your favourite mealtime?**
The next meal – whichever that may be!

**How do you decide what to cook?**
Whatever looks good when deliveries arrive.

**What inspires you?**
Eating.

**What is your favourite drink?**
Perrier Jouet Vintage Champagne.

**What are your likes and dislikes?**
I love chips (french fries) and I hate tripe.

**How can you inspire others to enjoy great food and cooking?**
By example and by eating together.

**How did you become a chef?**
I was inspired by my father.

**Do you have any favourite junk food?**
A burger and a pie on Chelsea Bridge!

**How do you feel about cooking for children?**
Love it.

**Can you give one piece of advice for the domestic cook?**
Think simple and be organized.

GUINNESS GRANDSTAND
VILLAGE
GUINNESS
GUINNESS
GUINNESS

* Cushions of Smoked Salmon with Cockle and Parsley Dressing
* Yorkshire Hotpot
* Breakfast Bread and Butter Pudding

## Cushions of Smoked Salmon with Cockle and Parsley Dressing

**Serves 4**

**175g (6oz) cooked fresh salmon**
**2 tablespoons crème fraîche**
**2 tablespoons mayonnaise**
**2 shallots, finely chopped**
**2 tablespoons chopped chives**
**1 tablespoon vinaigrette**
**1 tablespoon chopped spring onions (scallions)**
**4 large slices of smoked salmon**
**a little oil for brushing**
**salt and freshly ground black pepper**

For the cockle and parsley dressing:

**100g (3 1/2oz) cooked cockles**
**1/2 teaspoon Dijon mustard**
**1 tablespoon white wine vinegar**
**4 tablespoons olive oil**
**2 tablespoons chopped parsley**
**1/2 garlic clove, crushed**
**1 tablespoon finely diced skinned tomato**

Flake the cooked salmon into a bowl but do not break it up too much. Mix in the crème fraîche, mayonnaise, shallots, chives, vinaigrette, spring onions and some salt and pepper. Leave to stand for 10 minutes.

Lay each slice of smoked salmon on a separate piece of cling film (plastic wrap). Spoon the fresh salmon mixture into the centre of each piece. Pull in the sides of the smoked salmon to enclose the filling, then use the cling film to shape it into a ball. Push each one into a 5cm (2-inch) ring, joins uppermost, and put in the fridge to chill.

To make the dressing, mix together the cockles and mustard, then stir in the white wine vinegar. Add the olive oil, parsley, garlic and tomato and mix well, then season to taste.

Carefully take out the salmon from the rings, unwrap and turn each one over on to a serving plate. Pour the sauce around, brush the smoked salmon with a little oil and serve.

# Yorkshire Hotpot

**Serves 4**

**175g ($^3/_4$ cup) duck fat or dripping**
**1 small shoulder of lamb, boned and rolled**
**2 heads of garlic, cut in half**
**2 sprigs of rosemary**
**100g (7 tablespoons) butter**
**225g ($1^1/_2$ cups) carrots, sliced**
**2 large onions, thinly sliced**
**1 tablespoon vegetable oil**
**4 tablespoons thick lamb gravy**
**500g (18oz) small, waxy new potatoes, skin on**
**salt and freshly ground black pepper**

Heat the duck fat or dripping in a large frying pan (skillet), add the lamb and sear on all sides. Transfer the meat to a roasting tin (pan) and add the garlic and rosemary. Place in an oven preheated to 220°C/425°F/Gas Mark 7 and roast for 20 minutes. Reduce the oven temperature to 160°C/325°F/Gas Mark 3 and cook for at least 2 hours, until the lamb is well done and very tender. Remove from the roasting tin and leave to drain.

Meanwhile, melt half the butter in a pan, add the carrots and some seasoning, then cover and cook slowly until tender. In a separate pan, gently stew the onions in the oil for 30 minutes. Drain off any excess oil and add the gravy. Bring to the boil, then remove from the heat and set aside.

Slice the potatoes very thinly, using a sharp knife or a mandoline. Melt the remaining butter in a frying pan, add the potatoes and stew slowly for 3 minutes. Remove from the heat and set aside.

Remove excess fat from the lamb and separate the meat, keeping it nice and chunky where possible. Take a 15–20cm (6–8-inch) mould, such as a cake tin (pan), about 6cm ($2^1/_4$ inch) deep, and brush the base and sides with duck fat or dripping. Arrange a layer of overlapping potato slices in the base, then another. Add a layer of onions and then a layer of carrots. Mix the remaining onions with the meat, season with salt and pepper, then fill up the mould with the mixture, packing it in tightly. Place in an oven preheated to 200°C/400°F/Gas Mark 6 and cook for about 45 minutes, until thoroughly heated through. Turn the hotpot out carefully on to a plate and serve with purple sprouting broccoli or chunky spring cabbage.

# Breakfast Bread and Butter Pudding

**Serves 4**

**6 one-day-old croissants**
**100g (7 tablespoons) unsalted butter**
**175g (generous 1 cup) Californian raisins**
**100g ($^{1}/_{3}$ cup) apricot jam**
**150ml ($^{2}/_{3}$ cup) milk**
**450ml (2 cups) double (heavy) cream**
**1 vanilla pod (vanilla bean), slit open lengthways**
**2 eggs**
**4 egg yolks**
**50g ($3^{1}/_{2}$ tablespoons) unrefined caster (superfine) sugar**
**icing (confectioners') sugar for dusting**

Slice the croissants horizontally in half and spread generously with 75g (5 tablespoons) of the butter. Grease a large ovenproof dish with the rest of the butter and arrange half the croissants in it. Cover with the raisins and apricot jam, then lay the rest of the croissants on top.

Put the milk, cream and vanilla pod into a saucepan and bring to the boil. In a large bowl, whisk the eggs, egg yolks and caster sugar together. Let the boiled cream cool a little, then pour it on to the egg mixture, stirring all the time. Strain this mixture over the croissants and leave to stand for 15 minutes. Sprinkle with icing sugar and bake in an oven preheated to 180°C/350°F/ Gas Mark 4 for 30 minutes. Remove from the oven and leave to stand for a few minutes, then dust with more icing sugar and serve.

# forty five

# JEAN-GEORGES VONGERICHTEN

## Jean-Georges

Internationally renowned for his innovative cuisine, Jean-Georges Vongerichten has emerged as one of America's leading chefs. He introduced us to his 'vibrant and sparse cuisine', whose intense flavours and satisfying textures are created by eschewing traditional meat stocks for vegetable juices and fruit essences, light broths and herbal vinaigrettes. When he spent five years in Asia, he developed his love for the exotic and aromatic flavours of the East, something that is prevalent on the menus of all his restaurants. Currently he owns and runs eight restaurants in New York City and collaborates on ten other restaurants around the world.

**What are your favourite foods/tastes/flavours?**
Asian food, yummy-tasting, contrasting flavours.

**What are your favourite utensils?**
A great knife, a Japanese mandoline and a microplane grater.

**What is your most useful piece of kitchen design and equipment?**
Clean lines and great materials. A Vitamix blender.

**What is your favourite season?**
All four, but I have different cravings for each one.

**What is your favourite mealtime?**
Breakfast.

**How do you decide what to cook?**
Whatever I see that excites me.

**What inspires you?**
The whole world.

**What is your favourite drink?**
Anything with ginger and lime.

**What are your likes and dislikes?**
I don't like people who dislike before they even try to like.

**How can you inspire others to enjoy great food and cooking?**
By travelling and bringing back new flavours and combinations.

**How did you become a chef?**
By getting excited and inspired in my grandmother's and my mother's kitchen.

**What are your top ten ingredients?**
Ginger, chilli, lemongrass, truffles, caviar, berries, cardamom, Thai basil, all seafood and any vegetable.

**What are your kitchen secrets?**
Don't prep; keep it fresh.

**What are your top tips?**
Season with your senses.

**Do you have any favourite junk food?**
Any type of chocolate.

**How do you feel about cooking for children?**
I love it. They are fun and tell you the truth.

**Can you give one piece of advice for the domestic cook?**
Take the 'it's only food' approach, and cook with the seasons.

* Ribbons of Tuna with Avocado, Spicy Radish and Ginger Marinade
* Sirloin Steak Topped with Gingered Mushrooms and Soy Caramel Emulsion
* Gingered Crème Brûlée

## Ribbons of Tuna with Avocado, Spicy Radish and Ginger Marinade

**Serves 4**

**350g (12oz) very fresh tuna fillet**
**1 shallot, very finely diced**
**1 Thai chilli, very finely diced**
**8 tablespoons olive oil**
**2 ripe avocados, peeled, stoned and finely diced**
**juice of 1 lime**
**6 radishes, sliced 5mm (1/4 inch) thick and kept in iced water**
**chilli oil, to taste**
**salt**

**For the ginger marinade:**
**2 tablespoons lime juice**
**25g (2 tablespoons) caster (superfine) sugar**
**100g (3 1/2oz) fresh ginger**
**about 2 tablespoons olive oil**
**125ml (1/2 cup) champagne vinegar**
**125ml (1/2 cup) soy sauce**

To make the ginger marinade, put the lime juice and sugar in a small saucepan and bring to the boil. Remove from the heat and leave to cool, then strain through a fine sieve. Peel the ginger and chop it roughly. Purée in a blender until totally smooth, adding just enough olive oil to spin. Mix in the champagne vinegar, soy sauce and lime syrup.

Cut the tuna into perfect spaghetti. Gently season with salt, then mix with the shallot, chilli and half the olive oil, to taste.

Mix the diced avocados with the lime juice, remaining olive oil and some salt. Drain the radishes well, season with salt and toss with a little chilli oil.

To serve, place a generous spoonful of the avocado in each of 4 small bowls. Top each one with about 6 slices of radish and arrange half the tuna in a bundle on top. Add more radish, the remaining fish, then top with radish again. Spoon the marinade around and drizzle with chilli oil.

# Sirloin Steak Topped with Gingered Mushrooms and Soy Caramel Emulsion

**Serves 4**

**4 x 175g (6-oz) sirloin steaks**
**salt and freshly ground black pepper**

For the caramel soy emulsion:

**250ml (9oz) light soy sauce**
**6 tablespoons rice vinegar**
**1 large shallot, sliced**
**3 garlic cloves, sliced**
**1½ teaspoons black peppercorns**
**1 tablespoon honey**
**50g (3½ tablespoons) butter, chilled and diced**
**lime juice, to taste**

For the gingered mushrooms:

**100g (3½oz) shiitake mushrooms, diced**
**1½ teaspoons very finely diced fresh ginger**
**50g (3½ tablespoons) butter**
**50g (2oz) enoki mushrooms, cut 5mm (¼ inch) long**
**1 tablespoon chive batons, cut 5mm (¼ inch) long**

For the caramel soy emulsion, put the soy sauce, rice vinegar, shallot, garlic, peppercorns and honey in a pan and bring to the boil. Simmer until reduced by about a tenth, then remove from the heat. Leave overnight, then strain.

For the mushrooms, sauté the shiitake and ginger in the butter until caramelized. Add the enoki and toss until wilted, then add the chives and season with salt and pepper. Keep warm.

Season the steaks and cook to your liking. Leave to rest in a warm place for about 5 minutes. Meanwhile, finish the caramel soy emulsion. Reheat 125ml (½ cup) of it in a small pan, then gradually whisk in the butter. Season with salt, pepper and lime juice.

Put the steaks on 4 warm plates and arrange the mushroom mixture on top in a layer about 1cm (½ inch) thick. Pour the sauce around and serve, accompanied by sprouting broccoli and French fries.

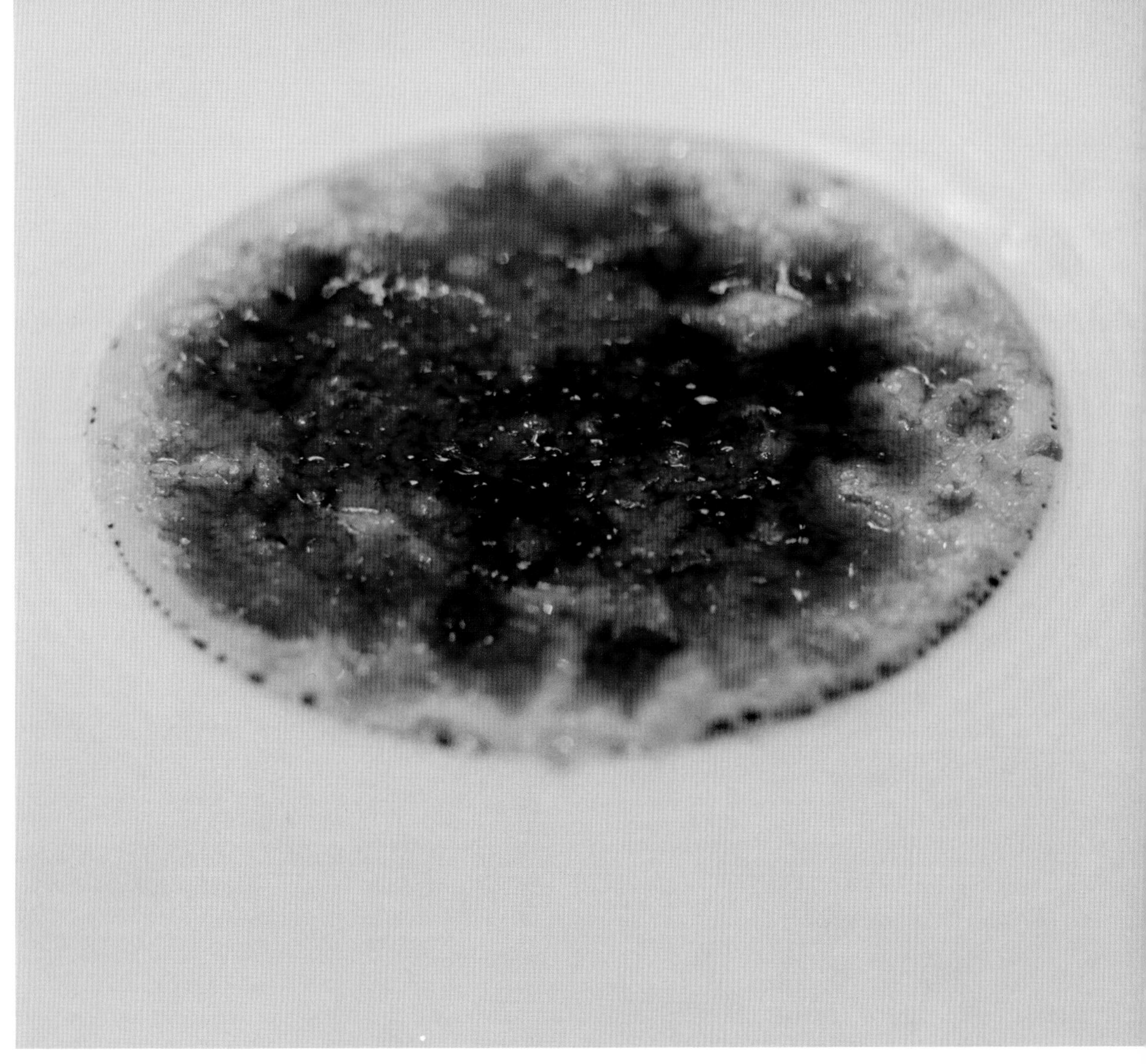

# Gingered Crème Brûlée

**Serves 4**

**500ml (2$^1/_4$ cups) double (heavy) cream**
**75g ($^1/_3$ cup) caster (superfine) sugar**
**100g (1 cup) fresh ginger, chopped**
**6 egg yolks**
**50g ($^1/_4$ cup) Demerara (light brown) sugar**

To decorate:
**12 raspberries**
**4 sprigs of mint**

Put the cream, sugar and ginger in a pan and bring to the boil, then remove from the heat and leave to infuse overnight.

The next day, whisk the egg yolks together in a bowl. Bring the cream mixture back to the boil and whisk it into the yolks. Strain through a fine sieve, then divide between 4 ramekins or other small dishes. Place on a baking sheet and bake in an oven preheated to 160°C/325°F/Gas Mark 3 for about 35 minutes, until set. Remove from the oven and leave to cool.

Shortly before serving, sprinkle the Demerara sugar over the crème brûlées and then caramelize with a blowtorch. Leave for a few minutes until the sugar hardens, then garnish with the raspberries and mint sprigs.

# forty six

# MARCUS WAREING

## Pétrus

Marcus Wareing worked at the Savoy Hotel and Le Gavroche before joining the starting brigade of Aubergine restaurant, where he worked beside Gordon Ramsay and won the accolade, '1995 Young Chef of the Year'. After stints with Daniel Boulud in New York and Guy Savoy in Paris, he became head chef at L'Oranger in London, gaining his first Michelin star at the age of 25. In 1999 Marcus opened Pétrus in St James's with Gordon Ramsay and regained his Michelin star within seven months. Four years later Pétrus relocated to the Berkeley Hotel and Marcus returned to the starting point of his career with the relaunch of the Savoy Grill. In 2003 the Savoy Grill also earned a Michelin star.

**What are your favourite foods/tastes/flavours?**
French cuisine.

**What are your favourite utensils?**
Non-stick pans.

**What is the most useful piece of kitchen equipment?**
Stoves.

**What is your favourite season?**
Spring.

**What is your favourite mealtime?**
Breakfast.

**How do you decide what to cook?**
It all depends what is in the cupboard and what fresh produce I have.

**What inspires you?**
A passion for food.

**What is your favourite drink?**
Tea.

**What are your likes and dislikes?**
I like cooking for people with an open mind. I dislike cooking for fussy eaters.

**How can you inspire others to enjoy great food and cooking?**
Lead by example.

**How did you become a chef?**
I followed in my brother's footsteps.

**What are your top ten ingredients?**
Potatoes, all vegetables, rib-eye beef, pork belly, all herbs, stocks, new salad herbs, lobster, foie gras, salt.

**What are your kitchen secrets?**
I don't have any.

**What are your top tips?**
Have an open mind and trust your own palate.

**What is your favourite junk food?**
Pizza.

**How do you feel about cooking for children?**
Love it.

**Can you give one piece of advice for the domestic cook?**
Follow recipes.

* ✱ Crab and Lobster Tian with Guacamole, Cocktail Sauce and Oscietra Caviar
* ✱ Boiled Pork Belly with Turned Seasonal Vegetables and a Light Bouillon
* ✱ Peanut Parfait with Chocolate Mousse and Chocolate Sauce

# Crab and Lobster Tian with Guacamole, Cocktail Sauce and Oscietra Caviar

**Serves 4**

**1 cooked lobster, weighing about 500g (18oz)**
**200g (7oz) fresh white crabmeat**
**2 heaped tablespoons mayonnaise**
**2 tablespoons finely chopped chives**
**2 tablespoons finely chopped chervil**
**a squeeze of lemon juice**
**a little vinaigrette, made with 4 parts extra virgin olive oil to 1 part white wine vinegar**
**4 teaspoons Oscietra caviar**
**sea salt and freshly ground black pepper**
**salad leaves, to garnish**
**Melba toast, to serve**

**For the cocktail sauce:**

**4 tablespoons mayonnaise**
**1 tablespoon tomato ketchup (catsup)**
**a squeeze of lemon juice**
**a dash of brandy**
**a pinch of cayenne pepper**

**For the guacamole:**

**1 ripe avocado**
**juice of 1/2 lime**
**1 tablespoon mascarpone cheese**

Remove the meat from the lobster, keeping the tail meat whole. Pick through the crab and lobster meat, making sure there are no traces of shell. Chop the lobster claw meat and put it in a bowl set over a bowl of ice. Bind with the mayonnaise, then stir in the herbs, lemon juice and some seasoning.

For the cocktail sauce, mix together all the ingredients, adjusting the lemon juice, brandy and cayenne to taste.
To make the guacamole, peel and stone (pit) the avocado and push the flesh through a fine sieve. Add the lime juice and mascarpone and mix well. Taste and adjust the seasoning.

To serve, place a stainless steel ring, about 7–8cm (2 3/4–3 1/2 inches) in diameter and 1cm (1/2 inch) deep, in the centre of each serving plate. Pack the crab and lobster mixture into the ring and level the top, the remove the ring. Finely slice the lobster tail, dress with a little vinaigrette and season lightly with sea salt. Fan out overlapping slices on top of the tian. Place the caviar in the middle, on top of the lobster.

Drizzle the cocktail sauce around the tian, then place dots of the guacamole around the plate – the easiest way to do this is to put the sauce and guacamole in squeezy bottles. Lightly dress the salad leaves with vinaigrette and place them around the outside. Serve with Melba toast.

# Boiled Pork Belly with Turned Seasonal Vegetables and a Light Bouillon

**Serves 4**

**2 large onions, cut into 5cm (2-inch) pieces**
**1 leek, cut into 5cm (2-inch) pieces**
**2 carrots, cut into 5cm (2-inch) pieces**
**2 celery sticks, cut into 5cm (2-inch) pieces**
**1 head of garlic, cut in half**
**20 peppercorns, crushed**
**4 star anise, crushed**
**8 sprigs of thyme**
**4 bay leaves**
**1.5kg ($3^1/3$lb) pork belly, skin on**
**sea salt and freshly ground black pepper**
**chopped parsley, to serve**

**For the vegetables (choose from the following):**
**turnip**
**swede (rutabaga)**
**carrots**
**potatoes**
**parsnips**
**beetroot (beet)**
**courgettes (zucchini)**

Put the onions, leek, carrots, celery, garlic, spices and herbs in a large saucepan and add the pork. Pour in just enough water to cover everything and bring slowly to the boil. Turn down to a simmer and cook very gently for 2 hours, keeping the temperature at about 90°C/194°F. Remove from the heat and leave the pork to cool in the cooking liquid. Strain off the cooking liquid and set aside. Trim the skin off the pork and take out the bones, then cut the pork into blocks about 6cm ($2^1/2$ inches) square. Keep covered, so it does not dry out.

The vegetables can be 'turned' [trimmed into barrel shapes] or just peeled and trimmed, if you prefer. Any firm vegetable can be turned and the technique serves a dual purpose: the vegetables cook evenly and the presentation is more elegant. You will need a specially designed turning knife with a curved blade, and, in the beginning, a little patience! The turned vegetables should be no larger than 5cm (2 inches) long and 2.5cm (1 inch) thick – cut larger vegetables into quarters first, if necessary.

To cook the vegetables, bring a large pan of water to a rapid boil over a high heat. Add enough salt so the water tastes faintly salty. While the water heats, fill a medium bowl about three-quarters full with ice, then add enough cold water to come just to the top of the ice.

Add the vegetables to the boiling water in batches, keeping the different types separate. Make sure the water doesn't lose its boil. Simmer the vegetables until they are tender but barely cooked. Test a piece by eating one. As soon as the vegetables are done, remove them as fast as possible from the water and submerge in the ice-cold water. Remove from the iced water when cold and set aside ready for reheating.

To serve, strain the pork stock through a very fine sieve or a piece of muslin (cheesecloth), carefully discarding the sediment. Put enough stock in a pan to cover the pork and bring to the boil. Add the pork and simmer for 5–6 minutes, until heated all the way through. Reheat the turned vegetables in the same way. Heat up the remaining pork stock, adjust the seasoning and add some chopped parsley to it. Place the pieces of hot pork in the centre of 4 bowls. Arrange the vegetables around the pork, pour in the bouillon, as you would a soup, and serve.

# Peanut Parfait with Chocolate Mousse and Chocolate Sauce

This recipe has several stages to it but the parfait can be made well in advance and kept in the freezer. Then all you need to do on the day is make the chocolate sauce and the mousse.

The quantities below will serve more than 4 but it's not really practical to make any less. Just store the extra parfaits in the freezer and the mousse in the fridge.

Serves 4

For the parfait base:

150g (1 cup) peanuts, chopped
75g ($2^1/_4$ cups) rice crispies
225g ($^2/_3$ cup) golden syrup (light corn syrup), warmed

For the sabayon:

2 eggs
2 egg yolks
75g ($^1/_3$ cup) caster (superfine) sugar
25g (1 heaped tablespoon) liquid glucose

For the Italian meringue:

70g egg whites about 3 egg whites but do weigh them, as it is important to use the exact quantity (US readers use $2^2/_3$ extra-large egg whites)
50g ($^1/_4$ cup) caster (superfine) sugar
50g ($2^1/_2$ tablespoons) liquid glucose

To finish the parfait:

**100g (6 tablespoons) crunchy peanut butter**
**4 tablespoons double (heavy) cream**
**250ml (1 cup) double (heavy) cream, semi-whipped**

For the dark chocolate sauce:

**240ml (1 cup) water**
**240g ($1^1/_4$ cups) caster (superfine) sugar**
**80g (1 cup) (unsweetened) cocoa powder**
**250ml (1 cup) double (heavy) cream**

For the dark chocolate mousse:

**200g (7oz) dark (semisweet with at least 70% cocoa) chocolate, plus a little melted chocolate to serve**
**100g egg yolks, about 6 egg yolks but do weigh them, as it is important to use the exact quantity (US readers use 5 extra-large egg yolks)**
**100g ($^1/_2$ cup) caster (superfine) sugar**
**350ml ($1^1/_2$ cups) double (heavy) cream, semi-whipped**
**50ml ($3^1/_2$ tablespoons) milk**

For the parfait base, mix all the ingredients together, then roll out on a baking sheet between 2 sheets of baking parchment until it is 3–4mm (about $^1/_8$ inch) thick. Place in an oven preheated to 160°C/325°F/Gas Mark 3 and bake for 4 minutes, then turn the tray around and bake for 4 minutes longer. Remove from the oven and leave to cool. Cut out 4 shapes to fit the ring moulds you are using for the parfait and set aside.

Using a freestanding electric mixer, whisk the eggs and egg yolks together for the sabayon. In a heavy-based pan, heat the sugar and glucose without stirring until they reach 120°C/248°F on a sugar (candy) thermometer. Gradually pour the hot syrup on to the eggs, whisking constantly. Continue to whisk until the mixture is cool and forms a thick mousse. Transfer to a bowl and set aside.

In the cleaned bowl of the electric mixer, whisk the egg whites until they form stiff peaks. In a heavy-based pan, heat the sugar and glucose without stirring until they reach 120°C/248°F on a sugar thermometer. Gradually pour this hot syrup on to the egg whites, whisking constantly. Continue to whisk until the meringue is cool and forms firm, velvety peaks.

To finish the parfait, mix the peanut butter with the 4 tablespoons of cream, then add it to the Italian meringue. Fold in the semi-whipped cream, then finally fold in the sabayon. Pour into ring moulds about 4cm ($1^3/_4$ inches) deep and place in the freezer.

To make the dark chocolate sauce, put the water and sugar in a pan and heat gently until the sugar has dissolved. Bring to the boil and stir in the cocoa powder and cream. Reduce the heat and cook very gently, stirring constantly, for about 3 minutes, until it is a smooth, thick sauce. Remove from the heat and set aside.

For the chocolate mousse, break up the chocolate and melt it in a pan set over a bowl of simmering water, making sure the water is not touching the base of the bowl. Whisk the egg yolks together in a freestanding electric mixer. Put the sugar in a small, heavy-based pan with a tablespoon of water and heat gently until the sugar has dissolved. Raise the heat and boil until it reaches 120°C/248°F on a sugar thermometer. Gradually pour the hot sugar syrup on to the egg yolks, whisking constantly. Continue to whisk until the mixture is thick and mousselike and has cooled to the same temperature as the melted chocolate. Fold this mixture into the melted chocolate, then fold in the semi-whipped cream and the milk. Put the mousse into a piping (pastry) bag with a large plain nozzle (tip).

To serve, pipe a border of melted chocolate, about 7cm ($2^3/_4$ inches) square, on each serving plate. This will hold the chocolate sauce. Pipe or carefully pour the chocolate sauce inside the square – not too much, as when the parfait sits on it, it will push the sauce out to the sides. Take each parfait out of its mould by warming it up lightly (you can just warm the moulds in your hands), then sit the parfait on a rice crispie base. Carefully place the base and parfait in the middle of the sauce. Pipe the chocolate mousse on top of the parfait.

**Opposite: Left, Boiled Pork Belly with Turned Seasonal Vegetables and a Light Bouillon; right, Peanut Parfait with Chocolate Mousse and Chocolate Sauce**

# forty seven

# JOHN WILLIAMS

## Ritz Hotel

John has been executive chef at the Ritz Hotel in London since June 2004, fulfilling a lifelong ambition. Previously he was chef-director at the Royal Garden Hotel and Le Crocodile, then joined the Savoy Group in 1986. This included a stint at the Berkeley before moving on to Claridges, where he became Maître Chef des Cuisines. As Chairman of the Academy of Culinary Arts in Great Britain, he works tirelessly to promote the education and training of young chefs. The proud recipient of a Pierre Taittinger International Award, Williams also received the Craft Guild of Chefs Award in 2000.

**What are your favourite foods/tastes/flavours?**
Lemon verbena, vanilla, grouse, lobster, langoustine and sea urchin.

**What are your favourite utensils?**
Grande Cuisine saucepans.

**What is your most useful piece of kitchen design and equipment?**
All-in-one wall and floor joined. A Thermomix.

**What is your favourite season?**
Autumn.

**What is your favourite mealtime?**
Dinner.

**How do you decide what to cook?**
It depends on the season and the temperature outside.

**What inspires you?**
The seasons and fresh, locally grown produce.

**What is your favourite drink?**
A good Claret or Burgundy.

**What are your likes and dislikes?**
I dislike pretentious, badly cooked food.

**How can you inspire others to enjoy great food and cooking?**
By frontline leadership.

**How did you become a chef?**
Through the enjoyment of food.

**What are your top ten ingredients?**
Vanilla, star anise, bay leaves, lemon verbena, lobster, langoustine, liquorice, lemon, chocolate, lime.

**What are your kitchen secrets?**
I have none.

**What are your top tips?**
Use the best-quality fresh ingredients.

**Do you have any favourite junk food?**
Hamburgers.

**How do you feel about cooking for children?**
I like to cook for youngsters.

**Can you give one piece of advice for the domestic cook?**
Have good preparation and stay calm in the kitchen!

* Carpaccio of Beetroot with Matjes Herring and Apple Salad
* Poppy-seed-crusted Chicken with Avocado, Tomato, Mango and Balsamic Dressing
* Vanilla-scented Roast Nectarines with Vanilla, Strawberry and Rosewater Sauce

## Carpaccio of Beetroot with Matjes Herring and Apple Salad

**Serves 4**

**500g (18oz) small raw beetroot (beets)**
**320g (11oz) Matjes herrings, drained and very finely diced**
**2 apples, peeled, cored and finely diced**
**1 teaspoon finely grated fresh horseradish**
**3 1/2 tablespoons plain yoghurt**
**100ml (7 tablespoons) crème fraîche**
**lemon juice**
**80g (3oz) mixed baby salad leaves**
**1/2 garlic clove, crushed**
**sea salt and freshly ground black pepper**

For the dressing:

**5 1/2 tablespoons groundnut (peanut) oil**
**4 teaspoons red wine vinegar**
**1 tablespoon finely diced shallot**
**2 tablespoons chopped mixed herbs (chives, chervil, tarragon, parsley and basil)**

Top and tail the beetroots, wrap them in foil and roast in an oven preheated to 140°C/275°F/Gas Mark 1 for about 45 minutes; they should still be fairly firm. Allow to cool, then peel them and slice very finely. Set aside.

Mix the herrings, apples and horseradish together and bind with the yoghurt and crème fraîche. Season with salt, pepper and lemon juice to taste.

Mix together all the ingredients for the dressing and season to taste.

Place a ring in the centre of each serving plate and spoon the herring mixture into it, then remove the ring. Arrange the beetroot slices, slightly overlapping one another, around the herring. Toss the mixed leaves with some of the dressing and place on top of the herring. Then spoon some of the dressing over the beetroot and sprinkle with a little sea salt. Serve at room temperature.

# Poppy-seed-crusted Chicken with Avocado, Tomato and Mango and Balsamic Dressing

**Serves 4**

**4 boneless chicken breasts (breast halves)**
**60g (1 cup) fresh breadcrumbs**
**25g ($2^1/_2$ tablespoons) poppy seeds**
**15g (2 tablespoons) sesame seeds**
**50g ($^1/_3$ cup) plain (all-purpose) flour**
**2 eggs, lightly beaten**
**2 limes**
**sunflower or vegetable oil for deep-frying**
**2 small avocados, peeled, stoned and diced**
**$^1/_2$ mango, peeled, stoned and diced**
**2 small chillies, deseeded and diced**
**1 tablespoon finely diced shallot**
**80g (generous $^1/_2$ cup) tomatoes, skinned, deseeded and diced**
**1 tablespoon chopped coriander (cilantro)**
**1 tablespoon chopped basil**
**salt and freshly ground black pepper**

**For the dressing:**
**$5^1/_2$ tablespoons hazelnut oil**
**4 teaspoons balsamic vinegar**

Remove the skin from the chicken breasts, along with any sinew. Cut the meat into thin strips and season with salt and pepper. Mix the breadcrumbs with the poppy seeds and sesame seeds in a shallow dish. Dust the chicken strips with the flour, then coat with the beaten egg, letting any excess drain off. Finally, coat them in the breadcrumb mixture, pressing it on gently to ensure that it sticks. Set aside.

Peel the zest of the limes and cut it into fine strips, then remove the pith of the lime and cut out the segments. Set aside.

Mix together the dressing ingredients, season with salt and pepper and set aside.

Heat some oil for deep-frying to 180°C/350°F and fry the chicken, in batches if necessary, until crisp and golden brown. Drain on kitchen paper towels.

Put the avocados, mango, chillies, shallot, tomatoes, lime segments and lime zest in a bowl and toss with the herbs and the dressing. Taste and adjust the seasoning. Divide between 4 serving plates and place the crisp pieces of chicken on top. Serve immediately.

# Vanilla-scented Roast Nectarines with Vanilla, Strawberry and Rosewater Sauce

**Serves 4**

**100g ($^1/_2$ cup) caster (superfine) sugar, plus 2 tablespoons**
**100ml (7 tablespoons) water**
**1 teaspoon rosewater**
**4 vanilla pods (vanilla beans)**
**4 large nectarines**
**300g (2 cups) Demerara (light brown) sugar**
**100g ($3^1/_2$oz) strawberries**
**20g ($^3/_4$oz) fresh ginger**
**a small bunch of mint**
**vanilla ice cream, to serve**

Make a sugar syrup by putting the 100g ($^1/_2$ cup) of caster sugar in a heavy-based pan with the water and heating gently, stirring occasionally, until the sugar has dissolved. Simmer for a few minutes, then add the rosewater and scrape in the seeds from the vanilla pods. Strain the syrup and set aside.

Flatten the vanilla pods with the back of a knife and slice them into very fine strips. Coat in the 2 tablespoons of caster sugar and place on a baking tray. Leave in a warm place, such as above the stove or in an airing cupboard, for about an hour to dry.

Roll the nectarines in the syrup and then in the Demerara sugar. Put them in a baking dish and pour over the remaining syrup. Place in an oven preheated to 200°C/400°F/Gas Mark 6 and cook for about 12 minutes, until nicely caramelized, shaking the dish every 4 minutes to coat the nectarines in the syrup. Remove the nectarines from the syrup and set aside.

To make the sauce, put about 100ml (7 tablespoons) of the syrup in a liquidizer (blender) with the strawberries and ginger and blend until smooth. Pass through a sieve and pour the sauce over the hot nectarines. Garnish with the dried vanilla pods and sprigs of mint and serve with vanilla ice cream.

# forty eight

# ERIC ZIEBOLD

## CityZen

**Prior to opening CityZen at Mandarin Oriental, Washington DC, Eric spent almost eight years at the world-renowned The French Laundry in California. Before that he held positions at Spago in Los Angeles and Vidalia in Washington, DC. He started working in restaurants when he was sixteen years old and hasn't looked back: 'I really fell in love with the lifestyle – the creativity, passion and commitment of those around me. It was contagious.' Eric has been named 'one of America's Best New Chefs 2005' by *Food & Wine* magazine.**

**What are your favourite foods/tastes/flavours?**
Just about anything with pork and high in fat.

**What is your favourite utensil?**
A stiff bowl scraper.

**What is the most useful piece of kitchen design?**
Sufficient worktop space and good sight lines.

**What is your favourite season?**
Autumn.

**What is your favourite meal?**
Breakfast, although I hardly ever have time to eat it.

**How do you decide what to cook?**
It depends on my mood in a lot of ways. When I'm tired, I tend to cook more grounded food; when it's hot, I tend to cook lighter food.

**What inspires you?**
Amazing products, especially ones that have a history or character you can draw upon and put your personality into by way of how you use them or cook with them.

**What is your favourite drink?**
The lemonade made with Meyer lemons by my pastry chef.

**What are your likes and dislikes?**
Dislikes are easier. I'm not a big fan of curry, and tend to avoid things that are spicy. I like salt, fat and red and white Burgundy.

**How can you inspire others to enjoy great food and cooking?**
Set yourself up to have the experience that you're looking for on that particular occasion and follow this simple guideline: 'the more the merrier, the fewer the better the food'.

**How did you become a chef?**
I used to wrestle when I was younger so I was always trying to cut weight. Since food was always on my mind, it seemed logical to get a job in a restaurant. I was fortunate because the restaurant I started at had a pretty great chef and an amazing staff, so I became enamoured with restaurant life.

**What are your top ten ingredients?**
Pork, thyme, coriander (cilantro), flageolets, butter, shirako, matsutake mushrooms, quince, artichokes.

**What are your kitchen secrets?**
Season as you go, don't be afraid of salt or acid - taste, taste, taste.

**Do you have any favourite junk food?**
My mother makes little pretzels that are covered in almond bark. They're the perfect blend of salty, sweet, creamy, crunchy.

**How do you feel about cooking for children?**

The same way that I feel about cooking for my sister – it can be difficult because they're bound to be picky, but if you make it taste good you may be surprised at the results you get.

**Can you give one piece of advice for the domestic cook?**

As I'm a chef, everyone gets freaked out cooking for me. The point of having dinner with friends is to have a good time. So stop worrying about everything being perfect. If you're not enjoying cooking it, then it's not worth it. If you taste something and you're happy with it, chances are everyone else will be too. If you overcook it, undercook it, overseason it, underseason it, or in some other way do something to screw it up, chances are the person that's eating it has too. So relax, and open another bottle of wine.

# Corned Beef Tongue Salad with Parma Ham, White Mushrooms and Périgord Truffle

**Serves 8**

**1 ox tongue**
**50g (3 tablespoons) salt**

For the brine:

**5g (1 teaspoon) sel rose, or red preserving salt**
**25g (2 1/2 tablespoons) brown sugar**
**5g (2 1/2 teaspoons) mustard seeds**
**10g (2 1/2 tablespoons) coriander seeds**
**2 garlic cloves, sliced**
**4 allspice berries**
**12 black peppercorns**
**1 bay leaf**
**225g (3/4 cup) salt**
**2 litres (2 quarts) water**

To serve:

**50ml (3 1/2 tablespoons) best-quality olive oil, such as Tattoli**
**2 teaspoons Banyuls vinegar, or best-quality red wine vinegar**
**1 fresh Périgord truffle, 1/2 finely diced, 1/2 cut into matchsticks**
**40g (1 1/2oz) Parma ham (prosciutto), cut into small matchsticks**
**8 small white mushrooms, lightly cooked**
**a handful of lamb's lettuce (mâche)**
**salt and black pepper**

To brine the tongue, dissolve the sel rose in 100ml (7 tablespoons) water, then mix with the brown sugar, mustard and coriander seeds, garlic, allspice, peppercorns, bay leaf, salt and water. Rinse the tongue in cold water, place in a container and pour the brine over it. Leave in a cool place, about 12°C/55°F, or in the fridge, for 30 days.

Remove the tongue from the brine, rinse it and place in a large pan. Strain the herbs and spices from the brine and add the spices to the pan. Add enough cold water to cover the tongue by 10cm (4 inches), then add the salt and bring to a simmer. Use a plate or something similar to weight the tongue and keep it submerged. Simmer for about 1 1/2 hours, until the tongue is tender. Transfer it to a container and pour enough of the cooking liquid over it to cover. Leave to cool completely, then chill.

To serve, cut 16 slices of tongue about 5mm (1/4 inch) thick, starting from the thick end. Place 2 slices on each serving plate. Whisk together the olive oil and vinegar, season with salt and pepper, then mix with the finely diced truffle. Garnish the tongue with the Parma ham, truffle slices, mushrooms and lettuce, then drizzle the dressing around.

# Braised Shoat with Cardoon Gratin and Roasted Pork Jus

**A shoat is a pig that has just been weaned. Ideally you would use 2 small legs of pork for this dish, but if you can't get hold of them use half a larger leg instead.**

**Serves 8**

**1 carrot, cut into 3cm (2$^1/_4$-inch) pieces**
**1 onion, cut into 3cm (2$^1/_4$-inch) pieces**
**1 leek, cut into 3cm (2$^1/_4$-inch) pieces**
**2 pork legs, weighing about 2kg (4$^1/_2$lb) each, from a 12–13kg (27–29lb) pig**
**500ml (2$^1/_4$ cups) white wine**
**chicken stock to cover**

For the roasted pork jus:
**2 tablespoons oil**
**1kg (2$^1/_4$lb) pork bones**
**1 carrot, cut into 3cm ($^1/_8$-inch) pieces**
**1 onion, cut into 3cm ($^1/_8$-inch) pieces**
**1 leek, cut into 3cm ($^1/_8$-inch) pieces**
**2 garlic cloves, peeled**
**3 litres (3 quarts) veal stock, or use chicken stock**

For the braised cardoons:
**2 litres water**
**100ml (7 tablespoons) champagne vinegar**
**100ml (7 tablespoons) lemon juice**
**100g ($^1/_3$ cup) salt**
**200ml (7oz) olive oil**
**24 cardoon stalks**
**$^1/_2$ onion, very finely chopped**
**4 garlic cloves, sliced**
**10 black peppercorns**
**10 sprigs of thyme**
**5 sprigs of parsley**
**1 bay leaf**

For the cardoon gratin:
**1 litre (1 quart) double (heavy) cream**
**6 sprigs of thyme**
**2 garlic cloves, peeled**
**3 large Yukon Gold potatoes, or other waxy potatoes, peeled and cut into 5mm ($^1/_4$-inch) dice**
**1 tablespoon chopped parsley**
**salt**

To serve:
**sel gris**
**chopped chives**

To braise the pork, put the carrots, onion and leeks in a heavy-based casserole large enough to hold the pork legs. Put the pork on top of the vegetables and then add the wine and enough chicken stock to cover by 10cm (4 inches). Bring to a simmer, then cover and transfer to an oven preheated to 180°C/350°F/Gas Mark 4. Cook for about 4$^1/_2$ hours, until the meat is tender. Remove from the oven and leave to cool at room temperature for 2 hours. Carefully remove the pork from the casserole, reserve the braising liquid and place the pork on a board. Gently remove all the bones and gelatinous material, then place the meat on a baking tray. Cover with another baking tray, put some weights on top to press the pork, and leave to cool.

Meanwhile, make the roasted pork jus. Heat the oil in a shallow casserole and brown the pork bones in it. Once they are evenly browned, remove them, drain the fat off and add the vegetables and garlic to the pan. Cook until lightly browned, then return the bones to the pan and add 1 litre (1 quart) of the liquid that the pork was braised in, plus the veal stock. Bring to a simmer, transfer to an oven preheated to 180°C/350°F/Gas Mark 4 and cook for 45 minutes. Remove from the oven and strain out the bones and vegetables. Place the pot on the hob (stovetop) and simmer until the sauce has reduced to a light coating consistency. Remove from the heat and keep warm.

To cook the cardoons, combine the water, vinegar, lemon juice, salt and oil in a large pan. Cut the cardoon stalks to the point where they're no longer hollow and then peel them. Slice them 5mm ($^1/_4$ inch) thick and add them to the pan. Tie the onion, garlic, peppercorns and herbs in a piece of muslin (cheesecloth) and add to the pan. Bring to a simmer and cook for 30–40 minutes, until the cardoons are tender, then drain well and set aside.

Once the pork has completely cooled, the meat should be very firm. Lightly score the skin with a paring knife and then cut each leg into 4 pieces. Place the pork in a sauté pan with three-quarters of the roasted pork jus. Bring to a simmer, then transfer to an oven preheated to 180°C/350°F/Gas Mark 4. Cook for about 25 minutes, basting every 5–8 minutes, until a nice glaze has developed.

Meanwhile, for the cardoon gratin, bring the cream, thyme and garlic to a simmer in a shallow pan. Season very well with salt and add the potatoes. Simmer gently until the potatoes are fully cooked and the mixture is quite thick. Add the drained cardoons and the parsley and spoon into a large, shallow dish. Place under a hot grill (broiler) and allow to brown for about 1 minute: slowly is better than quickly here.

To serve, divide the cardoon gratin between 8 serving plates and place the pork on top. Sprinkle a little sel gris and chopped chives over the pork, then pour the remaining jus around the gratin.

# Meyer Lemon Soufflé with Citrus Salad and Honey Sabayon

**Serves 8**

For the Meyer lemon curd:

**250g ($1^1/_4$ cups) granulated sugar**
**175ml ($^3/_4$ cup) Meyer lemon juice, but if you can't get Meyer lemons, use large organic ones**
**grated zest of 2 lemons**
**4 eggs**

For the citrus salad:

**1 ruby red grapefruit**
**2 blood oranges**
**2 navel oranges**
**2 Meyer lemons, or large organic lemons**
**125ml ($^1/_2$ cup) purified water**
**75g ($^1/_3$ cup) granulated sugar**
**1 Tahitian vanilla pod (vanilla bean)**

For the honey sabayon:

**1 egg**
**4 egg yolks**
**4 tablespoons Patterson Farms honey, or any delicately flavoured honey**
**300ml ($1^1/_4$ cups) double (heavy) cream, lightly whipped**
**salt**

For the meringue:

**10 egg whites, at room temperature**
**4 tablespoons caster (superfine) sugar**

To make the lemon curd, mix the sugar with the lemon juice and zest and whisk in the eggs. Place in a medium-sized heavy-based saucepan and cook over a medium-high heat, whisking constantly, for about 10 minutes, until the curd is thick and frothy. As soon as the curd starts to bubble around the edges, pour it into a shallow bowl and leave to cool, whisking occasionally. Once it is cold, put it in the fridge.

For the citrus salad, peel all the fruit, removing all the white pith, then cut out the segments from between the membranes and place in a shallow dish. Combine the water, sugar and vanilla pod in a small pan and bring to the boil, stirring to dissolve the sugar. Remove from the heat and leave to cool. Pour this syrup over the citrus fruit and chill.

For the sabayon, put the egg, egg yolks and honey in a bowl set over a pan of gently simmering water, making sure the water does not touch the base of the bowl. Using a hand-held electric beater, whisk until the mixture is pale in colour, has doubled in volume and is warm to the touch. Remove the bowl from the pan of water and continue to whisk until the sabayon is cool. Fold in the whipped cream and add salt to taste.

Butter eight 125ml ($^1/_2$-cup) ramekins and dust them with a little caster sugar. Make the meringue by whisking the egg whites to soft peaks, adding the sugar half way through. Gently fold the lemon curd into the meringue, then divide the mixture between the ramekins. Place in an oven preheated to 180°C/350°F/Gas Mark 4 and bake for 6–8 minutes, until the soufflés are well risen. Meanwhile, divide the citrus salad between 8 plates and put a spoonful of sabayon on top of each one. When the soufflés are done, serve them immediately, accompanied by the citrus salad.

# Index

# Conclusion: Hope for the future

There are 2.5 million people worldwide living with paralysis caused by spinal cord injury and it is conservatively estimated that over 130,000 people each year will survive a traumatic injury of this kind. The added tragedy is that spinal cord injuries primarily affect young adults, with more than half occurring among people in the 16 to 30 age group.

Spinal cord injury causes a devastating disruption to the lives of injured individuals and their families, who become pervaded by a feeling of helplessness. Healthy, strong, independent people must now rely on others and face a life bound to a wheelchair. The day Daniel Nicholls suffered a spinal cord injury in a swimming accident at the age of 19, his life and the lives of his family changed immediately and radically. David Nicholls has resolved to see Daniel walk again. Is this heartfelt desire realistic?

Twenty years ago it was believed that spinal cord injury was incurable and that regeneration of the spinal cord was impossible. In the last ten years, research into this area has made significant advances and overturned this belief. The result is a new optimism in the scientific community and a new expectation for people suffering a spinal cord injury. This optimism is fuelled by a more comprehensive understanding of the initial and secondary damage caused by spinal cord injury; the discovery of proteins that inhibit and support nerve regeneration; the number of new therapies that successfully support regeneration and/or remyelination in animal models of spinal cord injury; and the realization that regeneration of fewer than 10 per cent of the injured axons in the spinal cord is needed to support substantial functional recovery. Currently, the most promising experiments involve the testing of combined therapies. In the last year, several different combined therapies tested in animal models have been reported to be dramatically more effective than the individual therapies. The major question now is not if, but when, effective therapies for spinal cord injury will be available.

The challenges faced by an individual with spinal cord injury are not easy, but the injured have demonstrated their determination to reclaim their future and maximize their quality of life. Government and society, however, have not invested adequately in spinal cord injury research. It has been worldwide charitable organizations and the spinal-cord-injured communities themselves that have worked tirelessly and valiantly to fund it. This funding has led to the recent significant progress made in spinal cord injury regeneration and rehabilitation research. Because of the feasibility of developing therapies that will restore function in thousands of paralyzed people, there is an unprecedented level of urgency to identify and fund the most promising therapies for spinal cord injury and to accelerate clinical trials for them. The resolve and optimism of the Nicholls family and hundreds of thousands of others to restore function in paralyzed people can be turned into a reality.

**Juanita J. Anders, PhD**
Associate Professor of Anatomy, Physiology and Genetics
Uniformed Services University of the Health Sciences
Bethesda, Maryland